I Did Inhale

— Memoir of a Hippie Chick —

W. M. Raebeck

Library of Congress number 2015908822

ISBN 978-1-938691-00-3

At least 20% of the proceeds from this book go to protecting wilderness, wildlife, all creatures, and oceans from human violation, insensitivity, and ignorance.

This book is sourced from a responsibly managed North American forest, meeting the requirements of the independent Sustainable Forestry Initiative Program.®

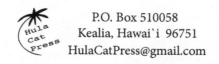

P.O. Box 510058
Kealia, Hawai'i 96751
HulaCatPress@gmail.com

Acknowledgments

"Words are cheap, but they're all I can afford," was my mantra when I started this book in 1977. Since then, the manuscript has kind of grown up with me. In no way does it resemble the first draft, the fifth, or even the initial intention (to record some adventures). Back then, the stories were recent and I'd hardly evolved beyond being that rascal. Now the urge to improve things, in life and in writing, continues, but it's time to let my little book go—while my crazy generation is still young enough to chuckle at ourselves, and while (amazingly) so many of us are still *here*.

I wish to thank a few people, who long ago were kind enough to critique my first attempts at writing a book (long before you'd ever find a contemporary female memoir in a book store). It's scary to bare one's soul and shabby behavior as I've hereby done, but the following individuals helped me at least bare better. All gave valuable commentary that was taken to heart: Max Scott, Rosario Perry, Debra Kingsland, Barry Raebeck, and Shelby (Skip) Raebeck.

Then in 2014 came Marcie Powers. With reverence for the written word, she had true compassion for the writer relationship to the material. Her enthusiasm and laughter, combined with her patience and gentle suggestions, were more than one could've hoped for. Many *mahalos* to Marcie.

And…anyone from the hippie times would be remiss not to bow deeply at the altar of the generation before us. Our parents never could've anticipated or prepared for what their kids would put them through or blame them for. Though mostly gone now, I only hope they were wise enough to know, or lived long enough to see, that our scorn mostly betrayed how inexperienced, spoiled, and arrogant we were. Blinded by idealism, and privileged enough to shout in the streets, we were heavy on finger-pointing, heavy on drugs, and light on the doggedness and lifelong dedication necessary to bring about real, long-term social reform and environmental protection. We knew little about hardship or sacrifice.

This book is lovingly dedicated to Charlotte H. Raebeck, my mother and guardian angel.

I never realized it was you keeping me safe.

Disclaimer

Forgive my trespasses, unscrupulousness was part of my early story. At least I've changed all the names (except Dad, Mom, Oma, Yanni, and the pets). If owning our truth frees us, and frees others to own theirs, here we go. I was young, and—compared to more sheltered, protected, and sensible sorts—maybe a little far out.

Please understand that I have always scraped the bottom of my essence for the most compelling direction. It has been about the journey, the bite, and the unknown. And, ironically, some of the worst experiences make the best stories.

In the end, you can't judge yesterday with today's reason or appetite. And that's what makes yesterday rich.

TABLE OF CONTENTS

PART IV ~ DESTINY

PART V ~ ISLANDS

Prologue

May 1974

Whenever I was traveling, I always looked for him in airports, in European railway stations. That's where I thought I'd see him again. We wouldn't coincide at a party, I would never hear from a friend that he was in town; I'd hear he was in other towns, other countries. So I looked for him in airports and in odd, out of the way train stations, or on boats to islands.

Sometimes I'd spot him and stop dead. Then the man would turn slightly and it was a different profile. Occasionally I'd hurry after someone on the sidewalk, holding my breath. Then, getting close enough to call out his name, the man would turn squarely into my expectancy. Oh no…no.

Visiting dear Oma in New York City was trying. One never quite knew why it was so draining. Departure was the worst, something so chaotic about getting out of that apartment. Too many last words, too many wrapped parcels, too many last-minute items crammed into bulging shopping bags or into those old purple Bergdorf Goodman boxes, too many unwanted last-second mittens and slippers one was forced to accept and carry between the teeth to the elevator door.

That afternoon, finally escaping my doting granny, I managed to bungle myself onto the downtown subway, arriving in Penn Station with nine minutes to catch the Long Island train. Like a donkey beneath the baggage, I didn't look as good as one, but stumbled along in the underground mob, anticipating the privacy of the back seat in the last car of the train. Approaching the juice stand, above where the stairs led down to the platforms, suddenly I saw him. For real. He was just picking up a suitcase, and the woman he was with was as long and as perfect as I'd expected her to be.

I'd heard he was coming in from Spain soon, with his German girlfriend. I'd hoped to see him after a phone call or at least after a bath. Not in Penn Station stew. Turning on my heels, I hobbled the other way, dodging commuters. He hadn't seen me.

I had to find a ladies' room to gain composure, and powder my elbows or something—as if I could eliminate Oma's encircling aura. I couldn't miss that train, though, that he'd also be taking; it was the last of the day.

It took a full five minutes to locate a restroom, and once locked in, I contemplated the filthy four-inch-square sink. With three and a half minutes left to get to the train, all I could really do was apply lipstick, wrap my head in a scarf, and hide my face with sunglasses. Feeling I'd blend in with the other passengers now, I pulled up my collar and did the Seventh Avenue shuffle back to the station, still transporting my grandmother's 'thrift store' in those God forsaken shopping bags. Hardly able to walk under the load, I desperately scanned the crowd for a pauper. Seeing an old woman, I passed off one of the bags with a benevolent smile.

Rushing onto the train, I concaved into the first vacant seat. From deep inside my coat, I slowly peered around, relieved to find he wasn't in that car. As the train eased out of the station, an uncomfortable anonymity settled into my throat. Suppose he walked into this car and looked straight at me. Would I just sit there and hope to go undetected? I could've been Richard Nixon under a disguise that thick. I would say something. I would probably have to say something…. Meanwhile, I just sat there and watched the bouncing door in case he entered.

But it was weird knowing he was so near after all this time. I should go and greet him, for my nerves if nothing else. It even felt a little dishonest to any remaining friendship to pretend I hadn't seen him.

At least I could now extricate myself from the baggage.

He didn't recognize me as I walked down the aisle toward his seat. (Last chance to pass by incognito….) But I lifted the glasses. He was surprised; moved over so I could sit. We spoke. He asked, I answered—I asked, he answered. All was fondness, warmth, as if we hadn't been through three years of global hide and seek, as if I was a friend.

I Did Inhale

— Memoir of a Hippie Chick —

PART 1 ~ FREE CANDY

- 1 -

Oma Corrupted Me

Durham, North Carolina, 1951

It was decided, by Dr. Spock and my over-achieved sister, that twelve months was a ripe old age to be weaned. Eighty-sixed from the milk supply, that dressed up like a secretary and marched out the door, I was left in the company of my cup-drinking sibling and Oma, my German grandmother. Unfamiliar with cows, vitamin D requirements, and life in general, I could draw no parallels between the sleepy elixir I got from Mom and the cold white stuff that wouldn't stay in the cup I couldn't hold.

As a psychologist, Dad agreed with Mom, Spock, my proof-of-the-fact sister, and Freud, that baby bottles were bad. These man-made inventions would only promote later oral dependencies: thumb-sucking, nail-biting, gum-chewing, and chain-smoking. Baby bottles were for suckers, and as low on my parents' list as candy, a word spelled not spoken in our house.

Oma, who lived down the hill and across the dirt road, there on the outskirts of Durham in the early 'fifties, had a more lenient slant on most issues. She figured I was safe from nail-biting and gum-chewing because I had no teeth, chain-smoking because I had no cigarettes. And thumb-sucking, my one vice, would actually be counteracted by introduction to the fake nipple. She smuggled in a baby-bottle of warm milk under her sweater when she came to babysit.

I took a keen liking to this sneaky old lady, and leapt in my high-chair at the sound of her footsteps on the porch. Mom was thrilled at my rapid adjustment to her part-time job, and recommended Dr. Spock to other working mothers in the neighborhood. "But I don't understand," she confided to Oma, "why she won't drink milk in a cup from me. She just cries and spills it on the floor.... She must like being fed by you."

"Yes, I sink so," Oma replied, wishing Mom would take a powder because it was too warm for a sweater. "Zey fire you, you know, if you're late."

Then one day Oma didn't come anymore. Mom stayed home. And to make matters worse, a thirsty little brother arrived. From God knows where. Clearly I was cut off for good and the only thing to do was move out.

"Mother! Mother!" Mom's frantic voice came through Oma's telephone, "I can't find Wendy anywhere. I'm worried sick. I've been searching everywhere and calling her. Where can she be?!"

"Vell, you von't believe zis," Oma bounced me on her knee and I gripped the bottle tighter, "but she came over here."

"But I didn't see you come and get her."

"She came alone."

"That's crazy, she can't walk."

"She didn't valk, she crawled. I sink she love her old Oma very, very much. Her hands and knees were coffered vis blood!"

"She crossed the road? She crawled down that long gravel driveway and crossed that dirt road?"

"I svear to Got in heaven she is right now here vis me!"

"What's she doing?"

"She, uh, she drinks a cup of milk."

"I'll be right there."

I was in no mood to relinquish the hard-earned prize, so it was Oma's turn to panic. Never short of resources, though, or German chocolate, she popped a morsel into my mouth.

And that was the turning point of my life: I discovered religion. Sugar would be my guiding force, and Oma the church where I'd find it. My addiction to my grandmother was regarded by Mom and Dad as a sweet affiliation—they didn't guess how sweet—and everything was divine.

♥ ♥

Littlefield, Ohio, 1957

Then we moved and Oma didn't.
So I turned to crime.

Raisin bread was the best thing you could find in our kitchen. So, at age seven, while wrestling with both the concept of honesty and the sugar blues, as a daily ritual I'd go into the neighborhood drug store and stand in front of the gum machine salivating. When no one was looking, I'd toy with the handle to no avail, or stare scientifically into the coin slot to invent a method for recycling those idle pennies inside. My primal impulse was to bash the glass bubble, grab all the gum I could, and make for the door. But how could I? So I'd go home, giving the gum machine a last longing look over my shoulder.

One day I gave the machine an 'I'll be right back' look and ran all the way home. "Do we have any cardboard?" I asked my mother, with a trace of urgency. She gave me a square of cardboard that looked just about right. "Mommy, can I borrow a penny, just a penny, I'll give it right back to you, I'm not gonna buy gum?"

"Okay," she agreed, without the usual song and dance, and handed me the penny.

"And a pencil? And a scissors?"

"Here you go." She gave me all the tools. "What're you making?"

"Money." I hated to blow it like that, but she'd be watching for sure as long as I had the big scissors.

"Oh," she said. Then, to my amazement, she walked away.

"What a great mother," I thought. The upside to having avant-guard parents was that they believed their high ideals were transferred by association to their off-spring.

The cardboard was perfect, the same thickness as the penny. I was joyous, thinking about gum, how good it tastes. I traced the penny onto the cardboard, making row upon row of new money, then tackled the laborious cutting. My thumb was killing me, but I needed the capital. When I was done, I decided to hold onto the real penny a little longer just to have some cash on me if I got busted. Putting the fresh counterfeit into a little purse, I set out.

Nobody ever noticed me in that shop, but still I had to be careful. I walked casually in and nonchalantly over to the machine, as always. Even more nonchalantly. I made sure my back was between their eyes and the coin slot—in case they suddenly took interest—and inserted a cardboard penny. It fit fine. I turned the knob. It turned fine. It went all the way around, and I was tasting victory… but no gum came out. And after a full revolution, the cardboard penny was still there. So I tried a different slug. Same problem. "Then they're not thick enough maybe," I thought, "even though they look thick enough." And I squished in another one on top of the first, making one real fat penny, and turned the knob again. It didn't turn as easily this time so I used both hands and turned with all my might. It went about halfway around and then got stuck. Then, no matter how hard I tried to turn it, it wouldn't go either way.

The combination of frustration and temptation finally got the better of me and I decided I'd brave the wrath of my mother later for one piece of gum now. (Addiction trumps honesty.) Anyway, maybe she'd forget about the loan. I went over to the man behind the counter and said in an annoyed voice, "Someone put fake money in the gum machine, and now I can't get any gum." I held up my real penny meaningfully.

"Did they?" He smiled and walked with me over to the machine, "Let's take a look." Sure enough, someone had definitely jammed cardboard money into the coin slot. He tried to turn the knob, and he couldn't do it either. So he gave a mighty thrust, and with a rattle and a shake, the knob turned. But so did something else. The man and I both stood back wide-eyed as a waterfall of gum came showering out the hole like confetti, spilling all over the floor and rolling in every direction.

"Oh my goodness," I said.

Finally it stopped. The machine was empty. "Well, well," said the man, looking at the mess. Then he looked at me, still standing there with my penny. I may have been foaming at the mouth. "You can have the gum if you want."

"I can?" I had to control my ecstasy. "It's not too dirty, is it?" I asked in such a way that forced him to say, "No, I don't think so."

"I'll get a box for you," he added, and disappeared.

I was dumbfounded. My ship had come in. How had such wickedness been so richly rewarded? Ah, proof that my religion worked—you just gotta believe! The man returned with a shoe-box that I wasted no time filling. Then I thanked him, made a remark about how dumb can a person be to think cardboard money would work, and headed home, stopping every five steps to admire and sample my hoard.

At home, I went straight to my room and carefully hid the ten-year stash, then went to find Mom. "Here's your penny," I gave it back to her.

"Did you buy anything with the money you made?" She was smiling, but I couldn't tell whether she was serious.

"No. Crumb. It didn't work."

$$

In second grade, two things happened.

One: Our entire family (now numbering five kids with teeth and one without) visited the dentist. "I've never seen children with such beautiful teeth," the dentist was genuinely impressed (a mother's finest moment). "Four of them have absolutely perfect sets, not a single cavity."

"Only four?" Mom raised an eyebrow.

"Yes, it's inexplicable…your second daughter has twenty-four cavities." I spent the next few months under tight surveillance and under the influence of Novocaine, while my nickel-a-week was reduced to a penny that went straight to a savings account to prevent tooth decay.

Two: Judy Wilson. Even on lock-down, I had to support my habit. I would've bettered my counterfeit technique had I not met Judy Wilson. I could tell by her Tootsie Rolls at lunchtime that we were going to be friends.

Judy led the privileged existence of having a working mother—her kitchen was unsupervised after school. And her mother believed in cookies. But not as many as me and Judy, so we accidentally broke Judy's sister's piggy bank and took our business to the candy store. It was so wonderful to walk out with a bagful of heaven that we agreed to set aside a portion of each day for reverent replenishment of our blood sugar. The following day we tackled my sister's piggy bank, then raced back to our place of worship.

When my sister, Cara, spied her hog half empty, she reported the theft to local authorities downstairs. It was then decreed that I would have no more association with a) money, and b) Judy's bad influence (her mother was divorced). Judy could still come to my house, for peanut butter sandwiches and general guidance, but I couldn't go to hers. And, from now on, my sister would handle all school-related expenses on my behalf, until the dentist verified I'd changed my ways. A loyal friend, Judy stomached the whole wheat bread and apples like a trooper, but we were both cold turkey.

It was Judy's mother, ironically, who finally came up with a permanent solution to not only the immediate problem but a host of future ones. One evening, Judy and her mother went to a carnival. "Wait for me right here by this game booth," Mrs. Wilson said. "I'll be right back."

"Okay, Mommy. Where're you going?"

"Just to the ladies' room, dear," she turned to go. "And don't steal any pens."

"What pens?" Judy wondered, shocked at the warning—she would never dream of stealing outside the family. She turned to see a jar of brightly colored pens on the counter beside her and promptly stole one. No one saw her do it, no one would ever miss it, and no one would ever catch her. She showed it to me the next day and we studied it and each other as the impact of the simple accomplishment blew the doors off the eighth commandment. And from that moment, money lost all significance.

I could comprehend the torture of the dentist's drill: though my baby teeth were going to fall out anyway, I deserved the pain, or something like that. And I tried to understand other punishments like piano lessons. But Sunday school was beyond me. The pancakes before it were righteous, the roast beef and gravy later were manageable, but sitting in a pew (who thought up that name?) and 'offering' precious nickels and dimes were against my religion. "Anyone can be like Jesus," I whined to Mom, "but who wants to? It's no fun."

Mom replied that there was great enjoyment in being good and that maybe if I tried harder I'd understand what she meant.

But I couldn't think of a single good behavior that would lead to high adventure or candy, and neither could Judy. We'd seriously considered it before her mother taught us to steal. So by the time our filching operations were getting streamlined, our rationalizations were pretty smooth, too: stealing was fun and therefore good because goodness was bad because it was boring. So life became exciting and Sunday ordeals were at least neutralized by Aunt Jemima.

I grew adept at my craft. And though Judy Wilson and Littlefield, Ohio were in my wake by age nine, America was bursting at the seams with candy counters and willing apprentices. Everything took a back seat to my chosen walk of life. Teachers echoed my mother, "You could be such a good student if you'd just try harder."

"Anybody can be a good student. Being a good student is boring." Anyway, you don't need math if you don't need money. After school was when I came to life; that's when I was committed and ingenious.

- 2 -

Up the Island, Up the River

Long Island, 1961

Adolescence started making demands along with my hypoglycemia, so I let my fingers do the walking in the Five and Ten, trying my luck with nail polish, mascara, and flowered bathing caps (the rage). Though previously an enemy and even a Christian, my older sister, Cara, was now in my club—she couldn't get bathing caps any other way, they cost five dollars.

There was no end in sight. The world was literally at my fingertips. Though dishonest about where I'd been, and generally dodgy with my parents, I appeared somewhat normal. Except at dinner. "I'm not hungry," I'd insist, seizing the opportunity to be truthful. I was skinny and nervous like any substance-abuser and filled to the larynx with Mars bars, but my parents just wrote me off as the runt of the litter, and held discreet meetings regarding whether or not I'd 'make it.' I didn't enjoy worrying them, though, nor a two-hour stalemate with a portion of peas contracted to leave the table inside my body. Luckily, Freud, our dog, wasn't fussy and knew his place under the table. About mid-meal, he'd nose my knee and I'd dumb-waiter the veggies to him. "What about dessert?" one might well ask. Answer: dessert was spelled not eaten in our house.

Aside from poor Cara, I'd also managed to corrupt a new friend who lived next-door. And my mother's casual observation one afternoon, "I wonder what that police car's doing in the Fontinis' driveway," had me and Cara feverishly packing for Australia. A phone call followed, that we listened to from our hide-out. Cara was reminding me through tears that it was my fault, and I was silently explaining to Jesus that I hadn't really meant He was boring, and that I knew the nickels and dimes on my father's bureau didn't belong to me and that they should be earned by ironing shirts. I told Him I'd give Him fifty cents next Sunday if He could please forget that I gave two Parcheesi pieces last week. As Mom and Dad called our names, we tried to summon the lies we'd rehearsed for if we ever got caught.

Our parents were basically heartbroken. Their two eldest children, the ones most familiar with lofty life principles, had turned out to be two-bit larcenists. They calmly refrained from eliminating us, opting instead for the humiliation method. We each had to send a dollar in an envelope to all the stores we'd stolen candy from and five dollars to the Five and Ten for the bathing caps. In each envelope, we were to enclose a note. So places like the A & P got anonymous contributions with blunt explanations, "For The Candy," "For The Bathing Cap." We were ironing for weeks, the family never looked so pressed before or since. The punishment was meant to cure us permanently. And it might have had we stayed in that small town.

Up the Island, 1962

I wasn't really a hardened criminal, just couldn't live within my means. Now, suddenly we were surrounded by shopping centers. Twelve years old and surrounded by shopping centers? All of thirteen, Cara moved on to grown-up sports like beer-drinking, but I didn't have a choice...I had to get my daily fix, and it takes time to get established as a babysitter. So roving from mall to mall, I was able to resume my Hershey's diet without missing a beat. In fact, this new turf was proving quite fertile.

As expected, Cara again came 'round to my viewpoint...when I refused to share my frosty lipstick. And we were just branching into 45's (records, not guns) and accessories when we had another unfortunate run-in. A librarian-like woman approached me in Woolworth's one afternoon and politely asked if I was shopping or shoplifting. She was hardly the type to confide in, so I said, "Shopping."

"Then where's that pink nail polish you had in your hand?"

"I put it back."

"Show it to me." I led her to the stand and pointed to another nail polish like the one in my handbag. "Let me look in your purse," she said firmly.

Who was this character anyway? A fellow thief had recently told me that it was illegal for a store to search your personal belongings, and the only way to catch you was as you were actually walking out the door with the goods. "No," I said to the lady.

"Your two friends have already admitted to shoplifting," the old prune nodded to where Cara and our friend Belinda were standing sheepishly, with assorted cosmetics in their lunch-hooks.

Great. Oh well, at least we were in it together.

Mom and Dad were less diplomatic this time. We were grounded forever. My dreams were shot. Imagine sailing around the world in your *bedroom*. Imagine Rhett Butler ever finding you in your *bedroom*....

The redeeming thing about parents, though, is that they forget. And of course baby-sitting was allowed, so we became proficient at diaper-changing, and before I perished of glucose deprivation, things returned to normal. I just avoided Woolworth's.

Didn't avoid Macy's though, or Abraham & Strauss. I give them full credit for my "best dressed" award senior year. Those places were like closets to me, I'd stop in sometimes just to change clothes. Everything I had was technically theirs, so it wasn't far-fetched to exchange old goods for new. Stealing clothes wasn't easy, but no other suburban pastime affected the adrenalin so directly—this was before glue-sniffing—so we had to stick with it, heed its calling...or get pregnant. In a word, the only way to stay a good kid was to be a bad kid. So Belinda and I were rotten to the core, but we looked terrific.

Simply snatching things was risky in department stores, except for small items, but no one had a clue that half the store was being sucked into a black hole marked "fitting rooms." In these unmonitored stalls, it was a numbers game. They'd hand you a plastic

'1' or '2' or '3' as you entered to try on clothes. So we'd snoop around the dressing rooms for stray garments to carry out in place of the ones now in our satchels. Or we'd part with something we were wearing—an old t-shirt stashed between two velvet dresses was Belinda's stroke of genius, or another velvet dress we'd had for a week. Another method of Belinda's, that I never had the patience for, was to spend an evening at home knocking out a batch of 'dresses' (two lengths of fabric sewn together) and smuggle them into the store as wampum. You could pass almost anything under the unassuming nose of a saleslady. "Oh, I'll take them back out to the rack myself," Belinda would beatifically volunteer.

We filched those number cards whenever possible; they were like gold, especially the 1's and 2's—then you could enter the dressing room with four items and exit with one or two. Plastic 3's and 4's, that we ended up with by default, were less useful—even problematic once we got home. "What are all those 3's and 4's in your room?" an observant matriarch might probe.

"The new math, Mom."

There was no down-side to being a shoplifter. Maybe slight peer group wonder and parental concern as to how we financed our expensive tastes, but the lies were as polished as the acquisition techniques.

Up the Island, 1968

Then, just at the age when it might've become awkward to be a rip-off artist (eighteen), lo, stealing became the fashion. Suddenly, institutions like Macy's were "corporate pigs," and the more you could get, the more points for our side. Anything in the hands of "the system" was better off in the hands of us, the love children, the ones with the pure vision of a perfect world.

One late-summer Saturday, I decided to prepare myself for my freshman year of college. Shoeless, braless, and careless, I carried an empty shoulder bag into Abraham & Strauss. Thinking I might be actually using money in college, the first thing I stole was a wallet.

After scoring socks and underwear, I then perused the sportswear section.

When the bag grew heavy, I went out to the car, off-loaded the loot onto the back seat, transferred my ID to the new wallet, then resumed my spree. As the second load became cumbersome, I decided to call it a day, and strolled out. Halfway around in the revolving door, an arm gently gripped mine. "Come with me," said a female voice, and around we went, back into the store.

"What is it?" I asked innocently. Uh-oh, 'up the river,' the place where bad kids from NYC and Long Island were sent, was suddenly looking real…if I even still qualified as a juvenile. At eighteen, it might be the Big House.

"You're amazing," the rather nice woman looked me straight in the face. "I've been watching you."

"What d'you mean?"

She wasn't letting go of my arm. "The clothes," she said, nodding at the recycled A & S shopping bag in my arms.

"Oh……I'll put them back," I offered quickly. Maybe she was as nice as she looked.

"Yes, you'll put it all back…but first you have to go to the office."

"Oh dear." She was steering me toward God knew what tribunal. "I'm really sorry. I know I shouldn't have done it."

"I'm sorry, too," she sympathized. "Now—you have a car, don't you?"

"Yes." (I'd save my lies for 'the office.')

"Let's go out to your car and see if there's anything in it you have stolen from this store."

Oy. "Why don't I just give you back the stuff and we'll let bygones be bygones?"

"I'm sorry, but I'm hired to protect the store. I wouldn't be doing my job if I let you go." At my car, she summarily repossessed the garments, then ushered me and all the booty into a back door, down some hallways, and into a grim anti-room probably affixed to a torture chamber. I then waited as she conversed with a male voice in the doom-room (after requesting I lift up my dress to prove I wasn't layered in lingerie underneath).

Summoned before the boss now, I saw my ex-new clothes stacked and folded on a desk. A not unpleasant man in a suit had itemized them by description and price. Now he was scrutinizing me. "This is quite a heist," he sighed finally. "How'd you do it?"

Fat chance I'd divulge trade secrets. With tears of regret, I explained that I'd never before stolen anything. "And I never would have," I went on, "but the cashier lines are so long in this store.... I was standing on line with a sweater and I was waiting and waiting, and then...I don't know what got into me, but suddenly I just *took* it."

"Well, that explains one sweater. What about the rest?"

"Well, then I...I...I guess I just went crazy."

"I guess you *did*. We've had some real professionals who haven't compared to this." But he could see that I was honest, and when he learned I was only seventeen (though I couldn't find any ID in my wallet), he said he wouldn't take any legal measures. He definitely wanted a word with my parents though. TODAY. "What's your phone number? I'll call them now," he said.

"They're not home," I said truthfully and gratefully.

"When will they be home?"

"Late this afternoon."

"Okay, I want you to tell them what happened and have one of them call me here before closing time today. Since you're a minor, and you've never stolen anything before, I'll leave the matter in their hands. But if they don't call today, I'll have to follow the customary procedures."

"They'll call you. I'll tell them."

Knowing that my parents' measures would be worse than anything ordained by the State of New York was almost as unsettling as having no new clothes. Macy's was on my way home though, so I recovered some of the losses.

But the afternoon was almost over. I phoned Belinda with my bleak tale and asked her advice. "Disappear," was her solution. And if a better idea didn't materialize *fast*, I might have to.

"Hello, this is Mrs. Raebeck. I'm calling about the, uh, shoplifting incident earlier today."

"Hello, Mrs. Raebeck. Thank you for calling. I assume your daughter told you what happened."

"Yes, I'm shocked. I am so sorry. And humiliated.... I really don't know how to apologize for her. I'm very disappointed. I had no idea she would ever do such a thing."

"Well, she said it was the first time."

"How do we know it was the first time?"

"Kids sometimes do these things. I don't think it's anything to get too worried about."

"I'm extremely upset. I must be giving her too much freedom. I'll have to punish her severely."

"Don't be too hard on her, Mrs. Raebeck. She's very sorry, you know; and she's really a nice girl. She's not at all like the usual type of person we pick up for shoplifting. I'm sure she'll never do it again."

"Well, I don't know." A long pause. "It's so very disappointing."

"I think she's learned her lesson. Don't be too hard on her."

"Well...thank you for being so understanding. I'll think about it. But please do accept my most sincere apologies."

Belinda was the only one who ever knew that I imitated my mother's voice.

- 3 -

Space in the Heart

Eastern Long Island, summer 1968

The sea was wide and high, the beach white and personal. I didn't need anybody. I was as essential as the land and ocean. It was ripe August, the sky was cool, the sun hot. My skin was dark and felt coarse and grainy like the sand. It belonged, it absorbed the salt water like food. My hair hung in uncombed scraggles, blonde from the sun. My nose was peeling. I lay on the frayed red towel of recent summers, in the worn red suit that was a trusty friend.

Around me and in the water were surfers, friends. One called Fatty, who wasn't fat, and Gene, were my pals there. We had fun, but they couldn't figure out why I was a virgin. The summer was flying past. We worked in restaurants and bars, danced at night, and spent our days on the beach.

That afternoon was a hum, no one coming or going, just being there wet against the burning sand. I was lying alone on my stomach, idly watching two shepherd dogs playing. Behind them sat a group of people. Someone from the cluster got up and came toward me. The white shepherd dropped everything to follow, and they arrived together and sat down. "My name is Jonah Rosa," the guy said, "and this is my dog, Sassafras."

I looked up into a pair of yellow sunglasses, pointless for the beach, and behind them two deep round eyes, direct and dark. The face was unusual, Mediterranean, not that of a surfer.

"Oh," I said. He stayed a few minutes, chatting lightly, then went back. I remained somewhat aloof since he was older and didn't really fit the jams-and-surfboard theme of the summer of 'sixty-eight.

I worked in a diner from five to midnight. So did Frances, my good friend. Everyone stopped in late at night because it never closed. Everyone including this Jonah, who even invited me to come listen to his band after work (playing guitar was his driving force). But watching musicians practice held little appeal to dancing fools like me and Frances; ten minutes of that was all we could handle. And this Jonah guy was too serious.

May 1969

In May of 1969, my amazing mother died. Though I'd had to hoodwink her since babyhood, I cherished her beyond words, respected her, and knew she was right about most things. And though she over-estimated my honesty, and gave me more freedom than I could wholesomely handle, and though she had shortcomings of her own, she was witty and brilliant, forgiving, ever-present, and devoted like the sky is to the earth. For better or worse, she was there for us. We were her life, and she was ours. Her heart had no boundaries, her lights were always on, and she never showed her pain.

And though I could never convince her of the value of chocolate, that issue shrank to nothing beside the vacuum of her death. The world was empty. And there was no answer, no solace, no fixes of any kind.

Time, I was told, was my only hope, but I didn't believe it. So I floundered in endless space. The floor beneath me was paper. And everything I said or did that appeared to be ordinary—like walking down the street or driving to a store—was a pretense. I wasn't with the living, I was with the dead.

But each member of our family would continue because we had to…. We needed each other as we never had before.

♥

July 1969

I was slaving away to save money because in October I was going to set sail. As a college sophomore, I'd been accepted by Semester at Sea, a floating school heading to seventeen countries. I waitressed myself into a frenzy, serving snacks and cocktails at a cabaret theater from five to midnight then dashing next door to the diner—struggling into my white dress in transit—to serve burgers from midnight to seven a.m. All the theater-goers bee-lined straight for the diner after the show, so of course I'd wait on them again. Being a waitress was bad enough, but sequential humiliation? "What do you really do?" patrons plagued me endlessly, suggesting I was already failing at life mere moments past my nineteenth birthday.

"I'm REALLY a waitress," I'd say. Or sometimes I'd pretend to be twins.

At seven in the morning, I'd stumble out of the diner and often drive right to the beach, struggling into my bathing suit in transit. At the early empty beach, I'd collapse against a dune and sleep till noon, then ride waves till it was show-time again.

Eddie Sherman was a perennial bartender who kept tabs on everybody. He was a gossip column, a rumor on the rocks. He loved the girls but they never fell for him—the chubby carrot-top in the cartoons. He was too red-haired, his glasses too round. Keen and outrageous though, he knew the latest scandal before even the participants, and it was his pleasure to inform the world at the top of his lungs, when the bar was shoulder-to-shoulder with scandalees. I liked Eddie.

On a rare night off, Frances and I strolled into Smitty's. It was late August, late night. Frances saw a boyfriend on the porch and sat down. I meandered in toward the bar. "Ah-ha! Just the little girl for my plan!" cackled Eddie. Everyone turned as I distrustfully approached. He then confided the scheme to me and the entire alehouse. "Do you remember Jonah Rosa?"

"Jonah Rosa? ...No."

"You don't remember him? Well he remembers you. Didn't you meet at the beach? Plays guitar, international playboy, Spanish gypsy?"

"Wait a minute…I think I know who you mean." (The Spanish-gypsy-playboy part had not been my interpretation.) "Does he wear yellow sunglasses?"

"You got it. Rides a motorcycle, handsome, beautiful—"

"I know who you mean."

"Anyway, he's back. And he's looking for a skinny little blonde-haired creature just like you. Or preferably a few years younger."

"Send him over to my father's house. My sisters are fourteen and fifteen."

"No, you'll suffice. He's staying at my house, so I told him I'd bring you over for him."

"Oh charming, Eddie. Well, I'm not interested. You have to arrange his social life for him?"

"He was here earlier, but got tired and went home to sleep. He just came in from Spain today. Maybe he'll take you with him next time. You'll make the perfect pair—I can't wait."

"Eddie, you're ridiculous." I went out to the porch.

Abe was sitting on the steps. He lived at Eddie's, too. He was a big guy, who ate a dozen eggs for breakfast with a pound of bacon and two Entenmann's cakes for dessert. Always wore a cowboy hat. Lying at his feet was a white shepherd dog who looked up as I sat down. "That's Sassafras," said Abe.

"Sassafras? Oh, that's Jonah's dog."

"That's my dog," Abe said possessively.

"Was he ever Jonah's dog?"

"Never was Jonah's dog, always was my dog. Right, Sass?" The dog raised an ear. "Oh, they hang out together—Jonah likes to think Sass is his dog, but Sass is my doggy, right, boy?" Sass raised an ear.

Frances had left with her boyfriend and it was getting late. I made a 'ready to move on' gesture and Abe said, "Don't you want to come over and help us with this?" he pulled a thick joint from his shirt pocket. "Jonah brought some great hash back from Ibiza."

"Well, I'd like to, but Eddie's trying to match me up with him and I know he'll make a scene, so I better skip it."

"Well, I just came from the house and Jonah's sound asleep upstairs."

"Oh yeah? Are you sure?"

The Voice then quaked the night, "Is Wendy still out there? She didn't escape, did she?" Eddie appeared in the lit doorway, "So you're gonna come? I knew you couldn't resist. Jonah always gets what he wants."

"Abe says Jonah's asleep, so it may be safe to stop in for a quick smoke."

"He won't be sleeping for long," Eddie raised his eyebrows twice, then went to clean up the bar.

I looked hesitantly at Abe. "Eddie won't wake him up," he assured me. "And Jonah's out cold."

Abe and I arrived first. The house was quiet. We poured some wine and put on a record. Eddie appeared shortly, then to my horror, tornadoed up the stairs calling Jonah's name. Too late to flee, I could only hope for the best. But Eddie soon descended in defeat—Jonah wouldn't get up. "This whole thing is in your imagination," I said to him, relieved.

Next day I woke late in the splendor of my bedroom. The sky was blue, so I went down to the beach near home. John, a friend from the previous summer, met me there, and we lay in the sand as the afternoon rolled past. Gazing toward the parking lot hours later, I saw a familiar red jeep pull up. Out of it jumped Eddie, who'd never been to this beach in his life. "Oh no," I shuttered. Then out the other side hopped Jonah. "Oh no-o."

I was momentarily comforted as they walked the other way toward the hot-dog stand. But once armed with food, they spun around and began scanning the beach. We were over to one side, but Eddie's piercing peepers plucked me out of the panorama, and the two marched in our direction. They'd shy away at the sight of John, I figured.

But for Eddie, John was added incentive. "Well, well, well," the town-crier called from afar, "what a coincidence! Look who's here— Little Wendy Raebeck." They arrived to tower above us. "Wendy, I'd like you to meet Jonah Rosa."

I looked at Jonah, still sporting the sunflower shades, and he at me. "We've met," I said. "This is John." Jonah plopped down onto the sand as though we'd been waiting for him.

Eddie spotted Frances and my delicious sisters, and trotted off to harass them as John and I regarded this unsummoned arrival, now in no rush to leave our cool company. "Don't yellow sunglasses sort of defeat the purpose?" I asked.

"They're great on bikes at night," was Jonah's reply. "You can see much more."

With no discomposure, it took only minutes for him to ignite a conversation about how what you've been through takes you up to where you are, drawing diagrams in the sand to illustrate the philosophical journey. And he somehow managed to hold us where his finger met the sand, emphasizing a power of the moment. His talk of travel became transient and even poetic. John and I were allured into his revelations, where life seemed vital and immediate. And where everyday thought was compelling, and everything belonged. Spinning a web around himself, he didn't seem to care where he was or who he was talking to.

He didn't stop, and we didn't really want him to. And eventually we reached a level, as in a climb. A smile all around. Jonah went in for a swim, then came back up the sand, wet and shivering. His body had a rightness about it—proportion and strong leanness. I noticed a long scar, an old one, running down his abdomen. Then he lay back down in the warm sand on his stomach.

In the background, all the lovelies were readying to go home now. Eddie, too, was picking up his towel. "Jonah," he called across the beach, "I'm leaving." He cast a proud match-maker wink at me behind Jonah's back as he strolled by with the girls.

"Can you drive me home later?" Jonah asked me.

"Okay." We were friends now.

Jonah, John, and I locked back into our session. So far the conversation had been triangular and fair. Sensing a common essence, every word expanded as we spoke. Jonah's mind had begun to feel earthy and familiar to me. I knew the place he spoke from and felt barefoot in his discoveries, grasping his meaning almost too soon.

Now the sun was going down. "Let's all go to my house," I suggested.

John and I both had cars, so Jonah came in mine.

"Do you want a shower?" I offered them back at the house.

"Love one," said Jonah.

"I really have to go," John said. Now it was awkward. I pointed Jonah toward the shower, then turned to John. "I'm sorry you have to go." We were both surprised by Jonah's staying power.

I took a shower myself then found Jonah in the kitchen, eating cookies with Mimi and Lily, and listening to the latter's exposition on the shortcomings of contemporary education. She was fourteen, earnest in what she considered her dilemma, and accurate in her observations. And Jonah was telling them about Siddhartha, the way Siddhartha learned. He'd recently read the book. "It was the first book I ever read," he said. "I always thought reading was a waste of time until someone gave me that book. Now I want to read everything."

"How old are you?" Lily asked in astonishment.

"Twenty-six."

"Didn't you have to read books in high school?"

"I didn't bother; I knew I wasn't long for the place. My parents sent me to a tight-ass boarding school in Colorado because I was too much trouble at home. One morning I woke up—fresh snow on the Rockies, beautiful powder—I put my skis over my shoulder and walked straight out of there. I wanted to ski. I didn't need books. I didn't need teachers. The mountains could teach me everything I needed to know. My parents went insane when they heard I disappeared, but they couldn't get me to go back. So, *finito la musica.*"

- 4 -

Jonah

Fall 1969

In the wake of my mother's death, I was lost at sea, searching for beams from any and all lighthouses....

Jonah was interesting, but older and not really connected to this beachy world of ours. His parents had a house here, but he was parachuting in from somewhere else, who knew where.

The morning after he crashed my date with John, a vehicle came blazing into the family driveway. With six relations plus two resident friends, one never knew who would next appear. I approached the screen door for a look, as that eager red Jeep came to a sharp stop and out bounced Jonah.

I stepped onto the porch as he sprang up the steps holding a slim paperback book. Like passing the stick in a relay race, he thrust it into my hands. "I don't want to see you again till you've read this."

I regarded the cover, 'Siddhartha, by Hermann Hesse.' I looked up, but, mission complete, Jonah was on his way. The jeep backed out, going for the gold, and I noted that the book was at least a short one.

Intrigued by both Hermann and Jonah, and not due at work till five, I rolled my assignment into my red towel and walked down to the beach. Scouting out a secluded dune, I hunkered in for a long read. What was it Jonah needed me to know?

As the sun glazed from east to west, I journeyed from west to east—to India, where I walked the soulful path of Siddhartha, an affirmative, fresh look into awareness and connection to source. Was I reading about Jonah, too? That spirituality mattered to him enhanced his profile. As bright and robust as my surfer friends were, the Far East for them was the Far East end of Long Island.

Jonah was slim, agile, restless, and excitable. He smoked un-filtered cigarettes, rode motorcycles, and was ever alert and poised for take-off. According to Eddie Sherman, who knew 'everything,' nobody was good enough for the guy. He was the privileged, ol-ive-skinned off-shoot of a renowned Spanish actor, and he held the keys to Europe.

In the other corner, we have this saucy nineteen-year-old ready for the universe, but grieving her mother's death. She's had one lover (two months ago). Then here comes this outsider, seven years older, who mocks the ordinary, seeks the extraordinary, and seems to say, "Come with me."

After adjusting to the fact that he didn't have a surfboard, I no-ticed Jonah was kind of cute. Not beach-y or collegiate, but a ramblin' musician with Mediterranean spice, round brown eyes, and a fetch-ing smile sparingly used.

The guys around town this summer were in no position to sweep someone off her feet—they had to finish college and show up at their summer jobs. Jonah, meanwhile, having denounced even high school, was sweeping double-time. When he showed up, the competition was more or less vaporized. Plus they all had to leave for school and Jonah didn't. He waited for me to take the bait.

Since initially he wasn't even my type, I remained guarded. But one night as we stood face to face in a doorway of Eddie's house, I let it go. Then everything that had happened before meeting him faded and my life seemed to start over....

But he was leaving for Mexico the next day, and from there he'd be in New York City, then Spain, then Austria. So, for me, the physi-cal part would have to wait. Emotionally, though, we both crossed the line. Something big and new and undeniable had selected us, signed us up for something together.

The next morning I woke before he did. He'd given me his winter address in Austria the night before, and my ship would be sailing in that direction. Now he was sleeping and I left him that way.

I continued waitressing for my shipboard tuition. It would be worth every penny to visit seventeen different countries while getting college credit. I had only one more month of burgers and juke boxes and wishing I was paid by the mile. At least it was September, and stunning beach days evened out the smoky, tip-counting nights. I could have worried and wondered about Jonah, but he was under my skin. Even when Eddie told me he was back in New York, and he hadn't come out to Long Island but only asked about me, I knew he loved me. I didn't need to second guess him.

Eddie was now gloating. But possibly concerned a little, too. He knew he'd fed me to the lions—I may be Jonah's physical type, but I was scarcely 19; Jonah, 27, had been around the block many times.

Mid-October the ship sailed from New York City. Crystal night of acute goodbyes. A sad family saw me off—one more leaving at a bad time. But there was renewal for me—I was off to see the world. And Jonah. The ship would be in Venice, Italy in a month—that would be the closest it would get to Jonah's Austrian Alps.

After stops in Istanbul and Greece, it was dawn when we languidly drifted into the unreal Venice mist. The morning was exquisite, like tears, and the fog still clung lightly as the city inched towards us. I'd been up for hours and stood on the deck squinting at the floating city, searching the water's edge for the place we'd dock. It was seven a.m., November, crisp, chilly, European, and exactly where I wanted to be.

In a 500-foot ocean liner, docking is a delicate operation, particularly in a city below sea level. As I leaned out over the railing, gazing at the liquid mystery vista and the people on the quay down below, suddenly I saw Jonah, who saw me at the same moment, neither of us quite believing it. We hadn't made a plan to meet.

"Get the hell off that boat!" he shouted.

In orderly fashion, students were lining up for their passports to disembark, as a teacher supervised the exodus. Involuntarily, I grabbed his coat, "I've got to get off first! I'll go crazy if I have to wait on this line." A few friends in the know vouched for my sincerity and the teacher transplanted me in front as the ship's big doors cranked opened. Walking steadily down the gangplank toward the waiting crowd, I didn't look right or left, but as my foot touched shore, two arms pulled me into them and Jonah was spinning me around and around. I was gone forever, lost in the middle of the world with him. Somewhere, somehow, we were there together. It could've been any-where. There was nothing but the two of us. Spinning around and around.

But it happened to be Venice, so we hopped in a gondola. He happened to have a Jeep and I happened to have a week, so we left shortly for Austria where he was spending the winter, impatiently waiting for ski season.

We drove for hours and hours into the night. The Jeep had no windows and no heat, so the snow and black night gushed in, but we couldn't care. We laughed about everything, not believing life could be so fine. "I can't believe you were standing there," I said for the tenth time.

"You should've known I'd be there," he replied for the tenth time. And, of course, secretly...I had known.

The two months hadn't mattered, we were deliriously in sync. This was as good as it gets. "I wouldn't care if the Jeep fell off a cliff right now," I told him. (And there was reason to fear it with him at the wheel.)

"I would care only because you might get hurt," he answered.

"But, I mean, death.... I wouldn't mind dying right now. It wouldn't matter at all. It might even feel good."

"Yes, it might even feel great."

We laughed.

We now had a week. A precious week of total us and anywhere our hearts took us. We were willing to risk everything. We had to, now that we'd met. And especially now that we'd found each other in a better place still. This week would cushion us and let us find out....

But it was scary. We had yet to make love. He had yet to realize how young I was; I had to learn he wasn't perfect. He had to find out that I wasn't going to stay, that I'd go back to the ship. I had to discover his pain about his art, his music. And we both had to grapple with the concept of needing someone.

He told me he needed me, and it wasn't until years later that I understood the level. I really didn't need him there and then, just to know he loved me. Just having him in my life gave me the widest expansion I'd ever felt, a freedom like flight that, strangely, offered me independence. It was like he'd given me wings— But he didn't understand. And I didn't understand that the seven years he had on me made him more ready. I was just being born and, with him in it, the world seemed so good.

We made love once that week, the first night. We tried again a time or two but it was strained. He told me he'd had stomach cancer that had spread, and I touched his scar and felt where it went all the way down. He said it was no big deal, luckily didn't affect his fertility. We dared not speak very much, and became overly sensitive, even estranged. Eventually we became silent, distant with each other, and took to writing notes. When we walked in the mountains, we talked only with our eyes and listened to the hills—all was positive, clean, and in harmony up there. When I did venture to speak, almost by mistake, it seemed like an echo of what we'd already wordlessly acknowledged; the mention of something almost implying a lack of trust. So we gave up words, and the affirmation soared. Until it was time to do something like cook or wash our clothes; then the poetry crumbled and we were spastic. There were no dirty clothes on our mountain and we didn't want to come down to do chores. Each self-reliant, we were clumsy with joint effort.

He then gave me a room of my own, saying the landlady frowned on her guests having guests. The room was good for escaping his intensity, but took us further apart. Scribbled prose came under my door, but I didn't know what to do about it. The days were being used up, the nights long, and our few words too abstract.... He seemed too old for me, knew more than me, yet he swore his love was open-ended. "You can always come back to me," he said more than once, "even with a husband and kids."

But that comment, however well-intended, rolled over in my mind.... Aside from being an unusual and unlikely premise, and even despite its 'unconditional' implications, it bore fatalistic undertones. Jonah wasn't saying, "I'll love you forever, no matter what," (also grandiose, but at least in the ballpark of lover speak), he was saying, "After we fail miserably, I'll still have feelings for you." There was no way around that interpretation…because if I've got a different husband (and kids), Jonah and I obviously bit the dust as a couple. (And why would I return to him?)

At the time, I surely asked, "What do you mean?" or "Why are you even thinking like that?"

To which he, no doubt, replied something like, "I just wanted you to know that." (Explanations weren't his forte.) But I never understood that remark, that somehow linked failed love and endless love, and that paired resilience with futility.…

Jonah grew up on skis, had walked from grade school directly to the slopes, pausing for a miserable year or two of high school. Now nine years had passed since he'd skied and this was the winter to make up for it. I had skied a total of five times. But Jonah spoke of nothing but snow, and watched out the window for the first flakes of the season. They didn't come. At times he even imagined them, "It's snowing! Come look!"

I'd look out expectantly. "Jonah, it's not snowing. It's not doing anything."

"It isn't?" he'd squint harder. "Are you sure? I thought I saw some flakes. Oh well. But as soon as we DO see snow, we put on our skis!"

"I don't have any skis. Or ski clothes. But it's not snowing so no problem."

"It's not no problem because it must be snowing somewhere. And we have a car. We gotta get you ready." He took me into the village and suited me up in a down jacket and mittens. Skis we could rent, pants were borrowed. I was set.

"But Jonah…I don't know how to ski." And I had a suspicion that these early arrivals ambling about town, looking constantly skyward, reading the stratocumulus like horoscopes, could. "This isn't my league, Jonah." We were standing side by side in our outfits before the mirror, a daily ceremony he insisted on. I looked like a joker in the red stretch pants lent from the elderly landlady. He looked pretty slick. "Thank God it's not snowing," I thought.

"It's REALLY snowing!" Jonah proclaimed one morning, gushing through the door after stepping out for cigarettes.

"No it's not," I said defensively and peeped out the window. "There's not a flake in sight."

"It's snowing at Kaprun."

"What's Kaprun?"

"Kaprun's a mountain that's higher than the others and it's snowing up there right now! Someone just told me. Let's go."

"Let's think about this for a minute first. This is a big mountain?"

"The biggest."

"This is the biggest mountain in the neighborhood, this is an Austrian neighborhood, and this is where we're *starting*?"

"Listen, it's not so bad, you know why?"

I did not.

"Because it's flat on top. It's like a glacier, and there's great snow up there, and we have to go anyway because it's the only place that has snow."

"How do you know it's flat on top like a glacier? Have you been there?'

"No, but trust me."

"Is there a lodge?"

"There's a lodge. But you're not going anywhere near the lodge. You're going to ski and get crazy and love it. It's not a serious slope." With my skiing ability, his carpeted floor was a serious slope. By this time, though, he was nearly dressed, and tossing long underwear across the room to me.

It was a forty-five minute drive winding around the valleys that were blanketed in fog. We couldn't even see the mountains, but there was no question as to their presence. I was gravely solemn, trying in vain to enjoy my last hour of life, lamenting that recent off-the-cuff death wish. Oh well, at least I was with him. And talking about snow—a multi-dimensional topic that could last days—was a reassuring switch from the silence.

We were getting close. Other cars and Jeeps outfitted with skis were appearing on the morning road. This crowd was serious. Their faces were serious. I looked at Jonah driving. He was serious. I was in serious trouble. We arrived at a parking lot where an assemblage of Olympians in expensive paraphernalia was unloading even more expensive equipment from their not-so-inexpensive vehicles. "Where's the mountain?" my quivering voice was muffled in the mist encasing us.

"It's up there," said Jonah, nodding toward the low white ceiling, while happily pulling the skis from the Jeep. I didn't know where we were going but we moved along with everyone else until we came to a cable car that was loading up. And I do mean up. The electric lines that would carry it into the firmament shot up at a ninety degree angle—an outdoor elevator, basically. I envisioned myself skiing at two hundred miles an hour down the razor face of a granite cliff.

There was a hush in the cable car as it ascended. I counted the passengers and there were forty in all standing tightly inside the clouds. Nothing could be seen outside. This was a far cry from the T-bar. We slid smoothly skyward. Maybe I could get straight to the Pearly Gates without having to stop off and die. Finally we landed—still nothing but clouds surrounding us, and no snow on the ground, if vertical stone walls are considered the ground.

"Jonah?"

"Look up."

Above us another perpendicular electric line vanished into the cotton. And a second cable car broke the whiteness as it descended to collect us. This ride afforded more of a view. We lifted out of the clouds and could see the rocky mountain sliding past. Patches of snow decorated and half-concealed the palisades. Still not a sound from our fellow ski-enthusiasts, as the probability of a cable car disaster upstaged the certain decapitation I expected later. We landed again. I hadn't glimpsed one inch of ski-able terrain, nothing even this-worldly.

"Jonah?" I was starting to squeak.

"Look up."

"Oh God." Another one. Mount Everest. We crowded in with the brightly-colored herd. Far from Planet Earth now, I expected to lose gravity shortly. Jonah was now jumping up and down excitedly, to the horror of the multitude. "Jonah, please. Don't rock the boat." This third cable car moved gracefully heavenward finally affording a view of real snow, and skiers below whizzing south. The cliffs were less threatening up here, the skiers adroitly avoiding them. I decided to adroitly avoid the whole experience. "Where do you catch the cable car back down?" I asked my ecstatic companion.

"You don't. You have to ski down to where we picked up the third car."

"What if I can't ski?"

"Listen, I haven't skied for nine bloody years; you're not the only one having cardiac arrest right now."

"Well, seriously, what are we going to do?"

He thought for a moment. "We'll play it by fear."

The car landed at the entrance to the lodge. Skiers bundled straight over to the benches to hurriedly attach their skis. Alternatives were few—slipping out the back would involve a chilly slide all the way to Northern Italy. "Bowl of soup," said Jonah, brilliantly. "Definitely time for a bowl of soup."

"I'll have ten bowls, please, and six cups of hot chocolate."

We ate our soup s-l-o-w-l-y. Finally we finished and both felt like crying. After several trips to the john, there was really little else to do up there. Time to join the choir invisible.

The lodge was teeny, teetering precariously on the top of the pointed mountain (not a glacier in sight). It had a tiny staircase that hooked it to the beginning of the "slope." From the bottom stair, would-be skiers were expected to leap out into the frozen whiteness, find their balance in mid air, maybe do a double flip, then breeze fancily down that first precipice to where it leveled off farther below. There one could adjust one's goggles, apply ChapStick, or in my case await the Red Cross.

All zipped up, mittened, capped, and weak in the knees, we hesitated on that bottom step, looking straight down upon a jagged, white, Alpine universe. Impatient skiers were piling up behind us. In a tight spot now, a few looks of terror passed between us. There was nothing at all to do but abandon all sanity and kamikaze through the frozen air out into the void then down, down, down to…our deaths.

"Do whatever I do!" Jonah cried out suddenly.

Putting both skis over one shoulder, he sat down, took a huge breath, then plopped off the bottom stair and slid down the sharp descent on his backside. At the base of that first ninety degree incline was a better place to start. I slid down behind him and we lay in the snow laughing as passing experts dusted us with powder.

Kaprun was supposedly a twenty minute run. It took me three hours on my stomach. Every now and then I would hear a "whoosh" and there would be Jonah, light and breezy, making up for the last decade in one day. Then he'd vanish again into the gauze, leaving me to my swear words and runaway skis.

Till now, falling off the world had been the least of my worries… but, as the hours passed, since I couldn't go up the slope, I made gradual, perilous progress down. The wide open spaces were fair game, because I could crash-land anywhere, but there were other hazardous little links surrounded by craggy nastiness. I came to a channel of sorts, slanting dangerously down and twisting violently right and left. I could either take off my skis and walk it—simply not done in the Alps—or wing it. I winged it, head first into the snow, only to horizontal myself directly across the path, blocking all passage. "Oh well," I was mortified, "just get up, put my skis back on and struggle along." I wrangled into a getting-up position, tottered momentarily, and rolled onto my other side. It was then I noticed a breathless string of blond, blue-eyed men clad in matching scarlet ski suits with yellow piping. They waited for me to roll one way or the other, but please clear the path. I couldn't bear the thought of erecting myself publicly only for a follow-up face-plant, so I flashed them a tortured smile and squirmed, worm-fashion, out of their way. That's when I spied the insignias on their jackets: "Austrian Ski Team." A dozen of the world's most physically perfect men passed me. Whoosh! Whoosh! Whoosh! Whoosh! Whoosh! Whoosh! "I bet they're real dumb," I muttered to the snow.

The following day I did the run in two hours and twenty minutes. Then, thank God, the snow melted.

Jonah and I had one more day together then I had to meet the boat down in Naples. He never actually asked me to stay, but as I packed to leave, he said, "If you loved me, you'd forget about the ship." This campus afloat had cost me a summer of waitressing and a bundle of cash. The ports ahead included Spain, North and West Africa, a south Atlantic crossing to Brazil, Argentina, then south to Cape Horn and back up through the Straights of Magellan to Chile, Peru, Mexico, and finally LA No one of sound mind would forgo a voyage like that.

I didn't know what was to become of us, but I believed. Jonah drove me to the Munich airport. Approaching the terminal, he said, "I want to tell you now that as soon as I say goodbye, I'm leaving. I don't like long goodbyes, so I won't be standing around watching you go." He grew increasingly restless as we got closer to the gate, then quickly hugged and kissed me. When I turned for a final look, he was gone.

- 5 -

To Spain or Not to Spain

February 1970

There wasn't much contact as my ship moved farther and farther from his mountains. I sent letters and presents, received stories and declarations of love, and then nothing. I waited. Two ports without news from him made me feel he'd evaporated. Aware of his mobility, for the next few weeks I could only wonder where he was. Then, in Lima, came a telegram.

> I WANT YOU TO KNOW I HURT.
> I WANT YOU TO KNOW IT'S EGO.
> I WANT YOU TO KNOW I LOVE YOU.

I had no clue what that meant, but it was a communication, he was alive. Still in Austria. All I knew was that I desperately needed his spirit and support. He'd freed me by showing me his freedom—I knew everything was possible by the way he lived his life. Even the pain I saw in him seemed to echo right choices he'd made. He inspired me and his life moved mine.

I stood on the pier in Los Angeles, my shipboard semester complete. I had nothing scheduled for the rest of my life. But this time no Jonah. He hadn't written, and I didn't know his plans now that spring was arriving. The west coast was new to me. Friends from the ship were going to stay in a house in Laguna Beach, so I went along. It was great to be on dry land. Guess I'd stay in California a while, maybe get a job.

A week after settling in, the phone rang early one morning. "What are you doing?" came Jonah's voice. (He'd learned my whereabouts by calling my home number.)

"Living here, checking it out. Where are you?"

"New York."

"Come here," I said.

"Okay."

"On second thought, I'll come there. I need to see my family. And I have to get some things at home. Then maybe we'll come back here together?"

"Okay, I'm waiting for you." He gave me the phone number of the apartment where he was staying in New York City. "Call me when you get here."

"Righty-o," I jotted down the number, "but it will be a while because I'm walking."

"What?"

"Well, I don't know how I'm going to get there, but I'll leave today."

"Call me when you get here. I'm waiting."

"Jonah, I love you."

"Me too."

"Well, looks like I'm leaving," I told my friends.

"You know," someone said, "Tommy's leaving today. He's getting one of those drive-a-cars. Maybe he can take you."

"Where's he going?"

"Pennsylvania. Call him."

I contacted Tommy, another shipboard student, just in time. "I'm getting the car this morning, then I'll come pick you up," he said agreeably. "I'm only allowed to take one extra passenger and now I've got three, but who cares?" Two hours later, Tommy pulled into the driveway.

"Holy shit," someone said, looking out the window, as I gathered my belongings.

Tommy marched in grinning, "They didn't tell me it was going to be a mobile home."

Tommy, Merle, Jerry, and I set out in the largest, state-of-the-art mobile home in existence. We'd be delivering it to a dealer in Erie, Pennsylvania—we didn't expect such a piece of crap. Barreling luxuriously to Route 66, then heading for Needles, Arizona, every possible thing went wrong with the vehicle, and all we could do was pay the repair bills and call 'Max,' our LA connection, to report the on-going bad news. After a couple of days, nothing seemed to work at all, the thing wouldn't even start. We couldn't find the battery, that had died, and neither could the few mechanics we managed to locate in the middle of the desert.

"Okay," said Max over the phone, "I'll come out there and check it out myself." We were scarcely into Arizona, meaning he'd be there in a few hours, so two of us had to vanish. Merle and I were the stowaways, so we volunteered. Arranging to rendezvous with the others "at the next Denny's on Route 66, wherever it may be," we hitched east under the hot sun. Fifty miles later, a Denny's appeared like a mirage, and we holed up there with coffee and good faith. About two a.m., the "fixed" mobile unit ambled in. The battery had been unearthed beneath the shower stall, and Max had thus returned to LA.

With so many delays already, we voted it would be nuts to pass right by the Grand Canyon without a look-see. So five days after departing Los Angeles, we were still in Arizona, now catching the sunrise over the Painted Dessert. Our faulty ride was moaning and ailing every ten miles so the sightseeing was curtailed by stopovers at every garage we came to, together with exasperating phone negotiations with Max, who thought the problem was us, not the vehicle. Then, not exactly disproving him, we pulled into a station with a low overhang, just for gas, and crashed off the skylight. (What a lemon.)

Due to all the cash we'd laid out for the mobile home, we were now down to one sketchy credit card. So Tommy, Merle, and I resorted to villainy (Jerry had been dropped off by then), acquiring our meals cheaply and cautiously at grocery stores whenever we approached a state line. We reasoned we wouldn't be chased over the line if caught in the act. Merle was hesitant about shoplifting, but I paid forward the coaching of Judy Wilson's mother, and he became invaluable.

A full seven days from LA, only halfway to New York, we reached dawning Oklahoma City. I thought I'd best give Jonah a heads-up to convey my earnest intentions. Dialing the number I'd scribbled, I waited for an answer in sleeping New York.

"Hullo?" an unenthusiastic female voice roused itself. Who was this?

"I'm sorry to bother you at this hour. Is Jonah there, please?"

"Who?"

"Jonah? Jonah Rosa?"

"Nobody here by that name. No Jonah."

I asked her if I had the correct number, and curiously, I did, but she'd never heard of him. For lack of an alternative, I tried the number again. The same woman was less than receptive, "If he wasn't here two minutes ago, lady, why would he walk in at five a.m.? I told you I don't know the guy." I climbed morosely back into the RV; there was no other way on Earth to trace Jonah. I was in touch with none his Long Island friends, who were all gone till summer anyway. And the only other person I knew in Manhattan was Oma. Jonah's parents had an apartment there, but they were in Spain; and he'd been banished from their place anyway.

So...now why was I going to New York if I wouldn't be seeing Jonah?

Moving northeast toward Madison, Wisconsin, Merle's depot, I set to work on the problem (no longer food, the fridge was stuffed). "I must've written the number wrong," I concluded after a meditation, and told the guys, "because Jonah wouldn't have given me the wrong number.... This means that I HEARD it right, and the correct number is in my brain somewhere, all I have to do is access it...."

"That's all you have to do," Tommy chuckled.

Yeah, that could take a little time.... But upon reaching Ohio, I concluded that the Case of the Incorrect Number might not be so complex, most likely a simple switching of two digits. But which two?

With no other recourse, I was forced to tap my intuition. For the first time, I took out the crinkled morsel of paper that preserved my written error. Looking at it as though from far away, I entrusted my third eye to ascertain which two numbers needed to change places. Then with curious confidence, I asked Tommy to stop at the next pay phone.

I dialed the reconfigured number. "Hello?" a different lady answered.

"Is there by any chance someone there named Jonah Rosa?"

"No..." she said slowly, and the disappointment coiled in, "no, Jonah's in California."

"What? But this IS where he— Where did you say he is?"

"He went to the Coast. Want the number where he's staying out there?"

"Oh, Jesus. When did he go out there?"

"Couple days ago." She gave me a number that I scrupulously notated.

"Just in case I don't connect with him," I said, realizing that in two days he could've circled the globe, "if you talk to him, could you please tell him Wendy called?"

"Does he have your number?"

"No, but there's no number."

Hanging up, I asked Tommy, "What the bloody fucking hell is he fucking doing in California?"

"Maybe he's looking for you."

"He could've saved me a long trip by sharing his itinerary." I dialed the LA number.

A girl answered. Just what I needed. "Is Jonah there, please?"

"Just a minute. Who's calling?"

Who was this woman in LA? (And who was the woman in New York?) "It's Wendy."

Then Jonah's voice, "Where the fuck are you?"

"Fucking Ohio. What are you doing in California?"

"You first, what're you fucking doing in goddamn fucking Ohio?"

"I'm trying to get to New York. To see you. But it looks like I'm going the wrong way."

"Where will you be tomorrow?"

"New York…. Where will you be?"

"New York," he made one of his half-second decisions.

"See you there," I said. "Call me at my father's when you get in. I'll pick you up."

"Perfect."

"Jonah?"

"Yup."

"Tomorrow's Valentine's Day. Will you be my Valentine?"

"Baby, I been your Valentine since the day I was born."

♥

New York. I arrived. The winter house felt funny. The family still crippled, but now awkwardly accommodating my father's 'girl-friend.' Mom had only been gone nine months. Hushed tones, as siblings unveiled opposing viewpoints on the prospects of "a more permanent relationship."

The new order worked, but tragically. Little sisters cooking and food shopping. The family was stronger, sweeter, more sensitive to each other, kinder than before; but our family as a family—craziness, madness, singing, dancing—was over. The albums stayed in their jackets.

The place was misty, but we could only cry like that, all together in the living room, once or twice. Then we had to start the new life. One by one, each of the seven survivors found their thread, a lead out. Our mutual neediness had to be resolved by each one independently.

So I returned to a termination. A crushed family, fighting for its life.

Then, just hours later, the impact of Jonah.

I saw him across the JFK terminal. The walk, the guitar case, the energy. We walked about a quarter of a mile toward each other, looking into what we were going to do next, what we were going to do about…us. Now there was no boat taking me away, no snow making him stay.

Just my red VW moving us along the Long Island Expressway. And the silence again. We had made love once. But the intimacy was still between us like a promise.

So we tried to be together. In the next few days, he waited for me to grow up fast, to become a sensual, responding woman, need him, take care of him. And I waited for him to talk to me, to communicate his vision of us, to laugh and play a little. I was nineteen— and grief-stricken. I had no future plan at all. But my hesitancy and loss for words he interpreted as coldness, my inexperience as detachment. My behavior didn't indicate the loyalty or intimacy a young woman should want. After three days of long looks, short talks, and not making love, Jonah came to the abrupt conclusion that our love was Unsuccessful. "Take me to the City," he ordered.

"I'm not driving you in. You can take the train if that's the way you want it."

"There won't be a train till tomorrow and I'm leaving now."

"You have to go this precise minute?" It was midnight and we were an hour and a half from New York.

"Look…it's not going to work. We're a million miles apart."

"You are! It's you. You're not doing anything. You're the one who's detached!"

"Take me to the City."

I realized the night could only get worse. Not knowing whether he was a spoiled brat or whether his immediacy was vital, I drove him in. Assuming this was our last ninety minutes, I delivered a heavy monologue that more than made up for the silences. I attacked his philosophy—what I knew of it—from every angle, and ended with, "What's the point of talking and thinking and loving someone, of trying at all, if suddenly after three days you're going to say 'Take me to the City'?"

"Are you through?"

"I don't know." I was disillusioned by his hardness, bewildered to see he didn't have answers for me, and sad to learn that his spiritual prowess didn't transfer to practical realms. Now I was dropping him off at a strange apartment with that same telephone number he'd originally given me. We said a goodbye that wanted serious separate time.

I wasn't going to push him. I would wait to see the change. I went back home, got a job, started saving money and reflecting on my ex-life gasping ghost-like from all sides. My loving mother's absence, combined with a failed first love were a heavy load. Some days I would drive out to the Hamptons where a winter cluster of summer friends waited for spring in the late night bars. Cara, my older sister, was a folk-singer in one of them. I'd listen, smile at the gossip and warm up by the fire, but I was only there for news of Jonah. These people were in and out of the City and some knew him.

One night Eddie Sherman remarked off-handedly, "I hear Jonah's going back to Spain."

"Who told you?"

"He did. I saw him in New York."

"When's he going?"

"Didn't you know? He said real soon."

"No, I haven't seen him in a while. But I want to before he goes." It had been six weeks.

"Don't tell me you've become yet another Rosa victim. I mean you fit the physical mold, but you're the only one who got as far as Austria. I was hoping he had come to his senses."

"Yeah, me too."

"Well, you better hurry if you want to catch him. He might be gone already."

Would he go without saying goodbye?

I rang the next day. "Jonah, it's me."

"Where are you?"

"Home…. I hear you're off to Spain."

"Yup."

"When're you leaving?"

"Couple of days…. I was going to call you before I left. How've you been?"

"Not bad," was all I could muster.

"Why don't you come and see me before I leave?"

"Well…." Loss of words…he was disappearing again.

"I want to see you. Come."

The power he had over me was hazardous to my health. "Okay. When?"

"Now."

"Tonight?"

"Tonight."

"Where will I stay?"

"Your grandmother's. Angie won't let me have anybody staying here. She's well, I'll tell you about her later.... She's a little uptight. Are you coming?"

"I'll come. It will be a few hours though."

"Call me when you get here, whatever time it is. I'll be waiting."

Damn him. I packed a few things and left. When I hit town I called him and he told me to come to this mysterious apartment, where he was living with, or being taken care of by, his brother's wife's mother—a sharp-shooter of fifty-five who didn't come out of her bedroom when I unhappily arrived. It was three a.m. but I heard her talking on the telephone.

Jonah and I sat in the dark living room, occasionally lit by Third Avenue fire engines. "Do you want to come to Spain and live with me?" he asked.

"I don't know."

"A little house, a car, that's what I want. I'm ready for that. Do you know what I mean? I've never had that. Are you ready for that?"

I didn't answer.

"You're not ready for that. I can tell by looking at you. Do you want to come anyway? Tell me if you want to come. I'm buying."

"You're not ready either. You'll last a week in your Castilian suburb."

"You're probably right," he had to smile. "But at least I'm going to try. It's time. Man, it's overdue. And you should see this fuckin' place. You'd fuckin' die. You get a donkey, you live like a saint on top of the village, take in the whole Mediterranean, little winding roads, no noise. You have a well and candles—that's all you need. At night you have the moon, full moon parties, the stars, and music. But fuck you...."

"Jonah, I want to be with you. If you're definitely going to Spain, then I guess I am too. Ideally though, I'm not in the mood to go live on the edge of a cliff somewhere playing house till the cows come home. What would we do in Spain day in and day out?"

"LIVE. Fuck our brains out. Swim in the summer. Play music… You're definitely not ready, woman," he looked at me pitifully. "But I'll take you with me if you want to come. Want to come? I want you to come."

"Do you love me?" I asked incredulously.

"Of course I love you. I'm offering you a first fucking class ticket. You don't want to go?" Pause. "Fuck yourself, I'll take someone else!"

"Exactly, Jonah. That's exactly what I figured you'd do. Fuck you. Creep. Take Angie. I wouldn't go as far as Kennedy Airport with you."

"You better go as far as the fucking airport, woman. The least you can do is take me to the plane."

"I've done a lot for you, you know. You probably don't even realize. Now…do you want me to come with you or not? And why first class?"

"Only the best for you, lady love," he smirked. "Let's think about it for a day. Go to your grandmother's now and come back tomorrow."

"Listen, if you really want me to come, I will. But I can't come in two days. Give me six weeks to pull it together and I'll join you over there. Go and figure out exactly where this romantic interlude is fated to take place, get your little house and your car, send me your address and I'll knock upon your door."

"Our door."

"…and I'll knock upon our door."

"What do you need six weeks for?"

"I'd have to keep my job a little longer so I'd have some money over there."

"Oh yeah, because that's really important work you're doing. You're carrying a lot of weight, you're NEEDED. More than I need you. Frankly, I think you've really hit on something. I think you should hold on tight to a demanding, challenging position like that."

I was a Foto-mate at Fotomat.

"Jonah, you're really a horrible person. Do you think I like wearing that little outfit? We can't all have trust funds. I have to make money, and no one's buying my 'art.'"

"What's your art?"

"My dreams."

"Listen, you don't have to worry about money. I told you a long time ago that as long as I have money, you have money."

I pulled one of my pockets inside out.

That prompted him to pull a wad of hundreds out of his.

"Well, guess what, Jonah, I don't trust you. How do you like that?"

"I don't like it at all. In fact I like it even less than you think. You're all fucked up. Listen, go to your grandmother's. There's no more to say. You wear me out, woman."

"What about a kiss?"

"One kiss."

Every time I saw him, I left his company in emotional chaos. I had no idea what was going on—he was simply a magnet that pulled me around the world. Somehow or other, I had decided the feeling was love, but it was setting a strange precedent—that true love was only pain, no pleasure or comfort or peace ever. I called it love, but it was agony.

The next morning, after breakfast, we resumed our negotiations. This time I was granted the courtesy of an introduction to this Angie, who was pleasant if not hospitable, and indeed motherly. Jonah had now confided that he was having "a scene" with her, but didn't elaborate. In a glance I resolved that if he was having a scene with her, it was his problem, Freudian or otherwise, and left him to it.

"You're just not ready for Spain, or for me, so you better stay in America where you belong," Jonah commenced.

"Thank you."

"No, I didn't mean it that way," he lied. "Listen, I'll go over, look around for a place to live on the mainland—I'm not going to Ibiza this time, too fuckin' crowded. Well, I might just drop in to say hello, but then I'm gettin' the hell out before summer—and then I'll let you know where I am and whether it would be good for you to come and join me. And you stay here, continue in your chosen field, improve your craft as a Foto-mate, and think it over. It's a tough decision, I realize, deciding whether to live in sunny Spain among the almond trees by the sea with someone taking care of you, or to go sit in a frozen booth in the parking lot of a Long Island shopping center every day dressed like a kangaroo, earning just enough to keep you alive and scared and going back for more. Good for you, you're doing just great. You're out of your fuckin' banana. Will you take me to the airport?"

"Yes, Jonah, I'll take you to Grand Forks, North Dakota, don't you understand? I'm literally at your disposal."

"Yes, I do understand, and I love you for it."

"Fuck you."

"No, I'll fuck you!" and he grabbed me and we went rolling across the shag carpet of Angie's living room to the sound of her phone voice in the next room.

I took him to the airport, so that he could continue HIS chosen professions...vagabonding about the Mediterranean, philanthropically distributing his wisdom, achieving fame as a lady-killer, streamlining the art of expensive spontaneity, and educating himself through his open pores. Driving along the murky highway to Kennedy, we were flip-flopping again about whether I should join him in Spain.

"I better go alone," he said at last. "I'll write to you."

I took a breather. "You know, Jonah, it makes me feel so much better. I'm not ready. I'm just not ready. I feel like I've just started my life. I can't go seal it up now on some romantic precipice. I have too much to do. I don't know what, but I can't stop the momentum right now."

"I love you," he said, and meant it that time.

We found his terminal. He bought a ticket, one way of course, with his parents' credit card, and I walked him to the gate. We didn't speak. At the gate he hugged me quickly, then patted me on the head, "Well, have fun. Sleep around a lot. And I'll see ya."

Six weeks later, when spring still hadn't come to Long Island, but my bank account at least was offering some alternatives, a post card arrived from the gypsy:

"The first is ? The second is how are you and the therd is that
    Im not going to be staying in Ibiza because its to crowded.
I will write you soon again -
    write to me to me in Madrid I'll be there in May
Love Jonah Ibiza has been good to me"

"Fuck him," I thought. My sister Cara and I were ripe for some hot sun, so we threw a little vacation plan together and next morning put out our thumbs. She had to be back for a singing gig in exactly one week, so we needed to make excellent time. We thought the Bahamas might be nice.

- 6 -

Sailing South

"When I settle down, I want to travel more."
~ Sister Mimi

We were moving right along, traveling light, and were just outside D.C. waiting for our next ride when we suddenly found ourselves in the back seat of a police car heading for the station. Our unfriendly chauffeur told us that hitching was illegal. "Where are you coming from?" he wanted to know.

"Long Island."

"Oh, runaways. Where are you going?"

"We're not running away. We're going to...Virginia Beach." Didn't want to upset him further.

"Do your parents know where you are?"

"Our father does."

"Well, we'll just have to call him up, won't we, and make sure he knows." At the cop shop, he instantly got on the phone and our father answered. "Uh, I've got your two daughters here, in Washington, D.C. Picked 'em up out on the highway hitch-hiking. They say they're going to Virginia Beach.... To the what? ...The Bahamas? So, you, uh, so you don't, uh.... Well, I guess if you don't— Well, okay, Mr. Raebeck, thank you very much." He took a long look at us. "Well, um, I'm just going to take you two girls back to the highway. You're not runaways," he confirmed. "But I want to make it clear that hitch-hiking is illegal, and it's against the law to do it." Back in the car, he drove to the exact spot where he'd found us, deposited us there with a final warning not to hitch, and zoomed off.

There wasn't much else to do by the side of the freeway with cars whizzing by at seventy miles per hour. So we resumed the journey as planned, spent the next night in the barracks of an army base in North Carolina, and hit Fort Lauderdale the third day. There, we went straight to the first travel bureau and bought plane tickets to the island of Nassau for thirteen dollars each. This was an extravagant cash outlay, but well worth it when we got an eyeful of the Caribbean waters below. We didn't know where we'd stay, had no intention of paying for a room, but decided not to worry. It would only be dusk when we landed, there'd be ample time to scope out the scene.

We found lodging on a boat in Nassau's harbor. But after only two days, Cara had to get home for her Friday night gig. I'd warned her at the onset that I'd probably stay in the islands, so she departed solo (and actually made it to her performance).

Meanwhile, I arranged to head south as a mate on a sailboat. The vessel's owner was an American called Buddy who welcomed me aboard for as long as I wanted. He and a peculiar couple were off to Puerto Rico via the Exuma Islands that run south from Nassau.

The couple consisted of a round man with the world's thinnest wife, aptly named Slim. She was the cook, and not a bad one considering our supplies—Spam, sardines, soggy Ritz crackers, or any combination thereof, three times a day. Slim would dish out meals—'sandwiches' of Ritz crackers with Spam or sardines on them— onto four plates. On her own there would be maybe one 'sandwich,' or just a single Ritz cracker, or a little blob of Spam. That was her din-din. Breakfast was black coffee, and for lunch maybe a bite of a sardine. One of our principle conversations aboard the 'Four Winds' was Slim's slimness, as we all made attempts to fatten her up and talk her out of her permanent fast. But she just looked on leanly as we grew corpulent from her 'cooking' and lack of exercise. She was slim on purpose, having once lost her head in college and gained fifteen pounds. That excess baggage she'd found so horrific that she soon took off thirty-five just to keep a safe margin. Now she was so pleased with her twenty-pound advantage over regular thin people that she'd made a career of emaciation.

Slim and her husband affectionately named me Spacehead, due to some of my as-yet-unpopular ideas. The hippie movement was still a movement rather than an industry, so one was expected to go to college, go to war, even go to church, and smoke cigarettes not pot. So I was put on the defense. However, my main problem on board was Buddy. He was nice; initially we got along well. He was a skillful sailor and we certainly traveled in and around the most beautiful islands I'd ever seen. But, by his calculations, two men plus two women (or one and a half) equaled two pairs, and I wasn't cooperating. So things became tense, especially at night, early in the morning, throughout the day, and whenever I wore a bathing suit.

He was persistent, and quite inconsiderate inasmuch as no terms had been stipulated, I was just a hitch-hiker. But when he stopped talking to me altogether, I realized the pressure wasn't going away, so probably I should. We reached Great Exuma on the tenth day, where the Out Island Regatta was under full sail. Tired of Spam, my nickname, and Buddy's testiness, I disembarked, leaving the trio to continue to Puerto Rico. (The following Christmas, I actually got a card from Slim, still in Puerto Rico, telling me that I'd been a great inspiration to her and that she no longer wore a bra.)

Great Exuma was the last in the string of atolls; there was nowhere to hitch to from there except far-off islands like Puerto Rico and Jamaica—month-long trips, regardless. After the "Four Winds," I was reluctant to sail off with unattached men, so I moseyed around on the pier a while, then poked my nose into a few of the slick cabin cruisers docked there. Everyone, it seemed, was going back to Nassau since the regatta was ending, so I accepted a ride back on an enormous Chris-Craft with a full crew and no passengers. Safety in numbers. And only a one-night sail.

The operator of this frilly enterprise was Captain Frank, a sixty-year-old who was "fixed for life" because all he had to do was make sure the ship was in good form when the owners took their annual two-week cruise. Otherwise the boat was his, to cruise in wherever his heart desired. He was paid handsomely merely to stay in reasonable proximity of it. So he docked it at Paradise Island back in Nassau, and gambled as much of the salary as he could, still finding himself uncomfortably wealthy. His eyes lit up when he heard I needed a lift. They would be happy to take me along, he said. They'd be leaving tonight at ten and would be back at Paradise Island by morning.

Great. I jumped on board, drank a beer offered by a steward, and proceeded to my designated bunk—only to be awoken, shortly after setting sail, by Captain Frank, who had shipboard romance on his mind. I was shocked—Buddy had been horny, but Captain Frank was a dirty old man! I couldn't believe that even older men wanted to have sex with me.

I flatly and firmly refused. But Captain Frank had assigned himself to the same cabin and, from his bunk across the stateroom, tried every conceivable verbal approach. After about two hours of everything from "I love you" to "I need you" to "I'm going to rape you," he came up with "I'll give you a thousand dollars, no strings attached."

"No, no, no, and no."

"You're not making it easy for me," he said. "Please don't make me embarrass myself."

"Aren't you embarrassed already?"

"You know what I mean," he said then. "Please don't make me do it."

"I don't know what you're talking about and I *don't want to know*."

"You can't leave a man in a situation like this. There's only one thing left for me to do, but it will be very embarrassing for both of us."

"I'm not 'leaving' you in this situation—I was never with you to begin with. I'm hardly going to jump overboard. And whatever embarrassing thing you're about to do, don't. I have now reached my limit with you, and I'm about to get up and go sleep on the couch. Which will really embarrass you in the morning when the crew sees me there."

"Well, what am I supposed to do?"

"Look, I don't care what you do as long as you don't involve me. You've been harassing me for about three hours now and I'm beginning to think there's something seriously wrong with you. If you have to embarrass yourself, embarrass yourself somewhere else." I punctuated my lecture with tears and sighs, mentioned my father, threw in a fiancé, and pointed out my captain's boundless potential for dangerous perversion. Finally he apologized for offending me, for masquerading as a kindly gentleman, and eventually promised me undisturbed sleep.

When I woke in the morning he wasn't there. I went above and there was our Captain, at the helm, his old self again, proudly dressed in his snappy uniform. He had a wonderful breakfast served for me and, as we motored into the port of Nassau, said that he was so sorry and so rich that he was going to give me the thousand dollars anyway because he wanted to prove he was really alright and besides I could use the money, couldn't I?

"No thank you, Captain Frank, it really isn't necessary."

He was feeling guilty though, and despite my refusals wrote out a check for a thousand dollars and handed it to me. I tried to hand it back, but he clenched his fists and stuck them stubbornly behind his back. "Keep it. I'm insisting."

"I don't want your money. You're forgiven. This isn't necessary."

But he wouldn't take it back, so I tore it into four pieces and tossed it into the Caribbean. At this, Captain Frank sadly shook his head, "That was a big mistake."

"You can easily void the check, it doesn't matter."

"No, it doesn't matter at all to me, whether you keep it or rip it up. A thousand dollars doesn't mean anything to me. Whether I give it to you or to the croupier in the casino makes little difference. I've got more money than I know what to do with. But there will be very few times in your life that someone will just hand you that kind of money for nothing. And that money could help you right now. There's going to be a day when you think back to this time and say to yourself, 'Boy was I dumb.' …Do you want me to write you another check?"

"Captain Frank, I appreciate your offer, and, sure, I could use a thousand dollars—who couldn't? But you say the money's for nothing, free money that I shouldn't refuse, and you're wrong—the money's to make me think of you as a nice guy and to forget about last night and remember you as you are now instead. And it's for your conscience, so you can remember me as someone you helped out rather than someone you tried to take advantage of—it's not for nothing. But it's not necessary because you've already shown me you're sorry. I accept your apology and I think we're friends now, aren't we? Besides, you also gave me a ride back here. And don't worry about me hitching around without much money—I'm doing what I want to be doing. I'm content. I'll get by."

I'd been away a month now and all I could think about was whether there was a letter from Jonah back home. It was early May, ideal time for the Hamptons.

Captain Frank set me up with another fancy ride back to Florida. A friend of his named Forty was leaving in a few days for Fort Lauderdale. "But…" Captain Frank warned Forty loudly, "I want her treated like a lady, like a first class passenger. Don't even talk to her unless she talks to you first." Despite the Captain Frank experience, I trusted Forty and accepted the lift.

When we got to Fort Lauderdale, Forty said the yacht would be docked there for a few days. He and the crew were leaving, but I should feel free to use it as base camp if I was staying around.

- 7 -

Flying North

May 1970

I walked to the ocean front and sat down at 'Lum's' for a coffee. I hated Fort Lauderdale and had to get out of there. Spring and the letter were surely waiting for me if I could just get back. But those long highways had even less appeal than Lauderdale. Oh, for a plane ticket....

A flamboyant young black man with a huge Afro at the next table started up a conversation with me, the typical traveling questions—where ya from, where ya been, where ya stayin'? In lieu of answers, I returned the questions. His name was Bernardo, he was a hairdresser from New York, and he was going back tonight.

"Flying?"

He was.

"Want to help me?"

His eyes brightened and he leaned forward. I told of my plan to stow away, and he said he'd love to be of assistance, got all excited about it, in fact. The Jimi Hendrix motif made him a less-than-ideal front man, but Bernardo had miraculously been delivered to me and I wasn't about to look a gift accomplice in the mouth.

"Ever done this before?" he asked.

"No."

We agreed to meet at the airport a little ahead of time. Then he regarded my battered, size eighty jeans, size ninety t-shirt, and bare feet. "Are you going dressed like that?"

"No way. I have to look spiffy so I'm not suspect." Though traveling light, I wasn't without makeup, a pair of heels, and other decoys for just these occasions. Returning to the boat, I transformed radically, then hitched out to the airport.

Bernardo was standing where he said he'd be. He watched my approach, surprised when I stopped beside him.

"Ready?" I asked.

"Oh, it's you!" he stared. "Wow. I can't believe it. You look really...different."

"Everything good to go?"

"Yeah, everything's fine, just fine," he approved of the renovation.

I had only two small bags—the scheme wouldn't have been possible if I'd had to check luggage. Now all I had to do was somehow get onto the plane. Fortunately, it wasn't a large airport, and in 1970, boarding passes hadn't been invented. Still, there was a guy by the exit door checking tickets before letting passengers walk out to the plane. An empty ticket folder, that I could flash at him, would probably work, so I scored one at the ticket counter. But we then saw that this guy was dutifully checking inside each folder for actual tickets. On the other hand, he was so absorbed in his task that I could possibly sneak out a side door and rejoin the line outside, where the people were filing onto the plane. Dressed like this, I could play the 'confused' blonde if anyone noticed and questioned me.

I synchronized this side-stepping with Bernardo getting his ticket checked; he would engage the guy by asking extraneous questions as I slid into the line outside.

So far so good.... We stepped into the plane and were just passing the greeting flight attendant when Bernardo, to my astonishment, took her aside and quietly confided, "You be careful 'cause you got a hitch-hiker on board. Understand? Just dig it."

The stewardess nodded and politely smiled as though another whack-job was run-of-the-mill. Concealing my horror, I moved quickly down the aisle behind Bernardo. Arriving at his seat, he cheerily tossed his case into the overhead compartment. "Bernardo," I whispered, *"why'd you say that?!"*

"Because that's what's happening and I want her to know so she don't say anything to anybody. I want her to have full com-pre-hen-sion of the sit-u-a-tion."

"Well, I don't want her to have ANY comprehension of the situation. Don't mention it to anybody else, okay?" Jesus.

The plane was fairly crowded but I was able to get a seat next to Bernardo. When passenger count was being taken, I went to the ladies' room, despite reluctance to leave my 'ally' unmonitored. In the restroom, I left the door unlocked so it read 'vacant' on the outside, and hoped no flight attendants would open it to look in. In case one did though, I hid behind the door so as not to be seen. "Please be seated for passenger count," then came over the intercom. I stayed put, holding my breath. And, sure enough, an attendant did open the restroom door. And didn't see me. About five minutes later, the plane slowly started to roll. I stepped out, and looked casually around. All seemed intact, so I retook my seat next to Bernardo.

"Let's order a drink to celebrate," he said, enthusiastically waving his arm toward an attendant. Next time I'd hold auditions for my aide. But as Bernardo ordered two martinis, I wondered why we'd stopped after taxiing instead of taking off. Looking over my shoulder, I saw, to my utmost discomfort, the stewardesses in back recounting passengers. As I slinked down into my seat, the plane did a slow and deliberate u-turn. Simultaneously, the pilot's voice came over the intercom, "We will be returning to the terminal for a few minutes… nothing to be alarmed about, just a matter of paperwork."

Yes, there probably would be some paperwork involved in my five-year sentence. The flight attendants, in a little cluster, were all visually scanning the passengers. When they then started asking to see tickets, I knew my number was up.

"What's the matter?" asked Bernardo, as I got out of my seat. "They don't know it's you."

"They'll find out fast when they ask for my ticket. I don't want to make a scene."

"Wait," he pulled my hand, "they might not catch you."

But I went up to the front where an attendant was alone by the door to the cockpit. "Is the problem that there's one too many passengers on board?" I asked her.

"Why, yes…how did you know?" She was young and seemed nice.

"Because I'm the one."

"You?"

I nodded.

"You don't have a ticket?"

I shook my head.

"How'd you do it?"

"I just snuck past the guy at the gate."

She looked at me for a minute then said, almost apologetically, "Well, I guess I'll tell the pilot that we've straightened out the problem. Wait there a minute."

She disappeared into the cockpit briefly then came out and said, "You're not going to believe this, but while you were out of your seat just now, the other stewardesses recounted and called the pilot to say they'd been mistaken and everything was alright. But it was too late because I'd already told them about you. I'm sorry."

"It's not your fault," I said.

"Listen," she said, "we're almost back at the terminal, so you better get your stuff." We came to a stop and the ground crew rolled the portable staircase up to the plane. I went to my seat for my bags.

"Well, Bernardo, thanks anyway. See you in New York." I didn't bother being annoyed with him.

"Good luck, kid. Sorry it didn't work out."

As I returned to the front, there was a man's face in the round window of the door that was about to be opened for my removal. "Is that the man you snuck past?" the stewardess asked me.

"Yes."

"Well, I'll tell you, that guy's a real bastard. He can be really mean. So if I were you, I'd just run like hell." Her worried look underscored the warning. The door then opened and the man stormed in meaning business. He rushed past us and into the plane in search of someone who looked more the part.

Quick thanks to the stewardess and I fled down the stairs then raced across the tarmac. The man was still on the plane. I didn't go into the terminal but around it to the front parking lot where I crouched in the dark between closely parked cars. There I pondered the issue…. By now, the gate man had surely learned that that unlikely blonde in high heels was not only the stowaway but got away. He'd be looking for me. So, nestled among the warm autos in the tropical night, I slipped off the dress and shoes and let my hair down. I climbed back into the salty jeans and t-shirt, grabbed my bags and crept to the closest ladies' room. There I washed off the Revlon facade and felt safe again—just another commonplace vagrant for which Fort Lauderdale was renowned.

Drugged by the smell of planes, I was still determined to fly. I had sixty dollars but needed sixty more. I went back into the airport and sat on a bench by the ticket counter. From there, I actually watched the gate man searching for me.

As the night trickled past in the tomb-like terminal, occasional men stopped by my bench. (Women took little notice.) "What are you doing?" guys would ask, registering the air of frustration I exuded. Everyone was kind-hearted and offered spare change, or even more generous contributions, but I said no thanks. I wasn't pan-handling really, just kind of being patient. Maybe some super-nice guy—a pilot, a magician, or a minister—would help get my not-for-profit off the ground.

At three a.m., a sleepy intercom voice announced that a flight was leaving for New York. After a futile attempt to talk the ticket agent into a discounted ticket, as his sister or something, I moseyed over to the departure gate. The area was empty and the door to the airfield wide open. I strolled out to the plane and climbed the staircase. A pleasant flight attendant greeted me at the top. The plane was nearly empty.

Too tired for tricks, honesty was my last resort. "I don't have a ticket and I can't afford to buy one, but I sure would like to fly to New York tonight," I said. The stewardess laughed. "Couldn't I just quietly take a seat? I don't have any luggage to check."

"No," she laughed again, "it's completely against the rules."

"Yes, I realize that." If it wasn't against the rules, this world would be altogether different.

"The problem is that someone would have to take responsibility for you, and nobody wants to do that," she told me. "Not that anything would happen to you, but if anything did, if you got sick or passed out or something, and it was revealed that you didn't have a ticket, whoever had let you on the plane would lose their job. If no one knew you were aboard, that would be another thing. But I do know, so I have to say no."

So the big empty plane took off for New York, and I returned to my bench.

Soon, three students drifted over and sat down. One named Tim had just flown in from North Carolina where he'd been expelled from college. The other two had come to collect him.

"Why were you kicked out?" I asked.

"I robbed a candy machine." My kind of guy. "It jammed when I put in a quarter that was attached to a piece of string. I was trying to fix it when the campus cop came along and formally ended my education."

"Total bummer. Did you at least get some free candy?"

"No, they took the candy AND kicked me out of school, can you believe it?" Despite these pressing concerns, he insisted I accept sixty dollars from him because his mother was "loaded" and it wouldn't make any difference to her.

I explained that my situation truly wasn't urgent, that I could easily take a bus but simply didn't want to, and that he had enough to worry about without taking on my case. But Tim was convinced that in the grand scheme of things this sixty bucks would be well employed helping a fellow candy thief, fellow drop-out, and weary wayfarer. So I caught an eight a.m. flight to New York.

There was no letter from Jonah waiting. But about three months later, I did receive a lovely note from Tim, and that very same day, I bumped head on into Bernardo strolling down the street in Southampton.

The Sunday Train to New York

That summer I got clique-y with my two sprouting sisters. With the family in splinters, we were three pieces of flotsam in choppy waters, trying to become a life raft. I wanted to be a supportive older sister, but providing the getaway car was my chief function. Plus imparting age-appropriate romantic data that they thirsted for. Savoring the details of my piece-meal love story, they also comforted my insecurities. We all knew my fairytale wasn't unfolding properly. Jonah and I had never even been to a movie, nor hardly shared a meal.

Meanwhile, I was *really* a waitress again, and wondering if I should just pull the plug on love and go to the University of Hawai`i. I sent for an application.

That summer, it was heartbreakingly clear that my best shot at helping the family stay connected was to stay connected to it. So I lived at home, body-surfed, and commiserated with my siblings, missed our mother, and skirted around 'Nadine,' the way you avoid poison ivy in the woods. Dad's new wife (accompanied by two young sons and a dog) wasn't evil, just had a clear agenda involving our father and our house. And not involving us or our three dogs. So we nine had to scramble; while Dad—key player and only possible link—was now inextricably paired with her. Or else he was off working or weeding the garden, or scolding us for not working or not weeding the garden. Though physically present and heroically durable, he just wasn't on our team anymore.

"What do you think I'm runnin' here, a home for retired teenagers?" he'd shake his head at what appeared to be laziness but what was actually mind-numbing shock over the new order and the rapidity of its installation. (He, too, of course was grappling—now having six kids and two step-kids all between the ages of eleven and twenty, plus four dogs, four cars, and three acres of vegetables.)

So, on a good day, Mimi, Lily, and I would leave the house around noon after lingering over pancakes and coffee. We'd then set out for the bird sanctuary and eagerly unpack the Milanos and diet soda we'd lifted from the local market. When feeling particularly deprived, we'd nab a Sara Lee chocolate cake for dessert. (Sara Lee was our new mother and Pepperidge Farm our new home.) Then we'd hit the beach for the afternoon and a Good Humor ice cream or two, then scoot home in time for dinner where we'd refuse the baked potatoes. "Eat 'em, they're good for you, fresh from the garden," Dad would say.

"We can't, we can't," we'd moan. It was a physical impossibility.

And on a bad day we ate a lot.

Meanwhile where was Jonah? No one in my network seemed to know. "Probably still in Ibiza...or somewhere else," was the general drift.

Eddie Sherman was again tending bar at Smitty's and making people squirm as he bellowed rude questions across the room. "Where's Jonah?" he'd call out every week or so. "Gee, and I thought I'd finally made the perfect match," he'd shake his red head.

One night the phone rang at one a.m. "Guess who's ba-ack...." came Eddie's voice.

"How do you know?"

"Uncle Eddie knows these things."

"No, tell me, Eddie."

"Someone just drove in from the City, said they saw him in Churchill's. And see how considerate I am? I get right on the phone and give you the news flash. So get ready...."

"Thanks, Eddie. You're not so bad after all."

"I thought you might be interested," he snickered.

At eight the next morning, the phone rang and I grabbed it, "Hi Jonah."

"How'd you know?"

"Grapevine."

"Christ, that was fast. I just got in ten o'clock last night. How're you?"

"Fine. How're you?"

"Very very far fuckin' out. It's good to be here. Ibiza was fantastic, crazy, fucked-up, beautiful. Crazy fuckin' place. Had to get out. Good to be here. How are you?"

"I'm fine. I'm really fine." It was good to hear his voice.

"Listen," he said, "uh-h, let's see…I'm going to come out there on the train this afternoon and…I'll call you when I get in."

"Uh, yeah…okay," I answered. What train? Which Hampton was he coming to? Oh well. "You know where to find me," I said.

"Right. Love you. See you later."

"Bye," I hung up limply and sat on the floor for an empty minute. It was too vague.

The phone rang again. I grabbed it so the whole house wouldn't wake up. "Wait a minute," said Jonah, "just wait one fuckin' minute. This isn't the way it's gonna be. I want to see you. Right now. Fuck these fuckin' trains. There's no train till four o'clock. So get in your red Volkswagen and come get me, woman. Fuck the train, come get me. I'm all yours and I'm waiting."

"Okay, where're you gonna be?"

"Meet me at Churchill's."

"Jonah, for you and you only I'll do it. I'll be there at one."

The City was a jungle to me. I never went there except for Jonah eccentricities or to visit my eccentric grandmother—basically abhorred the place. Now I was speeding along on the expressway.

Then I braked for a traffic jam and nothing happened. Terrific. I rolled directly off an exit ramp and into a well-placed gas station as the tin can car died altogether. I wasn't far from the City at that point and called Jonah at Churchill's.

"Get a cab," he said. "Just come straight here, I'll pay for it. Leave your junk heap there and tell 'em to fix it. We'll pick it up tomorrow."

As my cab pulled up to the bar, Jonah came out to meet me. We disappeared into each other's arms. He looked wonderful, a bit decked out a la Ibiza—handicrafted and scented with hashish and European coffee. We walked around in the street for a few minutes, then we tried to have lunch at Churchill's but couldn't eat. There was so much to say, but we couldn't talk. "Come on," he said, "let's go to my parent's place. They're not back from Spain yet, so we can stay there tonight."

When we got there, the doorman said, "Sorry, Jonah, but I'm under strict instructions to keep you out."

"What? What the fuck…they're not even in town."

"Please don't take it personally."

"Well, Jesus Christ. Listen, I'm going up for a few minutes then to make some calls."

"I'm sorry," the doorman held up a firm hand.

"What do you mean? I can't even go INTO the apartment?"

"It's worse than that, you can't even come into the lobby."

"They're nuts, those two people. They're out of their bleeding brains." Then turning to me, "Well, fuck 'em. We'll just go across the street and stay in the George Washington Hotel, see how they like that." Then to the doorman, "'Don't take it personally' my ass."

The G.W. Hotel was as seedy as pie, but Jonah wanted to be in smirking distance of his horrid parents, though they were in Spain. He wanted to make sure the doorman actually saw us check into sleezeville, that he accurately reported to Jonah's parents what their precious son had been reduced to.

In actual fact, it was nice in the hotel room that afternoon. It was clean and quiet, not hot like the rest of the city, and a yellowy light filtered in that was soft and restful. We were tired and tender with each other. This thing had been going on a year now, and we made love for the second time. In the realms of 'I'll do anything for you, go absolutely anywhere,' we were quite advanced. But in the here and now, not so skilled. This day was an exception, and we needed many more like it.

The next morning we picked up the car and made it out to the beach. Jonah's parents had a house there, too, obviously off-limits now, so I dropped him at Abe's.

Abe, Jonah's most loyal and generous friend, now lived in a little house in the woods. He mostly sat in the kitchen and received people like Jonah, Ribcage, and Tapioca. Abe had seen it all, including Eddie's performance as cupid the previous summer, and done a lot more. By trade he was a car thief, a secret known by close friends only. (And said friends drove *nice* cars.)

I was only half an hour into recuperating at home from the draining company of that high-strung crowd, when Jonah phoned pleading, "Come and save me. Ribcage just walked in here with a bullet in his stomach. Get me out of here, I don't have a car." (Abe's only friend that didn't.) I picked him up and took him to the beach. "I don't need that shit, that Ribcage shit," said Jonah. "I been through all that. Those people haven't changed at all." Later he talked me into spending the weekend at Abe's with him as a bodyguard, though I didn't need that Ribcage shit either. We went up to a makeshift bedroom in the attic where we actually made love two more times.

I thought things were maybe shaping up a little, as we went to the beach together the next day at my suggestion and attempted to act like the nifty couple Eddie had engineered. But the silent space had returned: the important things, I knew Jonah already knew, and less important things seemed too trite to mention. We felt pressured to do something extraordinary together, both scared to death of being normal.

Jonah was a natural on guitar, had been playing all his life. "You write the words and I'll write the music," he proposed that afternoon.

"Okay." Partnership and enterprise both appealed to me. Yet what worked for Simon and Garfunkel may not fly for us. "Who's gonna sing?"

"Not me," he winced.

"And not me."

"Well, we'll find someone," he said brightly. "Or maybe we'll learn to sing." He was always ahead of himself and wanted me to be there in his dreams. When I was, he was happy, but when I went back to myself, he lost me and all faith in us. He needed me right there, fully attentive, ready to respond, to be silent, to follow him, or at least take him where he was compelled to go next.

His father was a performer, too—successful, with ego to match—and Jonah couldn't compete with the Big Cheese. The trust fund took the edge off—he didn't necessarily have to 'make it'—but Jonah still grappled with the questions people in their twenties ask themselves. And when answers were sparse, he'd just buy a ticket out of the turmoil, usually to the peace, quiet, and afford-ability of Spain.

"I gotta get back to the City," he said after the weekend. "That's what I came back for, to play music. I gotta get back. I've decided that I'm gonna finally fuckin' learn to read music."

"You mean you can't read music?"

"No, always just played. I been lucky enough to find people who would play with me anyway. But now I gotta learn how to talk about music, have to learn the names of everything I play. Want to come to the City with me?"

"Oh Jonah, I couldn't live in that city. Especially in summer. Maybe in the fall. Are you coming back next weekend?"

"Yeah, I'll call you when I get out on Friday. Can you take me to the station?"

He got on the train. And then he just didn't call again, didn't come out. No one saw him around or heard about him. I was hurt, as usual, but not surprised. Eddie tormented me whenever I went to Smitty's, so I stopped going out altogether.

Six weeks after Jonah's disappearance, Eddie materialized on the beach one day looking for me with the headlines that Jonah had reappeared at Smitty's the previous weekend and asked for me. (Who knew why he so resisted the phone?) And I knew he'd be at Smitty's again the next weekend waiting for me. So I decided to arrive first and wait for him. I was certain he'd show up at precisely ten o'clock Friday night. And as the moment drew near, I stood waiting inside the front door. Seeing me standing by the entrance, Eddie asked what I was doing.

"Waiting for Jonah."

"When's he coming?"

"Ten minutes."

Ten minutes later, Jonah and Abe sauntered in. After a breezy hello, Jonah then proceeded to ignore me so loudly across the room that the whole crowd, spurred on by Eddie, began placing quiet bets as to whether or not we'd leave together. I knew this was Jonah's singular way of showing affection. To show mine, I danced with everyone else. Finally Jonah walked straight over, took me by the arm, and said imperially, "Let's go for a walk." Without a word, he led me out under the trees. As always I had a lot to say but wasn't going to say any of it. I'd let him start.

After a ceremonious moment of silence, he asked, "Are you my princess? I want you to be my princess. I want you to be everywhere with me. I want you to sleep with me, eat with me, stay with me. Will you? Will you be my princess?'

"Yes."

"Starting when?"

"Now."

"This very minute?"

"Yep."

"Okay. Let's go."

We went inside to get my sweater. Eddie was grinning ear to ear, cleaned up on the betting. "See this lady?" Jonah said to him, "She's my princess."

"I know," Eddie said, winking at me, "I picked her out for you, remember?"

We stayed together, and the next day he took me over to see his parents, whom I'd met once before. They had returned and granted temporary amnesty. His mother was one of those dark, elegant, European beauties. Her aura was one of complete grace and hospitality; her eyes sensuous, humorous and all-seeing. His father was a roundish troll with Jonah-eyes, ultimate dominion, little to no comprehension of English, and fair to poor comprehension of his youngest liability. No sooner had Jonah's mother mellifluously produced tea for four when Jonah launched a cascade of complaints to her. "I want her to be my princess and she won't."

"Yes I will," I said nicely.

"Why won't she?" his mother twinkled.

"I don't know, she just won't."

"She says she will."

"She says she will, but she won't. Can't believe a word she says." Everyone was smiling, but I just didn't get it.

After tea, we performed yet another episode of the Sunday Train to New York Departure Series. I wondered if Jonah would be gone a week or a year. "See ya next weekend," he chirped, as though he hadn't missed a Hampton weekend all season.

♥

- *9* -

Spain, Anyone?

The following Thursday morning, as I lay drowsily considering a short stack, there came a knock upon the door followed by Lily's voice, "Siddhartha's downstairs."

Toothbrush in hand, I went down to the kitchen.

"So, I'm going to Europe on Sunday," Jonah said, as though wrapping up a two-hour conversation. "You coming?"

I stopped brushing. "What did you say?"

"Going to Europe on Sunday. Ibiza." Then enunciating, "Are. You. Coming?"

"Uh…" Let's see, did I want to lose him forever right now or lose him forever once we got to Spain? His foot was tapping so I had to make a quick decision. "I don't know."

"Yes or no."

"Let me go finish brushing my teeth."

"Just nod or shake your head," he called after me.

Annoyed, I swallowed the toothpaste and turned back to him, "Are you overdue at the Oval Office?" Then I went upstairs. Friday, Saturday, Sunday…that was three days. Siddhartha downstairs probably filling ashtrays by the dozens, and did I want to go to Spain? Hadn't this happened once before? Hadn't he made this suggestion already? In fact, hadn't he once said he was *taking* me to Spain? And then, the last minute, didn't he go without me? "Uh, Jonah," I called down the stairs, "I'm having déjà-vu up here in the bathroom."

I went back down and poured four coffees. Mimi and Lily weren't going to miss this for the world but politely kept their eyes on their pancakes.

"Yes, I did at one time tell you I'd buy you a ticket to Spain if you'd come, and you said no."

"Bullshit, Jonah, I said yes and then you left without me."

"Bullshit. If you wanted to come you would've come."

"Horseshit. I didn't have any money and you didn't want me to come."

"You coming on Sunday? You're buying this time."

"I'm buying the tickets for both of us? We better choose a nearer island then, how about Coney?"

"You're buying yours…and that's letting you off easy, woman."

I looked at my sisters for support. They were staring wide-eyed at this alien in our kitchen.

"Yes or no?" Jonah put down his cup and headed for the door.

"Where're you going?"

"Well, lady, if you're not coming, I gotta tend to business."

"What, finding my replacement?"

"No, there's only one you, thank God. But I got things to do, so…."

"I AM coming."

"You are?!!" Mimi and Lily were joyous.

"No you're not," said Jonah.

"What're you talking about, Jonah? You ask if I'm coming, I say yes, then you say no?"

"Okay, you're coming? You're definitely going to be on that plane from New York to Ibiza on Sunday?"

"Yes."

"Okay, see you at the airport," he turned again to leave.

"For God's sake, Jonah, what's the problem? It's bad enough you only give me three days to fund-raise and totally reprogram my life, and then you just say, 'Fine, see you at the airport'? How about a flight number? How about a terminal? Or should I just look around for you at JFK? Do you want me to come or not? Because there's a new lifeguard at the Main Beach who isn't too bad." (Total fabrication.)

"If you want to come, I want you to come. I'll find out the wheres and whens and I'll call you," was the first normal statement out of his mouth ever. (And quite possibly the last.) "And if you want to bring your lifeguard, that's fine, too—you might need a life-guard."

When he'd gone, the fans went wild. "Are you really going?!"

"Boy, you two sure are happy. Aren't you gonna miss me? Aren't you going to miss my driver's license? Yeah, looks like I'm going…but don't tell Dad, okay? He won't want me to go. But I'm going. We'll just tell him shortly before I leave so he won't have time to think about it."

By dinner time Saturday night there was a distinct hum in the air that someone was getting ready to go somewhere. As the salad was making its way from hand to hand, twenty hands to be exact, my father opened with, "So, what's this I hear about a trip to Spain?"

Silence all around the table. Sneaky looks circulating. "Pass the salad please," I requested, seeing it would take a while to get around the table. Maybe someone would change the subject.

"Looks like rain," Mimi nodded toward the golden sunset in the window.

"Someone going to Spain?" my father asked again, as though for the first time.

"Spain anybody?" my brother Sonny offered, as if there was some delicious Spain in one of the pots.

The angle of my father's head discouraged another wisecrack.

"Will the real Spaniard please stand up," Cara whispered to me.

"Yeah, Dad, I'm going."

"You're just going to Spain, you're not going to ask me if you can go to Spain?"

"Nope."

"Oh." Then the sound of ten forks resuming the meal. Then a pause. "Would you care to elaborate at all about this trip you've so firmly and independently decided to take?"

"Sure…. I'm going with Jonah. Tomorrow."

"Is Jonah buying you a ticket?"

"Oma said she'd give me five hundred dollars. The ticket's two fifty."

"That's not what I meant."

"Oh."

"I just want to know if he is taking responsibility for you, or is this something you want to be responsible for yourself?"

"Well I just turned TWENTY, Dad."

"And?"

"Well, I don't *want* to be responsible for it but I'm going to be because he's a creep."

All forks had stopped. There was a long, slow-motion moment in which the whole family watched me officially grow up.

"So," my father said, "you're going to Spain tomorrow. With Jonah. And you've made up your mind that this is what you want to do…. Do you love him?"

"Yep."

"Then I guess that settles it," said Dad.

All I knew about Ibiza was that it was Jonah's dream-land where he had friends and knew the language and where I'd know not much. The last time he'd spoken of little houses and happily-ever-aftering, this time he was withholding even the flight number. I packed some island clothes and the lifeguard. I speedily made that business trip into the city to convince Oma to support this rad romance. It wasn't easy—she'd never met the gentleman in question. But it would've been impossible if she had. Plus there was the issue of the college education being scrapped.

"Und vhy isn't zis fellow paying for your ticket?"

"Uh, he is actually," I lied, "the five hundred is just so I have some money when I get over there. Just in case." Just In Case was going to be my middle name on this excursion.

"Oh, he is? Vell, zat's goot. Do you sink five hundred is enough?"

It wasn't. "Of course it is." It was a miracle, that's what it was. Thank God Oma loved Europe. And thank Him Jonah wasn't feeling fancy, or I'd be playing the spoons on Fifth Avenue for first class fare.

$$

The flight was delayed a few hours and we were confined to waiting. Jonah's approach to everything, including boredom, was to get thoroughly into it—don't turn your head from side to side, don't read or look at anything, don't speak. Slumping down in one's chair was permissible if done lethargically with caution here not to fall asleep. Staring at the departure screen to near-blindness was also recommended, required in fact. I failed miserably at all of the above.

When we finally took off, in a plane almost devoid of passengers, the first thing that happened was a full lunar eclipse outside my window. Jonah ignored it, of course, but to me it was another ominous indicator.

We got to Ibiza just as the evening sun was going down. The island truly was magnificent. Millions of farms with white farm houses called *fincas*—low mountains, close mountains giving up the skyline now to the night. We took a cab straight to Robby's house where Jonah was always welcome. Jonah, now back to abnormal, was jumping all over the back seat, elated to be there, leaning out the window then back in shouting, "Far fuckin' out! Far fuckin' out!"

Being a newcomer, I wasn't made particularly welcome at Robby's. Jonah could've helped me out here, but didn't. There was a tight community of foreigners who'd been coming to Ibiza for years and years. Their cold attitude of "it's our place" was somewhat justified considering the many who passed through only to spend money, take pictures, and make noise. The snobbery guarded the special life they'd created for themselves on this sensational island—a life of sun, candlelight, well water, bare bodies, see-through cloth draped around Europe's most beautiful women, music, full moons, remote stone houses isolated and basic with spectacular views of mountains, cows, stone fences, and the sea. Those were the sweet aspects of it, along with an unsurpassed high that one inhaled daily from bottomless pipes of hash. But from the first night, there was another feeling that prevailed all too strongly, an eerie quality in these same outwardly glamorous people with whom Jonah securely belonged. A detached look in eyes that vacantly proclaimed superiority. The actual day-to-day living in Ibiza slowly proved to be, granted, an entrancement with the natural beauty of the place, but also a fantasy played out well past enlightenment, and a hide-out for many from responsibility or the law. (Even a place of exile for some). And speaking of boredom, these folks had it down, and with such style that it was considered boring not to be bored. Underlying it all, of course, was a drug dependence I wasn't aware of until much later, because the Spanish police were so militant it had to be on the down-low. Plenty of heroin was in circulation.

In Ibiza I touched the earth. Here one would eat fruit off the trees or buy local-grown food in the shops. Everything one used came from the island. Because many foreigners and fashionistas had clothing shops in town, an elegant simplicity had become the island's trademark—texture, color, and comfort. Skin and nakedness were part of everything. You didn't even notice if people were dressed or half-dressed in their houses or at the beach. You didn't notice if you were. It was refreshing in that sense, to say the least. Empty rooms, silence, skin, and lengths of sheer muslin swaying in open windows.

From the moment we got to Robby's, where about ten people were staying and a few more came over for the evening, Jonah, for all intents and purposes, ceased knowing me. I don't know why, except that he was older, well-traveled, familiar with the island and the people, always stoned, and had *beaucoup* unresolved adulthood issues. We all sat around outside the house that first night, smoking and listening to guitars and flutes. Left to my own devices, I eventually went up onto the roof, up above the talking below, and gazed at the full moon—that looked back at me like a caring far-away companion. Kevin, a friend of Jonah's from before, joined me up there.

"What's wrong?" he asked, appearing to maybe be from Planet Earth.

"Nothing."

"You came with Jonah today from New York?"

"Yeah."

"Have you been together a long time?"

"No. On and off, but not really."

"Yeah, well, I've heard about you before from Sherry."

"Without seeming like a complete idiot, who's Sherry?"

"Oh. U-uh, well, they're not together anymore so don't worry, but Jonah lived with Sherry when he was here this spring. She's an American from New Jersey."

"Is she still here?"

"Yeah, she's here. She's a friend of mine. She's a little uptight about seeing Jonah again. She knew he'd be back, but she didn't know he was going to bring you with him."

"Well, tell her not to worry about that because I'm not *with* Jonah."

"Listen, don't let Jonah get you crazy. I mean, I really love him, I consider him a good friend and he's a good person—he's a great musician, too—but he's also insane, and can be kind of…mean. I love Jonah, but I don't understand him and not too many people do, so don't let it get to you."

Kevin and I became good friends. He was the only person in Ibiza that I ever really trusted.

He went back downstairs and Jonah came up.

"Jonah, what's going on?" it took some courage to ask.

"What do you mean 'what's going on?' Can't you feel it?"

"I mean what's going on with us?"

"Nothing."

"That's what it feels like. Why didn't you tell me this yesterday? You could've saved me the trip."

"You had to take this trip. You needed this."

"Is that why you took me here?"

Adios

A motorcycle careened around the corner at a ten degree angle. Pedestrians dove for safety. Afternoon snacks were coated with dust, but the sidewalk cafe tables were otherwise unharmed. Jonah had caught my eye. Moments later, he returned and parked the sweaty beast by my table. "May I join you?" he sat, ordering a *cafe con leche*. Lit a cigarette.

"Where's what's her name?" I asked.

It was rumored that Barbara was off turning tricks in Barcelona.

"Barbara's in Barcelona. Goes there sometimes." The attraction Jonah had to her had at first been difficult to fathom. Later it was impossible. Barbara was large, seemingly gay, facially handsome, clad in mostly leather, and paired usually with a gorilla-sized Harley. But that was perhaps the key to the affair—in no time Jonah had the key to the bike.

He now studied me. "It's good to see you…. You're doing alright, aren't you?" We'd been on the island a month.

"Of course I'm doing alright." Thank God my insecurity wasn't manifested as acne; a tumor is easier to hide.

He sat in silence a moment. "You know something?" he commenced with vigor. "Everyone on this island is nuts." Was he finally coming around? "Except me." Guess not. "And you."

"Kevin's good," I defended my one friend.

"Kevin's bananas."

"No he isn't."

"Nuts, I'm telling you. A child."

"Yeah, he's seventeen, give him a break."

"You and me are the only sane people on this island," Jonah repeated.

"Well, you're accurate about me. And you're accurate about everyone else. Why has it taken you so long to realize? You've been coming here for years. Took me about five minutes. What happened—I thought these were your darling friends?"

"Friends? I don't have any friends here. Everyone I know is out of their skull. Zulus. This place is really off the deep end. It's good to see you. Good to talk to someone from the real world."

"What about Robby? I thought you liked him."

"A complete zombie."

"What about Barbara?"

"A maniac. But she IS a real woman. You should take lessons from her."

"Bite the wall. I'm sure she'd consent to giving me lessons. What about Sherry?"

"Out in space, they're all out in space. I'm dead serious, woman, you're the only sane person on this island. What are you going to do about it?"

"Get the hell out. What are you going to do about your INsanity?"

"I'm just going to keep on playing my music. Been doing some nice new things. You should come over and listen. And I'm going back to New York soon, gotta get off this crazy island. New York's the only place to be if you got something to do and I got a lot to do. Want to come to my place and listen to me play?"

"I didn't know you had a place."

"Barbara's place. We're together."

Off we sped. Evil Knievel nearly doing us in on every curve. I had reason to be nervous—the things you see in cartoons were the things Jonah did on motorcycles. His narrow escape stories went right off the edges of cliffs.

Barbara's place was just that, a place—part of a house or possibly an apartment, and close to town. It was without the mountain views Jonah had claimed so essential to the senses, and for the hundredth time I wondered why he'd abandoned our original plan to live here together in a fabulous old farmhouse in the mountains. A month later, here we both were, more disconnected than ever.

Inside, Jonah lit some candles, poured some water and pulled out the guitar. He began playing in his way. You could trail his eyes through the sound as he found clean spaces in the tune. Each moment grew into another sound, his face following or leading the notes. A burning cigarette stayed in one corner of his mouth, the eye above it squinting. His jaw muscles clenched to the beat. The music itself was melodic and soft, telling of a Jonah who rarely surfaced. Eventually he wound down, then stopped. He went over to the bed, canopied with mosquito netting, took off his clothes and lay naked on top of the sheets. I took off mine and laid beside him. We listened to the evening outside and the voices of the neighbors. We didn't touch. Wanting to, neither of us could move. We just lay still watching the black ceiling.

In the morning he got up and made coffee. We drank it black. He had some chores to do in town and suggested I ride back with him. As we approached the shops and cafes, I noticed his jaw tightening again. Ibiza streets were paved with eyes. "Should we ride into town together?" he asked me, "or do you want to split up here?"

"Let's split up here," I said, sickened by the question. I hopped off, kissed his cheek insincerely, and Barbara's bike vanished.

"That does it," I said to the cloud of dust.

Later that afternoon I found Jonah sipping drinks with a couple of friends. He readily accepted my discreet invitation to a private conversation, suggesting a walk to the end of the pier. When we got there, I said, "Jonah, I have two things to say." He watched me and waited. "The first is that I love you."

He swallowed and then said, "And I love you.... It's a mutual feeling, it's nice."

"I'm not talking about pals and buddies, I really love you."

We scrutinized each other. "And the other thing is that I'm leaving tomorrow."

He was quiet.

"Where will you go?" he asked then.

"I've got a boat ticket to Barcelona," I said.

"And then?"

"Paris."

"Train?"

"No, hitching."

"Why Paris?"

"Because obviously I have to go to a city. London isn't foreign enough. And since I studied French, that leaves Paris."

"What will you do there?"

I was hoping he wouldn't ask. "Live…just live. You don't have to worry about me. If you did, I'd be insulted. Anyway, that's all I have to say. We can go now."

The next evening, in the port, we sat and had a drink together. "Before you go to Paris," he began, "I just want you to consider one thing… I want you to consider going back to New York."

I considered it the way you consider jumping in front of a subway train. "Jonah, if I wanted to be in New York, I wouldn't be here."

"Just wanted you to know that if you wanted to go to New York, you have a ticket. And if you want to change your mind about Paris, you can."

I'd never wanted to make up my mind about Paris in the first place. But all he was offering was a guilty conscience. "No thanks, Jonah."

The next hour was not fun. Loving someone you hate is a nightmare. Hating someone you love is hard work. But eventually we got to chatting as dear friends do. We spoke vaguely about the foggy plans neither of us had, complained once more about Ibiza, praised Ibiza, and basically waited for the boat.

It came and I wasted no time. The pull was now the mainland, not Jonah, suddenly the gentleman, carrying half my stuff up the gangplank.

"If you want to write…" he handed me my basket, "or if you need anything…."

I shook my head.

"…Well, you know where I am, either in New York or here."

I looked in his eyes and shook my head again.

"Anyway," he said, "I'm around."

"So am I."

He kissed my cheek, then disappeared into the crowd.

From the prow of the ship I looked with resolve at the island I'd leave behind. A Crosby, Stills, and Nash island of candlelight, well water, nakedness, and hashish. Of straw baskets and white stone houses that kept the coolness in and the heat out. And I swore by that island, by the moon above, and the sea below, that I would never move toward Jonah again. "If we ever meet again," I vowed out loud, "it will be by his doing or by chance."

PART II ~ EUROPE

- 11 -

Andorra

Funny how your fears shrivel when you face them. For weeks I'd been afraid to leave the island. Where would I go? Now, suddenly, I was getting on the boat. Everything ahead was wide open. No matter how alone and cold or poor I got, I'd have the comfort of knowing I'd survived love. My father had predicted I'd return home about this time, deflated and heart-broken. Instead I was going to Paris, deflated and heart-broken. Paris wouldn't have open arms, but neither would my pragmatic father and chilly stepmother, who, when it came to off-spring, enjoyed nothing better than a nice, long-term goodbye. So I faced reality and faced the Continent. By comparison, home seemed a lame alternative. I had every advantage and knew it: I was healthy, stealthy, and wise, had two thumbs, not much baggage, and long blonde hair.

Barcelona was a madhouse after the small-island tranquility, but I was just passing through. Within a few hours, I met a VW van containing four Australian musicians leaving immediately for Amsterdam via Paris. All male, they cordially invited me along. But Jonah had suggested that, while traveling north, I not miss the Republic of Andorra, nestled in the Pyrenees Mountains between Spain and France. The quaint natural beauty, he'd said, was worth the extra mileage. Determined to go there now, I had to forfeit this great ride. And, reluctant to hitch through the dry, expansive Spanish plains, I decided, instead, on a long bus ride as far as Andorra, that included an overnight stop at a roadside inn.

Stepping down to the sunny sidewalk of Andorra's capitol the next day, I was ready to use some of my newly acquired Spanish and do the town. Indeed, the Pyrenees were magnificent, and what better time of year than late September? But as the bus lumbered away, I saw one of my baskets gliding into the distance in its back window—camera, passport, travelers' checks, the works. Dumbfounded, I looked around frantically, then dashed into the nearest store. In handicapped Spanish, I tried to make my predicament understood, only to discover that Spanish isn't used in Andorra—they speak French. Fine, I'd sat through five years of it in school. But in a matter of moments I learned that Rabelais, Voltaire, and the boys were of no assistance with today's colloquial French. So, as the bus disappeared for points east, west, or north, I wept instead.

A kindly looking man in a suit spoke to me through, a thick Spanish accent, in what must have been French. "I don't speak French," I found myself saying, in Spanish, though moments earlier I'd thought it was Spanish I didn't speak.

"Oh, you speak Spanish?" the man then asked in Spanish with a French accent.

"No, actually I don't, but better than French." This realization was more than disconcerting, now that I was halfway to Paris with no Plan B. So I did a tragic jig of sorts, pointing down the road, holding out a crinkled ticket stub, and stammering, "My basket, my basket." This '*baskette*,' this '*chose pour porter quelque chose desdans*,' this '*valise du papier*,' '*cosa para vender frutas*' now making its way to Iberian extremities, was not only unlabeled but wide open.

A sad day for me, so I wept some more.

"Don't worry, I will help you," the man made himself understood, producing a clean white handkerchief. "Will you come with me? You do not have to worry. I think I can help you."

Dabbing at my sniffles, I followed him to a shiny car that he opened for me, and we drove away. (In the opposite direction the bus had gone.) We arrived shortly at a two-bit bus station and both went inside. At the counter, he asked a series of questions in Sprench that were answered accordingly. Looking optimistic, though he had from the start, the man led the way back to his car. "You mustn't worry," he conveyed. "I think you will have your basket returned.

But we must wait one hour and a half. Will you have lunch with me?"

"I don't have any money (*je n'ai tengo pas dinero*), but I'll stay with you since you seem to have the inside scoop and since you haven't killed me yet," I communicated.

"I will buy you lunch. It will be my pleasure." We were slowly exchanging hand signals, broken Spanish, broken French, and in my case broken English as a last resort. Gradually I retrieved my patchwork, elementary Spanish after the man convinced me he was actually from Barcelona but had been living in Andorra so long he'd switched to this local French dialect. Thus, we became friends. Driving back to town, he took me to a lovely restaurant with starched pink tablecloths and violin music, where we dined for an enchanting ninety minutes. By the second course we were in jolly conjunction, laughing hard at my misfortune. By the third, my financial ruin was a huge joke, my carelessness hysterical. And by dessert, it was time to go to I didn't know where, but he had a definite strategy for retrieving the basket.

We drove out past the bus station we'd stopped at earlier and continued along a pleasant country road, this guardian angel periodically checking his watch. Having trusted him from the onset, I not only kept the faith along this heavily wooded lane deep in the Pyrenees Mountains, but felt lucky and blessed. Soon we turned off the lane and into an even more isolated spot—a clearing with a barn and a vast yard containing a league of dead buses. Not a soul on the premises.

"*Uno momento*," said the gentleman, and vanished into the barn. Seconds later he reappeared, idly swinging my basket in one hand. All the contents were in order, now transforming my hectic charade into one splendid afternoon.

"Are you still going to hitch-hike to Paris now?" he asked.

"I must."

"Well, let me take you back to the main road and to the edge of town where you'll have the best chance of getting a long ride." My repeated thank you's were hopelessly meager in light of his graciousness.

Reaching the chosen spot and exchanging a touching farewell, I found myself roadside again, thumb extended, as my chum waited nearby in his car to make sure I didn't leave my basket on the grassy knoll.

The first vehicle to come around the bend was a VW van—always a good target for hitchers. Spotting me, it slowed down, and there were the Australian musicians waving excitedly out the windows. Jubilant, I ran back to the Spanish man and shared the great news, "Mis amigos! Mis amigos!" Incredulous and glad for me, he drove off feeling more reassured about my future than I did.

Shocked to see the Aussies again, I bungled aboard their camper and they passed me the wine and a fat joint. "What're you guys doing in Andorra?"

"Well, after you told us about this place, we couldn't get the idea out of our heads, so we decided to come up this way instead. And we were keeping an eye out for you!"

Kisses, Grapes, Trains, and Hugs

I didn't know a soul in all of France and hadn't even made inquiries as to where I might hang my beret. Now I was being dropped off in Paris, and quickly had to pick a part of town in which to live out my days. The Australians helped me locate a tiny hotel on the Left Bank that someone in Ibiza had scribbled onto a scrap of paper. On a narrow, hidden street a block from the Seine, a small blue neon sign identified it.

"You sure you don't want to come to Amsterdam?" the guys asked one last time. They felt unkind dropping me at destiny's door like this, a new-born in a basket being placed on a stranger's porch.

But living in Paris seemed like one of those life prerequisites for the creative. Even the words, "living in Paris," suggested writers and photographers weighing their brilliance against failure, artists and lovers pinning hopes against broken hearts, everyone half-forlorn, half-found by bare winters, baguettes, wine, cold rooms, and hot coffee. "Living in Paris"—where basic human needs were secondary to architectural splendor and the Seine running through, bridges built to be stood upon and gazed from. The heart of humanity, crossroads of history and culture, fashion and charm, liquid language, poetry of palette, and the quaint unknown. You were supposed to arrive with nothing and figure it out, find your way. That's what Paris was *for*—pain and art in its very mortar. It wasn't Dallas or Berlin, Calcutta or Cairo, it was…*Paris*.

I took a deep breath, giggled, shrugged, and stepped out of the VW camper….

I'd been there briefly once before and fully grasped that no one spoke English. So I'd just have to sink or learn better French, and I didn't mind those unAmerican odds. I had more pressing concerns: no job, money to last three weeks tops, and the first signs of a sore throat....

Prepared for the worst, I slipped inside the little hotel. But *quelle surprise!* it was adorably French. Standing in the foyer, I negotiated a weekly price with a small, quadrilingual blind man of about seventy-five. Driving an easy bargain, he asked three dollars a night. Also '*compris*' was continental breakfast each day—an enormous pot of fresh coffee, steamed milk, two croissants, butter, and jam. That would sustain me till evening. I signed on for a week, tickled at this delightful intro to Paris. The blind man led me to my third floor room, feeling his way before me with one hand on a guide rope strung against the walls of the stairs and corridors.

Drifting out into the Latin Quarter, I was instantly assaulted by a horny onslaught of relentless North Africans. This continued till I mastered the art of rudeness. Aside from an abundance of these young Arabic men, my other instant awareness was that the shopkeepers, likely native French people, weren't speaking French. Well, not my kind of French. Whether I spoke to them or they to me, the reaction either way was a blank stare. Within hours, I acquired a phrase book—somewhat retro for a supposed student of the language—and cursed my teachers for passing me. So what if I'd read Andre Gide, I couldn't buy a stamp, couldn't use a phone, and had to hold out a handful of change for salespeople to take the amount they needed. I didn't even know how to say "What'd you say?" Where were all the Ugly Americans when you needed them?

The situation was just daunting enough that the impending pneumonia might prove a simpler option. It welled up inside. The second morning, I stood up and literally fell back down on the bed. And there I stayed, not even able to manage my free breakfast. The all-seeing blind man sensed my infirmity and gave me directions to a "Drugstore" for orange juice. Fighting the chill, I trudged slowly through the churning neighborhood, then made my pilgrimage back to my antique room.

Each morning at eight o'clock sharp, the blind man would delicately deliver my breakfast tray. I'd hear him wending his way to each chamber with one tray at a time, and then all the way back downstairs to pick up the next of these breakfasts that his old wife prepared one by one in the kitchen. As the week progressed and he sensed I wasn't eating much, he inquired about my condition. He'd even bring up a glass of juice with breakfast out of the kindness of his heart. And there was a little shower in the hall for which you had to pay a few centimes for the key, but the blind man insisted I take free showers. He made a point of telling me not to let his wife know.

I was getting thin and didn't have much to spare, but at least the malady was postponing the crunch of bankruptcy. Terrified of my French future and winter on the way, I was hiding under a Bubonic cover.

One morning my non-seeing ally amazed me with a suggestion as to how I could save three dollars a day: "If you kiss me every morning, you can stay here another week for free." Goodness, even old men were into that?

"Let me think it over."

Astounded, I thought about it all day. I considered the saying, "Love is blind," and decided I was, in fact, capable of the transaction. This blind suitor wasn't exactly what you'd call attractive, but I could muster up an early morning peck. What was the implication though? With a mixture of pity, survival, fascination for the bizarre, and keen rationalization, I accepted his offer. If nothing else, it would be novel. Anyway, wasn't Paris supposed to be romantic? With a gymnastic imagination, this might qualify. Our deal was to commence first thing in the morning, "but not a word to the wife," he reminded me. (As if I'd knowingly break up a working fifty-year relationship.)

Next morning I anticipated his arrival with a vague nightmare followed by a preparatory brushing of the teeth. Then, on schedule, Romeo arrived, bearing the tray and the ruby red lips. He felt around for the shelf on which he set the tray as I volunteered a "*bonjour*" to help him establish my whereabouts in the room. Sensing the pointlessness of being evasive or coy, I planted myself squarely in front of him, allowing him to take me by the shoulders, and we neatly kissed. That was that, and gracefully he left.

Feeling rather pert after the simplicity of what I'd dreaded as an ordeal, I devoured the continental breakfast and put the tray on the continental shelf.

As the week ended, the kisses developed, as kisses do—longer ones that I found arduous but couldn't legally refuse because our agreement hadn't specified duration. But, although intent on milking the situation, he was basically well-behaved, and rather than assert himself unfairly, he made a new proposal, "If you kiss and hug me every morning, you can stay for another free week."

Oh God.

Money was really low now. I wished I had an alternative. But if nothing rescued me from this week of hugging, I'd have to proceed....

In Paris, as in all of Europe's major cities, the American Express Office was the information hub. As well as picking up mail, buying Travelers' Checks, and exchanging currencies, this was where long-hairs of the world swapped travel and job tips and sat on the curb with signs begging for rides. It was also where VW vans heading for London or Morocco or Afghanistan would swing by for a last passenger or two.

Flu in remission, I bee-lined down there.

The word on the sidewalk was that grape-picking was the go-to gig for immediate cash. With grapes in season, this vetted vagabond opportunity was in full swing in every vineyard in France. You'd be given tent space, thirty-six francs a day, plus food, and you just picked and picked and picked till your fingers dropped off. Sounded like something okay to do once in your life, particularly when your other option was off the charts.

I was also apprised that at about one-thirty a.m., the last train out of Paris could be ridden for free. Apparently, the conductors went home instead of getting on that final one-way train that then chugged out to the countryside. So you only had to show a ticket as you boarded the train, but not on board. Thus, you could purchase a ticket to the first stop, and stay on as long as you pleased.

I also learned about The American Centre for Students and Artists on Boulevard Raspaille—the general gateway to freak-friendly

Paris. Not too far from my hotel, this was the place to find job post-ings, apartment shares, and classes. I decided to go there as soon as I returned from the vineyards with my bundle of cash.

So, I made my midnight way to Gare du Nord and waited, with some hesitation, for the last train to load up. Though all the stops were clearly posted, I'd never heard of any of them, and didn't have a map. Still, with the amount of wine produced in France, the back-country had to be practically carpeted with vineyards. I flashed my cheap ticket (one way to a nearby suburb) at the gate-man.

Around 1:00, the drowsy train crawled out of the station. I peered out the dark window, watching the lights of the great city become gradually more sparse, as did the number of passengers around me. As fatigue crept in, it was obviously time to gather some geographical pointers. But the car I was in had now emptied.

In the next one, I found a suited young Frenchman riding alone with a briefcase. "Where is this train going?" I queried in French, after mentally practicing the sentence.

"Where are *you* going?" was his response.

"Well, where is this *train* going?"

"Well, where do you *want* to go?" He wasn't cooperating.

"To the grapes," I said, not having rehearsed this part, but 'grapes' must be the same as in English. So I just pronounced it the French way with the 'a' as in 'father,' the French 'r,' and a silent 's.' (Grop.)

"To the *grappe*?" he repeated it back.

"Yes."

"What *grappe*?"

"I don't know which *grappe*…. Any *grappe*."

"Well, *where* are you going?" he tried again.

"I don't know," I was forced to confess. "When the train stops, I will get off. Where is the last stop?"

"*Les Boir Noirs*," (The Black Woods), he said, or something to that affect, sending a cool breeze up my spine.

"Well how many hours is that from here?"

"About fifteen minutes."

Oh dear. "Is there a hotel there?"

"No, no, just a small village and some houses."

"Does the train then go back to Paris?" Defeat was already setting in and I was just setting out.

"In the morning."

"Do they have *grappe* in that village?" I asked hopefully. I could last the night maybe under a tree if I knew employment would commence in the morning.

"I don't think so...."

"Because I want to...." I made a picking gesture.

"I don't understand," he said politely.

Something was really wrong here....

I didn't find out till later that the French word for 'grapes' is pronounced 'ray-zaaa,' and spelled '*raisins*'—and the French word, '*grappe*,' that I was actually pronouncing properly, means 'bunch.' So here's this tired commuter bouncing along, being drilled by an out-of-place American looking for a bunch.

"I just want to...." I mimed the picking gesture again on an imaginary grapevine.

"I'm sorry," the man said, "but I don't understand what you are trying to do or where you are trying to go. I am getting off at the next stop, where I live. I'm going straight to bed, and first thing in the morning I'm going back to Paris to work. You are welcome to stay at my house, and it seems to me that you are on the wrong train and you are going to have to go back to Paris anyway to get the right one. So, if you want, you can come with me and then take the train to Paris tomorrow, or perhaps get another train from where I live that goes farther east. You can trust me, I am very tired. And I must go immediately to sleep so I can get to work tomorrow."

I couldn't understand all the words, but the gist was that I was up the creek without a paddle. And this offer looked like the last, and therefore the best, I'd get tonight. "I'll think about it," I said, tapping my temple in case I'd said that wrong, too. But the train was slowing into the station, so I simply picked up my bag and stepped down with the gent, who wasn't displeased at an unexpected overnight lady guest.

I found out why when the door to his flat opened to a tightly packed single room with one smallish bed in the center. "Don't worry," he reiterated, as I paused in the doorway, "I won't try to make love to you."

He didn't succeed at even a kiss, but he did try. He tried till the sun came up, till the toot of the train resounded through the rooster-filled air and we were both compelled to make haste to the station. But I'd survived another night, and now, grape-less, bunch-less, was going back to Paris.

In Paris we bid each other an unsentimental farewell.

The blind man took me back with open arms. He led me excitedly to my same room and made a hit-or-miss attempt at a sneaky hello-hug, but it was harder for him to hit than miss, and I held him to the morning-only terms.

But it was good to be home. My little blind man, now insisting I call him Tony (rather ordinary for such a dandy), must have had a lot of practice with blind passion while I was away, because he had a sizzling new line of maneuvers requiring fancy side-stepping on my part. Three days into this second week, he threw himself at me so dynamically that I ended up sandwiched between him and the bed. As I squirmed for air and freedom, what caused him to scramble hastily to his proprietary self, frantically straightening his tie, was the sound of someone in the hall. The wife!

At the American Centre was an ad for work as an *au pair* girl for an American family from Washington, D.C. The father's glossy post at the American Embassy entitled them to a palatial domain in the coveted Eighteenth Arrondissement. And, in the nick of time, providence removed me from Tony's charms. I was given a private room in the fourth floor attic with my own entrance and the single task of baby-sitting two or three nights a week. In exchange, I would eat like a pasha, enjoy the family's plush pad, and accept a small salary.

$$

- 13 -

Clint and Phoebe

Fall 1971

Aside from travel, was there anything more compelling than black and white photography? The darkroom was where the magic happened. So, in conjunction with becoming an *au pair*, I joined a photography co-op forming at the Centre. There, after I apprenticed a while, I could dabble in the darkroom to my heart's content.

The mastermind of this cool collective—in which we each paid a few bucks a month for chemicals in exchange for 24-hour darkroom access—was a photographer named Clint. But meeting him first, before being introduced to the other four members, did instill hesitation about being the only female. In a wide-brimmed black hat, Clint was skinny with shameful posture, his undernourishment underscored by decrepit black t-shirts, falling-off black Levis, and a manicured strip of black beard linking lower lip to Adam's apple. Even after meeting the others—where it was agreed I'd accompany each one on a shoot, then back to the darkroom to process film and make prints—I wasn't eager for my session with Clint. The mere sight of him induced cravings for vitamin B.

But a month later, I was not only amazed at how each photographer's vision, approach, and technique varied, but at how little I resonated with any of their work. All were more concerned with their equipment (tons of it) and the myriad technical details, than the content or composition of the photographs. I got the darkroom drill down, but no inspiration, or even techniques I'd ever use.

I now knew Clint enough to see he didn't lack humor or heart, just bore a ponderous intensity regarding how much there was to film in the world vis-a-vis how little time and money to do it. Un-

like the others, he was all about visuals, concept, emotion, and pushing the limits of his equipment and film. When I eventually hit the
streets with him, it was really fun.

This guy had no pretensions. His aim was to slide unnoticed
through the electric underground he'd discovered in the nightlife of
Pigalle, the red-light district. Low-key and moving fast, he would fire
off six shots before anyone gleaned he had a camera. Then he was
gone. (Thus the dark clothes and slinky stance.) He would reel down
the sidewalks, shooting from the hip, to immortalize unguarded
moments of the seamy Parisian under-story. Full documentation in
black and white was the intention—not always in focus, a-wash with
action and motion. His off-center shots were flashes of shoulders,
cleavage, legs, lipstick. A blurred hand across a stubborn pout. Lit
cigarettes between fingers or lips speaking a sensuality all their own.
Compromised eyes, vacant stares, chipped nail polish straightening
tight skirts.

He'd have no idea what he'd recorded until later when we'd scru-
tinize the contact sheets in the darkroom. Then, selecting the most
intriguing frames to enlarge, he'd dive into the chemicals, bending
over the tray almost getting his face wet watching the images come
up. Clint withheld no part of himself from his photography. Both
hands in the developer, he'd rub the photo paper to coax the images along. (That technique made no difference, I later learned, after
adopting the funky habit myself. But submerging in the chemicals
and rubbing prints felt like being a midwife or magician, birthing
photos from nothing at all.)

A huge movie camera was another prop he wore like an ap-
pendage. He'd slither through the deserted nights near Montmartre,
high on the hum of secrets in unlit corridors, filming everything,
shooting in pitch blackness half the time. He didn't compose, but
captured. And whatever he got was fair enough—swaths of blonde
or black hair sweeping across painted brows and powdered cheeks—
the chance faces of desire and desperation. It was real, the streets
were real.

Clint had been poor as a child and felt he owed poverty something, he didn't know what. He had clean, bright blue eyes that
showed his vulnerability and kept him just centimeters outside the

degenerate demographic he filmed. He was a loner. He played guitar late at night, slept by day, and never ate. His fridge was empty, except for darkroom chemicals; all resources going to art and assisting other artists.

The authenticity was rare and attractive. And, since his troubled side was addressed and expressed adequately through his photography, Clint was ironically easy-going, and actually...nice.

In time, we became unkempt lovers in his unkempt Pigalle flat. But in order to retain employment, I steered him clear of my *au pair* arrangement.

As a life companion, he perhaps left something to be desired—more meat around the rib cage—but he was a straight-up guy and a true artist.

And it was he who introduced me to Phoebe.

One day I was on the mail line at American Express and noticed a rainbow of a person. A frail strength was rigged up in Moroccan harem pants and a handmade, multi-colored vest, with a purple cape. She had an open, clown-y, child's face, chaotically cropped blonde hair, and sparkling things on her fingers, wrists, and ears. She was knitting as she waited in line.

A few days later I saw her again at the Artists' Centre, and again the full-spectrum energy. I asked Clint if he knew her.

"Yeah, her name's Phoebe. I wanna sleep with her."

"I'd like to meet her."

"Okay," he said, "we'll go to her place and you can meet her and I can have sex with her."

That evening we popped in. When Phoebe saw me she said, "I saw you the other day at American Express. I wanted to meet you but I didn't know what to say."

"Well, I felt the same way and that's why I'm here. Clint wants to have sex with you and that's why he's here."

The apartment was incohesive, with Phoebe in benevolent command of about seven third-world wannabes decked out along the walls, all either living or dying there. Even Phoebe now slept on the floor, having donated her bed to the one couple of the pack. This slice of humanity had woven itself together in a vague quarter of Paris beneath a huge white silk parachute covering the ceiling and draping down the walls. I couldn't see the connection Phoebe had to these unrelated hash-smoking, 'non-contributers' (to coin a term of my father). She basically didn't even know any of them except one, a heavy-set lug soon to be reduced to a heap of digesting food in a corner, who was her lover. "Whose place is this?" I asked her.

"Mine," she said, "…sort of, I think."

"But don't you care?"

"Well, it's not really mine—I'm just staying here, so I don't have a right to mind, but I did used to get uptight. Now I just go to the library at the Artists' Centre when I want to be alone so I don't get crazy anymore."

"Who pays the rent?" Really sounding like my father now.

"Well, everybody pays who can, but nobody ever can so I think we're getting evicted." She giggled, "But that's okay, too, because I think I'm ready for a change."

"You must be. I'm ready for a change and I've only been here five minutes."

"Come with me into the kitchen," she said, "because I think something's burning." We went on talking as she produced a peasants' feast to be silently and thanklessly devoured by her lackluster roomies.

"I don't think I quite understand all this," I told her. "I mean I understand IT but not you in it."

"I don't either," she admitted, "but it's not as bad as it looks. They're not bad people. Just…."

"Just what?"

"Just…they just smoke. But they might get it together. I think they will someday." That night went on and on. The pipe went round and round with mint tea as a chaser. Phoebe insisted Clint and I sprawl among the ruins of the meal and sleep with the masses, bribing us with tomorrow's croissants and *cafe au lait*.

Her philosophy was self-sacrifice and good faith. She had a stronger sense of obligation than anyone I'd ever met and a better way of hiding it, never letting anyone feel they were imposing or taking up her time, yet she gave continuously. So much, in fact, that she would then have to schizophrenically disappear for hours and hours to libraries, with her books and crochet hooks, to seek balance in isolation. Sometimes she'd crochet on benches in the park, knowing that strangers would afford her more peace than the orphanage she'd founded. She was almost twenty-seven though and finding out the charitable way that her philosophy and making money mutually negated each other. Consequently, she was very thin, an ingenious hustler, and had a buried grudge against men, choosing for lovers the most undesirable specimens in France. They ranged from parasites to married deceitfuls to 'carriers' who wouldn't look her in the eye. Not that our wintry Paris offered a dazzling line-up of Valentinos, but even Clint wasn't scuzzy enough for Phoebe, and they had Chicago in common.

Phoebe herself was a mid-western cheerleader, Queen of the Prom—modified by a five-year freak-out in Manhattan. The result was a corn-fed whirling dervish with a passion for dance. She took and taught classes at the Artists' Centre and had me spinning around with her in two days flat. She taught me how to dance, I taught her how to steal candy, and we became fast friends.

Both seasoned junk food junkies, we were borderline diabetics and embraced our malady. It became an instant bond. And Paris was a sweet tooth's paradise. The French don't even debate nutrition—if it tastes amazing, it's good for you. Resisting sensuality is not part of the national portrait. And who couldn't love a country with mouth watering bakeries on every corner? Phoebe and I never passed one by.

Phoebe had a mentor of her own to match my Jonah attachment. Hers was a female dance teacher who had inspired her but somehow left her empty. So we were both under spells that still haunted. What these people had suggested to us about life we'd accepted as gospel, but now here we were without them, finding loopholes in their preachings, and sadly acknowledging that we weren't going to become more and more like them, but less and less. We had graduated from their schools. We missed, loved, and thanked them, but not having them to answer to was actually a relief. In fact, we were so enjoying our freedom from them that we began to suspect they'd been cramping our styles.

Phoebe's ability to amass a fortune also paralleled mine. She wanted to get paid for having fun and was working long hours to figure out a way. Meanwhile, crime would have to pay. She, too, was in possession of a sweetheart grandmother, a sort of life insurance one could tap into before lying down in the gutter. Knowing somewhere in the world there was a bed you could go lie in for free gave the mind a caress. So what if you had to say German prayers out loud before she'd turn out the light? The material support was a bit more abstract…a five dollar bill in a letter twice a year, a package no way near Christmas or your birthday containing an old letter from Aunt Helga to Uncle Ernie, a bar of black soap, forty-six stamps from Finland, and a gray sweater that had spiraled around the extended family for a decade. The guilt about what to do with these semi-precious objects was what one ended up with, plus the duty of gushing appreciation onto paper and raising the cash for postage. I'd ask Phoebe if she could use the gray sweater or the black soap, and she'd say she'd just received some gray soap and a black sweater from her own grandmother but could I use eight Indian-head nickels or a signed photo of Teddy Roosevelt?

Insolvency loomed large around the edges, but we just laughed. This wasn't the way it would be, just the way it was right now. We had no shortage of scams, and our ears worked overtime for new ones. By the time our friendship was ten days old, we were manufacturing metro tickets in the kitchen to solve the nagging problem of subway fare. Phoebe's neighborly French, too, was a perfect compliment to mine. She knew all the swear words and hip jargon to get us in and around the younger set, and I, by then, was recollecting enough conjugations, tenses, and formal courtesies to give us a leg up around the older folks, shopkeepers and the like.

- *14* -

The Free Train

When I dropped the grape story on Phoebe, she instantly got my continental drift. "You wanna go somewhere?" her eyes lit up.

"Yeah, where?" I mused. "Somewhere far but not too far...."

"That leaves Amsterdam," she said. "Going there might be a good way to test this free train, maybe even on a weekly basis if it works."

"You obviously haven't been to Amsterdam. That's the last place I want to go."

"Amsterdam has GREAT museums."

"Phoebe, in case you don't know, I have a blanket repulsion for museums, statues, fountains, palaces, cathedrals, ruins, and government buildings. It's residue from my first trip over here with my grandmother when I was sixteen."

"What else is there in Europe?"

"That's what I'm trying to find out."

"What about Rembrandt? He's in Amsterdam."

"He counts with museums, and I've already been to the Riches-museum at least twice. It's like the Grand Canyon, you can't get around it."

"Well, Rembrandt Schmembrandt, I've never been to Amsterdam and I'd like to go. And I know some people we can stay with there."

It turned out the last train, the free one, didn't go anywhere near Amsterdam, so we'd have to stow away instead. (At least we could then depart a few hours earlier.) Equipped with an ill-gotten horde of Swiss chocolate, we purchased tickets to the first stop, boarded, then urgently sought the shelter of a freight car. A mail car carrying dozens of large packages, French Christmas presents for little Dutch cousins, offered unexpectedly good cover. We constructed a cubic igloo, complete with peephole, into which we sealed ourselves optimistically. By the first stop, though as yet undetected, we were already nauseous after vigorous consumption of the feast. By the second, our legs and necks were begging for a bigger igloo, and by the third, we'd lost all sensitivity in the extremities due to arctic temperature and igloo failure. We leaned dejectedly against each other under Phoebe's cape, depleted, with a long ride still ahead. Somewhere between midnight and dawn, we took an enfeebled stroll through the passenger cars, and finally stumbled upon a sleeping wagon.

Feeling relatively safe, as travelers were tucking into their bunks, we searched unsuccessfully for an empty compartment. Then we spied two Spanish gents preparing for bed in a compartment for six. "Uh, *parlez-vous français?*" we approached them.

"*Oui, oui.*"

In French, we asked them if the other beds were occupied. When they said no, we asked if they'd mind if we hopped in. They looked at each other, shrugged, smiled, and said sure, why not.

"Good, thank you," said Phoebe, "that's very nice. But this is only for sleeping, you certainly understand, not for other things."

"Oh, no, no," said the embarrassed gentlemen, "only for sleeping. We're going to sleep *toute suite*, we're extremely tired." They settled into the lower berths, meaning we could achieve maximum security in the uppermost two. By squishing tightly against the two opposite walls, we hoped to go unnoticed by railroad personnel.

We woke next morning to a ticket collector standing in our cabin asking the gents for their tickets. We exchanged a visual 'holy shit' and did our utmost to become the wall itself. Below, in sleepy confusion, our shills were fumbling through their rumpled pockets. We held our breath. The conductor stood waiting for what seemed hours, then approved the men's tickets and left.

Close one! And quite fine of our bunkmates not to spill the beans. Now…should we return to the postal fort that might not even be there anymore, or just move from car to car avoiding ticket takers? Amsterdam was only forty-five minutes away. Oh God, the conductor again!

Of course he now saw us, sitting on the berths with our feet dangling down. "Oh," he chuckled, "I didn't even see you two up there." He stepped into our cabin. "Can I see your tickets please?"

"No speak French," said Phoebe politely. "English. English."

"Tickets," said the uniformed man in distinct English.

"Oh! Tickets!" we looked at each other and laughed. "Of course, ha ha, one moment." We obligingly explored our bags for the tickets, but for some reason they just didn't seem to be there. So we hunted some more, under the pillows, inside our boots.

"I just don't understand this," said Phoebe, rifling through her hat and scarf, as I simultaneously ransacked my own campsite. We had previously conspired that if caught, we'd say we'd boarded the train much closer to Amsterdam so if we had to pay, it wouldn't cost so much.

"Where'd you get on?" the conductor asked.

In unison, we rattled off the practiced name of some obscure Belgian whistle-stop where the train had paused at four-o-eight a.m. to pick up one letter. "What were you doing there?" he inquired, losing patience.

"Visiting relatives," I said, as Phoebe said, "Touring," both of us forgetting we didn't understand French while our Spanish friends pretended not to know us. The conductor went off to fetch a superior who'd decide what is done to riders without tickets. We could only pray the train would stop or slow down so we could dive into a passing snowdrift. But in moments the superior was in the doorway demanding we pay the fare, and not from the mail stop we'd claimed as origin, but from Paris.

This personage, of the constipated persuasion, had no mercy and told us blankly that since we wouldn't (couldn't) pay for our tickets, we could and would be met in Amsterdam by Dutch police who'd tend to us accordingly. He assigned us two seats and remained to guard us safely into the station.

As promised, we got the police escort, two in the front seat of the squad car and one in the back with us as we admired the canals.

I nudged Phoebe, "This might be your chance to see one of Amsterdam's historic government buildings."

It was a short hop to headquarters where we were passed off to a new batch of authorities and instructed to sit on a bench and wait our turn. (Almost no one in Amsterdam at that time was following the rules.) Another case was in progress. Two young Englishmen were unhappily paying a ticket for illegally parking their houseboat, and trying to talk their way out of it. They were told not only to pay the ticket but to be out of town by sundown. "Oh well," they said, "we were planning to leave anyway. But what are you two doing here?" Our saga amused them and they decided to stick around and witness our decree.

The Amsterdam police, who didn't find us fetching, announced in cold and perfect English that we would either pay for the train tickets or be sent to the United States. Tonight.

"But who will pay the plane fare?" we asked.

"The American Consulate, and you will reimburse them in America." A simple matter.

"But we don't live in the States, we live in Paris. Can't you send us back to Paris?"

"You are American citizens and you will be sent back to your OWN country. Europe does not welcome or sponsor unsavory individuals like yourselves."

"Well, it looks like we're going to be home for Christmas," I said to Phoebe. We had a total of maybe six dollars. "I have some money in Paris," I ventured to the officer. "Can I somehow send for it?" (Surely I could get an advance from my *au pair* family.)

"You have to pay now. If you didn't have enough money with you, you shouldn't have gotten on the train."

We wanted to just forget the whole thing and be friends, they didn't. So we went back to our bench to mull things over. Suddenly New York was the next stop and wet, wintry Paris looked sweeter and sweeter. The Louvre, how we'd miss it, all those fake metro tickets we hadn't used yet.... The Englishmen listened as we waxed nostalgic—the Notre Dame, the Seine at twilight, Clint le Miserable, Gare du Nord.... Paris, our Paris. The Englishmen then said it would break their hearts to see the Dutch police and New York City come between us and our beloved city, and that we must accept their offer to pay our train fare.

We, of course, refused, secretly praying they'd insist. And they did. Such good will. And a shame they'd been ordered to vacate. Grateful goodbyes all around, as we were released and the Englishmen went off to get their boat in gear.

Loose in the streets now, we wondered whether to chance a free meal in the nearest candy store or go straight for an afternoon.

Amsterdam was unchanged—still the drug capitol of Europe, hippie heaven. People dropping acid in pubs, cheap anything-to-get-you-high on every corner, maroon night spots littered with beat down-heads attached to foot-long joints, Rembrandt—Phoebe convinced me to give him another chance—bicycles, houseboats, gray cold air, and grubby, woolen scarves around the necks of would-be students. Twee town houses and cute canals, but the atmosphere was quicksand, and I favored a quick exit. Phoebe soon got an ample dose of it, possibly irritated by my disinterest, and after three days we hit the road, not the rails. Nine hours of hitching and we were home.

(See photos on back cover.)

15

Brussels

I had two days to practice. Then, Friday afternoon, I met Tina (a Canadian acquaintance from the Centre) and we marched into the grand old theater.

It was dark inside except for the stage, on which a confettied assortment of about twenty young people were gathered to audition for "HAIR." Tina and I joined the group, now seating themselves in two rows on the floor. She insisted this was not strictly a call-back, though it was for her.... "At least hear out a few attempts before you flee," she urged.

"Who do we audition for?" I asked her. There was no one else around except a band set up to accompany the singing attempts.

Tina pointed to someone coming up the stage steps. He was tall with skinny denim legs and an overly long matching jacket, possibly concealing a protruding middle. He looked about fifty, had curly, black, uncombed locks and a look on his face that combined fascination, delirium, and condescension. He had a light step, and nearly trotted to where our two lines of consolidated fear congealed on the floor. Coming closer, he bent forward from the waist with hands behind his back and slowly walked down the line scrutinizing each face as though we were curios in a souvenir shop on Saturn. Then he carefully inched his way backwards to where he'd started. I shrank as he passed again, that look penetrating each of us. Looking into my eyes, he stopped, "You're first."

The crowd as one released a sigh and I timorously followed him across the stage to a microphone, where three musicians were all tuned up. "Do you speak French?" the man asked, leaning down toward me as though I were microscopic.

"*Oui,*" I squeaked.

"*Vien avec moi une seconde,*" and he led me off to the side. The following conversation then took place in French, his lines spoken delicately as if I might break. (After three months in France, I could now actually converse.)

He: You are a Pisces?

Me: No, Cancer, but my moon is in Pisces. And you?

He: I'm Sagittarius, but my moon is also Pisces. It's nice having moon in Pisces, isn't it?

Me: Yes, I like it.

He: You are American?

Me: Yes.

He: But you live in Paris?

Me: Yes.

He: And what do you think of Paris, of the French?

Me: Not bad.

With my character profile complete, he then asked me to sing a song into the mic. Well, I'd just do it, that's all, I'd just stand there and belt it out in front of all these strangers (not to mention the entire cast of the current Paris "HAIR" show who'd just finished rehearsing and were now watching our auditions from audience seats). No big deal, do it every day.

Right, here we go. I told the Sagittarian the name of my song, "Frank Mills." He stepped several feet back and the music started. No turning back, I sang in English...quietly.

"Can you sing a leetle louder?" he beckoned my faint voice with one hand, still regarding me as though I were six and in my mother's clothes. "Good," he said as my voice rose. "Now can you dance as you sing?"

Oh, give me a break.

Why did I have to be first?

I began treading water to the beat.

"Uh, okay, stop a minute," he said to the band.

No formalities needed, no sad farewells, just let me out of here. Let me get home to my *au pair* job before I blow that, too. I had an imaginary foot out the door and a real one poised in mid air. "Can you sing another song?" he asked.

He was giving me another chance—it was considerate and kind, but....

Well, it just so happened I did know another song from the show. I named "Easy to be Hard" and the band picked up the tune. I was growing accustomed to the discomfort now, but not to the dancing, that this Frenchman was actively promoting with both hands. "Really dance! That's good, that's good." Good? I was moving like the Eiffel Tower on a windy day.

"Okay," he cut me off in the middle again and led me back to our conversation spot. The last thing I needed was elderly advice about singing lessons and dance classes. "I'd like you to be in the show," he said. "I 'ave a part for you. Can you come to Brussel on Monday?"

I had to laugh, but of course said yes. (Pisces moon is flexible and spontaneous.) The man said his name was Gilbert (pronounced *Zheel-BEAR*), and he'd see me Monday in Brussels.

Oddly, the only two chosen from the audition were Tina and me.

Pulling out of my *au pair* gig was relatively easy because the father was the Cultural Attaché at the American Embassy and 'HAIR' was definitely American culture. Plus Phoebe agreed to fill in until my replacement was found.

Gilbert went all the way to New York and back over the weekend and still beat me to Brussels. He was standing in the studio when I burst upon the scene. It was a steamy room, the floor thundering under the feet of twenty-three dancers-to-be. Good casting, I thought, scanning the crowd. It looked like a Halloween party.

The choreographer was from New York's West Village, a small, gay Filipino dressed for war dance in beads, braids, headband, and moccasins. "That is Dimayo," said Gilbert. "The others are the company." Seventeen countries were represented in this troupe. There were yellow ones, green ones, red ones, Tunisian ones. Dimayo spoke English that a young boy translated into French, for no one's benefit, lastly the three who spoke only Japanese. Music sessions were separate and we were taught the French lyrics by an American who didn't know French.

Initially, I was somewhat disenchanted. Not with the work or the concept—though from an American viewpoint, HAIR was now several years old and not the big controversial deal the Belgians made it out to be—but with the "consciousness" of my fellow players. Few were political. Half didn't understand the words they were singing, and the other half didn't care. Beneath their outer freakiness, there was no grasp of the social importance of the play. They truly didn't know that long hair or the show were part of a rebellion. They weren't from the U.S.—just a bunch of kids, half probably runaways—and the last thing on their minds was an American war in Southeast Asia. I thought of my draft-dodging friends in Canada, my fellow drop-outs scattered in the wind, my traveling comrades exploring their dreams, and imagined how wonderful it would be if they were here doing the show. They'd be so grateful to channel their political frustration and Utopian intentions into something more than odd jobs and the compromises of the corporate world they were fighting. But, alas, this wiggy sideshow instead.... Still, like a patchwork quilt, the sum was equal to more than the parts; this tribe learned the songs and dances and certainly looked like dissenters, and the audience never knew the difference.

And HAIR truly was a fabulous show—even though the message was watered down with the burning of the Belgian rather than American flag, and referencing the Vietnam War in Flemish. Here, in the heart of Brussels, was a full-on Broadway show with all the costumes, lighting, singing, dancing, and glitter—complete with the joyous message of love, freedom, and peace. In two and a half hours, every night, HAIR transformed the audience from frightened voyeurs threatened and irritated by our manginess, bare skin, long hair, and torn clothes, to laughing-crying hand-holders clambering onto the stage to join in our final song, hug and kiss us, and dance with us. Every night. They couldn't help themselves. They'd leap from their seats and rush up onto the stage with us at the end to sing "Let the Sun Shine" and dance their brains out until the curtain finally came down. And we loved them for it.

Whenever Gilbert was around, everyone felt calm and sure that ours was the best HAIR show anywhere, from Munich to Sydney to Honolulu. He'd sprinkle patchouli on our untidy tresses and remind us, with or without words, that nothing mattered except how we felt about life, about each other, and about what we were doing. If our souls were in this, we couldn't fail. When talkative, he spoke exclusively of "lucidity."

But then he'd disappear to Amsterdam or Venus for two weeks, and instead of his encouragement before each show, we'd get scoldings and lectures from Dimayo, insisting we adhere to the original format rather than humoring ourselves with in-jokes and ad-libbing. "I swear to God," Dimayo cried one night a few months in, after keeping us like school children for hours after the show, "you've carried this free license so damn far that no one in the audience tonight understood one minute of the thing! Why can't you just perform the show the way it was written? It's a good show, it doesn't need improvement. I mean really, what's the point of wearing belts and boots for the nude scene? And, sure, it's hilarious to throw a water balloon on Danielle during his solo, but the audience thinks it's part of the play! And Martine, I'm not trying to inhibit you, God forbid, but it does detract from the effectiveness of the nude scene if you're naked for half the show. Can't you wear something part of the time, for Chrissake? Milo, why did you walk across the stage carrying a ladder during Tina's song?"

"I, uh..."

"Yeah, bad idea, get rid of it…. Megumi, why were you wearing an ape costume for the whole second act? It read very badly in your Black Boys solo. I've really had it with all of you. This is the most difficult HAIR show I've ever worked with."

"Gilbert says we're the best."

"Well I have news for you, Gilbert tells every show they're the best, how do you like that? He thinks it's essential for morale. I think it's essential that you shape up. You're all very unprofessional. (No kidding.) And one more thing, if you want to take drugs, that's your business, but could you get together on which drug you're going to take and include the band in your hand-outs? Because when they're stoned and all of you are tripping, it's like two different shows going on up here." This provoked some giggling. "If you could see this mess from out there you wouldn't think it was so funny."

Poor Dimayo. Then Gilbert would wing in from San Francisco, appear on the stage like an apparition somewhere in the second act, pass around some Acapulco Gold, and vanish again leaving a note in the dressing room that we were great, that he loved us madly, and that he was off to solve some problems for the show in Rome.

Gilbert didn't live anywhere. His idea of music was a 707 taking off. Each time he left, he went in a different direction (making Jonah an agoraphobiac). He buzzed around Europe checking up on his numerous HAIR enterprises, and back to Paris where he kept an apartment for his two step-sons, or to New York to see his young daughters, or to Amsterdam "to think." He appeared and reappeared always wearing the long denim jacket, dungarees, and a white shirt. He had one other accessory—a tiny brown alligator suitcase, the smallest I'd ever seen, that he never unpacked. In it, he carried one or two fresh white shirts, some socks, perhaps a newspaper, and a few drugs. He had no winter coat, no address book, and once scribbled my Long Island number (in case we ever lost touch) in his passport.

Winter in Brussels was terrifically grim. And the provincial Belgian mentality made me lonely. Jonah seemed less horrible now, and Gilbert's visits were refreshing and uplifting—he was the only spark of originality or worldliness in the entire metropolis. I began to think lucidity might be a good bet.

"Lucidity," Gilbert explained to the troupe, "is being able to sit under a tree weez ants crawling all over you, even in your nose and your hears, and not minding...and not trying to get zem off."

"But Gilbert," someone would say, "Dimayo says lucidity's irrelevant."

"Don't you realize it's all bullshit, love?"

"What's all bullshit?"

"Everything. And everyone." Gilbert's way of saying this revealed an inner certainty that couldn't be argued.

Not by me anyway. I became his disciple, possibly because I was the only one who could understand his thick French accent. After he'd speak, then drift off into the audience or the ethers, inevitably a few cast members would approach me, "What'd he say exactly?"

"He said 'It's all bullshit, love,'" I'd explain. And they'd nod slowly, not sure what exactly was all bullshit (everything and everyone?), but warmed that they'd been given the password to the gardens where the ants ran wild. But I personally agreed with Gilbert. "It's all bullshit"—what a great answer to any question. No matter what your issue was, trite or overwhelming, Gilbert assured you it mattered not at all in the greater scheme of things. Eastern philosophy in a nutshell. Meanwhile those sapphire, mirror-ball eyes peered into your bone marrow.

Gilbert's millionaire status helped keep him from being considered insane. Where people had trouble with his philosophy, they had none with his generosity. Though, for Gilbert, the two went hand in hand—he believed in giving all one has all the time.

The cast began to wonder about Gilbert and me. They couldn't compute how I understood him. I was American and twenty years old, he was from Corsica and about fifty. But, in fact, we were both from New York and recognized each other as 'real' hippies. For us two, HAIR was a critical message.

Gilbert looked in on the entire world from the outside and found it hilarious. And, having never met anyone so unaffected by gravity, being with him lifted me off the ground, too. Soon enough, I could say "It's all bullshit, love" as convincingly as he, and in response to almost everything. Eventually, it was assumed we were lovers. Appalled by this, I did my best to Ajax the lowly hearsay. How could anyone think I'd have an affair with an old codger twenty-five years my senior?!

$\mathscr{LSD}$

Arriving in Brussels, I was living on air basically, until I could accumulate a few HAIR paychecks. The production didn't offer us anything in the way of housing, so I was temporarily encamped in a depressing and crowded household of Belgian redheads. One of them was in HAIR, but only by the red hair on his chinny-chin-chin and not for long, and the rest were in the middle of absolutely nothing except the calendar and buckets of henna.

Andy, a peripheral personality not in the show, was an English musician from Trinidad. The color of his hair was returning to its original brown and with that change, he thought a new address might follow accordingly. Having outgrown his attraction to the crimson meal ticket he shared a room with, he neatly packed his pigeon and waited for me to come home from rehearsal. The evening before, we'd confided to each other that neither of us aspired keenly to the life of a redhead, particularly of the stoned, poverty-stricken, Belgian variety, and we'd then collaborated on the order of our escape. Andy knew of an empty apartment and had wangled a key. "Why don't you come with us?" he spoke for himself and his winged companion. "There's room if you don't mind sleeping with me. And you won't have to pay rent."

Even if you did have to pay rent, I'd have accepted the offer—from the cutest thing on wheels. Despite being young and morose, he was near-perfect. In moments, we were a perky couple taxiing to our new home, prepared for the winter ahead with a bird in the hand, a guitar, and a pair of worn espadrilles each. The flat that awaited us wasn't anything you'd find at the end of the rainbow—but it was at the end of a long, dark alley.

We worked hard at our "relationship" for a week and a half, me domestically cooking gallons of onion soup and Andy out stealing the onions. But within those same few days, (that hadn't altered Andy's despair), Gilbert was gradually graduating from friend and boss to escort. And I was coming home late from places like the opera, and pointedly avoiding onion soup in the better restaurants of Brussels.

Andy, too, believed Gilbert and I were lovers. And because I was so starved for the open-minded and worldly company my employer provided, I couldn't resist hanging out with him when he was in town. "We're just good friends," I explained over and over.

Then one night, Gilbert, appealing to my vegetarian palate, suggested we have dinner at his hotel because they had great salads. Arriving there, he asked if I'd like to eat in the restaurant downstairs or in his bridal suite. Without alerting him to the gossip from the ranks, I went for the public option. But afterwards, we went upstairs for coffee so he could make a few hundred phone calls.

There my naiveté was shot to hell—I was down before the coffee came up—Gilbert literally pounced! I was stunned. Another Captain Frank on my hands, another out-of-the-question, aging Casanova jumping my bones. But the conflict here was that I adored Gilbert, just didn't want to catch his prehistoric cooties. He was hot for my little inexperienced ones though, his weight pinning me to the bed.

"Gilbert, I have to go! I'm leaving right now!" I wiggled and squirmed and seeped out onto the floor, leaving him panting into a pillow.

"No, no, no, no, no."

"Yes." I stood up determinately, clutching my clothing should he make a final dive. He looked solemnly into my face as though losing all faith in me.

"You're a fool," he said quietly. I just looked at him. There was no way I could stick around. I went to the door, opened it, and turned around to say goodbye. "You're a fool," he said again.

I left.

I walked to the elevator and pressed the button. I stood there waiting. Something about the look on his face…. The elevator came and I got in. Rode to the ground floor. When the doors opened, I didn't get out, but just stood there. Then I pressed the button again and went back up. Slowly I walked to Gilbert's door and softly knocked.

"Come in."

I entered and stood just inside the door. He hadn't moved, was still sitting on the bedside, rumpled and leaning forward. "I'm not going to stay," I said. "I just wanted to tell you that you're right, I am a fool."

Then I left again.

I then rented a no-income apartment around the corner from where a lot of other cast members did the same. It was furnished in '50's cheap modern—bland and lifeless. And, from the start, I couldn't wait to get out of there. An acid trip convinced me how sordid the whole environment really was.

We'd all been out dancing after the show one night and some-one had come around offering acid. Having refused the stuff for about three years, I suddenly decided now was the time. I figured if the trip got bad, I knew enough about the pros and cons to tell my-self it would wear off and I'd survive. James, my gay, black, Amer-ican buddy, was sitting next to me. "Do you want to do some with me?" I asked.

"I would but I'm too tired."

"I'll take some," volunteered Clyde, another gay, black, Ameri-can—just a kid really, but up for anything. So he and I each dropped a tab. And James asked Clyde to watch out for me since it was late and my first trip.

Before it came on, we moved on to a restaurant where the cast was meeting at one o'clock for a customary late supper. Sitting at the long dining table in a small upstairs room, Clyde was at one end and I at the other. I had no appetite and didn't order. But the room seemed to be getting smaller, while all the eating grew busy and claustrophobic. Suddenly the table started stretching and Clyde was a block away. Then it came back and he was super close. "Clyde," I called down the table, "how are you? Is the table stretching?"

"It sure is," said he with a huge smile.

"Do you feel like going outside?"

"Sure."

We went out into the 'old town' where the streets were cobbled and glistening in a light rain. Clyde, who was extra tall, was wearing a turban with a fat jewel twinkling on the front, and a long cape that hung in a wide triangle. The wetness on the cobblestones created more jewels on the road, and everything appeared fairylike, sparkly, and wondrous. Giant smiling Clyde was a good genie ushering me along. He then suggested we step into a gay bar around the corner where some of the cast were regulars. I was more or less game, but inside it was dark and the phosphorescent light was blue and eerie. A carnal hunger seemed hard and obvious.

Clyde, though, easily melted in. Not wanting to disturb him, I waited through a few of his flirtations before suggesting we go back outside. He was agreeable, but once we started walking and the glitter everywhere verified that the trip was well underway, he announced he was tired and going home to bed, meaning I'd be alone throughout the night. And Brussels didn't offer much in the way of late-night thrills. So I walked Clyde home then proceeded gingerly back to my sketchy neighborhood. Without a companion, the streets became silent and creepy. No one was about, not even traffic, as I crept along....

Becoming fearful, I picked up the pace, checking doorways for lurkers as I passed. Alone and vulnerable, I made for James' place, just around the corner from mine. Usually when I went there, I could ring any of the top three unmarked bells, and someone from the show would let me in—a bunch of them lived up there and the party never stopped. But I didn't know which bell actually belonged to James, and now I didn't want to wake up anyone else. As I stood there deliberating, a scruffy young Belgian appeared from nowhere and stood tentatively beside me, pretending he, too, was visiting someone in the building. His skinny, junkie status was apparent as he waited for me to press a bell, gaining entry for both of us. I hesitated.

"Who are you here to see?" I asked in French.

"It doesn't matter who," he replied, and waited for me to press a buzzer. Since James was on the sixth floor, I didn't see the sanity in getting stuck in the corridors or elevator with this specimen, so I turned and ran. I dashed around the corner for my own building as fast as humanly possible without looking back. I thought I heard pounding footsteps catching up. With my hand in my pocket, I grappled for my keys. There were two—one for downstairs, one for upstairs—and they were nearly identical. I felt them both and chose one, praying it would fit in the downstairs door, and quickly.

I reached the glass front door panting, jammed in the key, still not turning around but feeling a chase, and the door opened. Slamming it behind me, I raced to the elevator and pushed the button, igniting a tiny red light that glowed into the darkness. Only then did I turn to look at the translucent door to see if there was a silhouette out there on the front step.

Framed there in the glass, I now saw a black shadow surrounded by the red glow. The figure had two large curved horns on his head and was trying to open the door. The Devil!

The elevator came, the red light went off, and I leapt in, petrified. I rode upstairs telling myself aloud that the enclosed space would not actually be getting smaller even if it seemed to, and that it would only be moments till I reached my floor—not to mention convincing myself that the Devil couldn't get through that downstairs door.

But getting inside my apartment was no relief. There was nothing about the place I could relate to, nothing I liked, nothing I even owned. At least the Devil was locked out. I sat in a chair for a while wondering what to do, then finally figured I might as well try to sleep. But all the hallucinations were now monstrous, graphic, and horrifying, so the rest of the night was a relentless and frightful movie.

At long last came the light of dawn, and I went to the window. The glowing sky brought back the kinder aspects of the acid, and all became a cartoon down below—casual dog-walkers and bustling business men. I watched little taxis zooming around, all very Yellow Submarine. When the morning light grew bolder, I sat in the kitchen and painted with watercolors. Then at noon I was finally able to sleep. But I decided that Clyde was a schmuck, and that the sooner I got out of Brussels the better.

17

Overcoming Prejudice

It now seemed I either had to consummate the friendship with Gilbert or avoid my only friend—the former meaning venturing beyond the realms of Captain Frank and even the Blind Man into God-knew-what dimensions of decrepitude, and the latter unthinkably lonely.

Gilbert was cheery and stoned as ever when next we met. And though he looked a tired fifty, I comforted myself with the recently acquired datum that he was only an exhausted forty-five. Again, he invited me to dinner.... Hating my silly prejudices, I resolved to overcome them.

"I'm going to make you ze woman I know you are," he cooed slyly over the wine glasses.

"What?"

"I'm going to make you ze woman *I know you are.*"

I didn't probe that one. We were seated at a long, crowded table in a tiny restaurant. Other HAIR associates—assorted, hip Euro business men and women of Gilbert's senior set who had been flown in to check out our show—were having drinks around us. Gilbert carefully emptied out a cigarette to be refilled with grass. He busied himself with this as waiters fussed around on all sides. "Gilbert," I warned, as he licked the ends of the freshly-made joint, "do you think it's cool to smoke here?" We both glanced at the waiter, who was inches from Gilbert's lit match about to light the joint between his lips.

"Do you think he smokes?" asked Gilbert.

"I don't know. Maybe. It's hard to tell."

"So we ask him?"

"What if he says no and there you are sitting there with the joint?"

"Well I don't care. I'll do zis: I light it, and I ask him if he care to join us. If he don't know what we talking about, zen no problem, and if he do know what we talking about, it's fantasteek for him because he will be very, very 'igh." Gilbert then held the joint invitingly to the waiter, who, thinking he was being offered a puff of a cigarette, politely declined.

"What about all these people we're eating with?" It wasn't my paranoia, but amazement at Gilbert's lack of it. "Won't they notice?"

"Zey all work for me, love. No, zey don't notice. Zey never notice nothing." And he died laughing. "Zey just do what I tell zem and take ze money, can you believe it?" He was almost falling out of his seat.

I labored over the last course, not exactly mobilized by the cradle-grave affair destined to commence shortly after the last spoonful of chocolate mousse. "Come, daahling, we go now." He whipped out a phial of patchouli oil and gave me a fond dab where earlobe meets mandible, then took my arm.

Back to the 'otel.

I was embarrassed. I didn't want him to take off his clothes. I'd never seen an old man naked. But he had no inhibitions whatsoever, and for mine he produced buckets of champagne, little packages of poppers, half a kilo of Peruvian Red, strong espresso with lemon, and should all else fail, more chocolate mousse. He consumed these in rotation, mixing me in amongst them. And the night passed, not unpleasantly, with Gilbert repeatedly asking if there was anything I'd like.

Was anything yet undelivered? The Philadelphia Philharmonic? "Everything's fine," I kept telling him.

"Are you 'appy?"

Curiously, I was. Unwilling to engage at his emeritus level of substance abuse, but ironically serene, sprawled messily on the snowdrift sheets and pillows in the shameful disorder of the elaborate suite. Room service was just arriving with Gilbert's latest request, hot chocolate, and as he answered the door *au natural,* I dove behind an armchair.

Soon Gilbert and I were going steady. He was determined to show me the ropes, figuratively of course, as I trespassed into another generation.

He was married I found out. His wife lived in New York, accounting for the racy sprints across the Atlantic and his 'I know something you don't' air. (A novice at adultery, I read his physical distance from his wife as a failing union, rather than the accepted lifestyle of seasoned over-achievers.)

He had two step-sons, two daughters, and a third daughter on the way. "How do you know it's going to be a girl?" I asked.

"Because all my life I wanted three little girls and I already have two."

The last night we spent together, he'd just returned from Amsterdam. "What'd you do there?" I asked him.

"Well, I 'ad to go. I 'ad to go zere to be alone to sink about ze world. Can you imagine, I 'ad to go all ze way to Amsterdam to be alone!? I took an 'otel and stayed in my room for two days without seeing no one. I read ze newspapers all day and all night to figure out exactly what is 'appening in ze world."

"Did you figure it out?"

"Yes...I did."

"Well...what do you think?"

"It is frightening, love, just frightening."

"What do you mean?"

"Well, my daahling, ze people that are running zis place are very, very clever. Zey are so clever zat it's frightening."

"The people that are running the world?"

"Yes, love, zey are way ahead of everyone."

"Who do you mean, the heads of corporations?"

"No, zey are just the pawns. I'm talking about ze master-minds controlling everything. No one knows 'oo zey are or where zey are. Most people don't know zey even exist, but I know it...." He took a pensive pull on the joint he was smoking, drained his wine glass, sipped his espresso, then exhaled. "Zey 'ave ultimate control—zey know everything zat's 'appening. Zey are even controlling ze revolution. Zey know what will 'appen with ze war, with ze stock market—zey control us all."

"But, if they know everything, that means they even know that you know."

"Exactly! And zat is why I never travel without a bodyguard."

"Are you serious?"

"Daahling, I just told you—I take a big risk going alone like zat to Amsterdam, but no one knew I went zere, I make certain. Even you didn't know where I was."

"I never know where you are. But it's nice to see you when you get back." And we jumped into the bathtub where he lathered my toes with soap then licked them off, blissfully foaming at the mouth.

Eventually our conversation turned to the show and Brussels. We'd both had it with the whole scene. "It's too American, and it's already 'appened in America," said Gilbert. Ticket sales were dropping and he'd decided to close the show. "I don't care about it anymore and I'm going to do other things," he said. "Would you like to go to another show?" he offered. "Paris maybe?"

"Gilbert, I just want to go south. Morocco."

"But I want to 'elp you."

"If you want to help me, you can let me leave a week early."

The next day he called a meeting and before luring us into serenity, he announced the final closing date, then went down the cast list one by one. Nina and Megumi would go do the Paris show, this one to Germany, two to London, one to Rome, one to Montreal. "And Wendy, all she want is to leave early, so she goes after tonight."

Gilbert and I had soared through those last weeks. It would've been hard to say goodbye if it wasn't such a habit. To quell emotion, we planned an April first rendezvous in northern Morocco. "Where will we meet?" I asked.

"Wait a minute." He called a travel agent and asked, "What is ze name of ze nicest 'otel in Tangiers?" then put down the phone. "We will meet in ze Velasquez 'Otel. I think it's good for us."

After my last show, I went directly to the station and took a sleeper train to southern France.

18

Tricks of the Trade

Waking up in sunny southern France worked fine for me. Fueling up with *cafe au lait,* I then hoisted my thumb and headed south to Spain. My sister Cara had recently written saying, "Five months ago Frances was somewhere in Morocco." Less than vague but enough to go on—my old pal might still be there. I'd find her if she was.

But after my ride to Barcelona dropped me at the same quaint hotel I'd stayed in after leaving Ibiza, I realized I left my passport in his glove compartment when we were stalled at the France-Spain border. The driver had continued down the coast, highly unlikely to discover my passport in time to save me the ordeal of applying for a new one.

So the next day involved treks to the American Consulate, Spanish police headquarters, the photo place, then back to all three. I was ultimately issued a legal note permitting travel only inside Spain, during the two-week wait for the new U.S. passport.

Might as well wait in Ibiza, it was such a laugh riot last time. I grabbed the next boat and twelve hours later was sailing into that familiar harbor. It was only March, so no one was around except a few desperadoes who couldn't afford to leave. So I continued on to Formentera, the tiny island next door, and rambled around the stony hills fantasizing about renting a house and paying homage to the wind-swept desolation. A box of fresh organic donuts for sale on the counter of a small Spanish *tienda,* suggested a tiny foreign population resided here despite the rocky remoteness.

Returning to the cloudiness and cold wind of Ibiza was plain depressing. The drug-induced idleness of the non-natives made my second week beyond tedious. And when the passport finally arrived, I flew instantly to Alicante, south of Barcelona on the coast. My Moroccan mission beckoned.

In 1971, Corporate America and Capitalist Pigs were the enemy. Under the flags of Love, Peace, and Moral Superiority, one could better the planet by exploiting and swindling power moguls. Anti everything status quo, hippies upheld the rationale that negatively impacting 'bad' people was good. In Europe (and before American corporate globalization), American Express was the off-shore mascot of capitalist pigotry, a reminder of Richard Nixon and all we'd fled from Stateside. Though we all used Travelers' Checks, and reliably received mail there while roaming foreign capitals, pulling the wool over Amex's eyes was considered another point for our team.

I had six hundred dollars in Travelers' Checks and believed I could double the amount by having them 'stolen.' Others who had done the scheme made it sound easy. There were two methods: one was to get a partner to steal your checks and cash them in another country at the exact moment you were reporting them missing (but the profit had to be shared); the other option was to go it alone.

With only six hundred bucks, the first approach wasn't worth the trouble. But going it alone had geographic challenges. I'd have to make it appear that I was in one place while the checks were cashed elsewhere.

I decided to pretend I'd flown to Morocco from Spain, and report the missing checks in Casablanca. In fact, though, I'd go overland at lightning speed and cash the checks in Algeciras, the Spanish port where the ferries left for Morocco. When cashing the checks there, I'd wear a light disguise, forge my own name, grab the boat to Morocco, then tear down south to Casablanca. The next morning I'd report the checks stolen, and it would seem impossible I'd come that quickly by land. If anyone did by chance investigate— by actually questioning the cashiers in the exchange places I went to—my disguise would safeguard me.

Algeciras reeked of hustlers. Had I not been up to no good, I'd have been one of a kind. And I was definitely the only traveler in town without hashish in their boots. Scores of currency exchange places were doing heavy business as droves scrambled on and off the boats to Africa. So I donned my outfit, aiming to be a nondescript neutral nobody. Straight jeans, boots, a leather jacket zipped all the way up, dark scarf concealing all my hair, and cheap sunglasses.

Then, in the space of twenty minutes, in four different exchange kiosks, I cashed all the Travelers' Checks, shoving bundles of pesos into every pocket, my underwear, notebook, and Spanish dictionary. A stuffed pillow, I then ferried across the Mediterranean to Tangiers, sorting out the crumpled bills in the flooded privacy of the on-board lavatory. In pesos, six hundred dollars seemed like six million.

Phase One complete.

Tangiers was an assault from the first step off the gangplank. Quick-footed Arab boys made laborious attempts to flog everything from love beads to lasting friendship to a compact derivative of manure promoted as hash. I walked into town with a band of mini peddlers harping at my heels, doubling in number every fifteen feet. Spotting a row of yellow buses parked in the town square, I approached two knapsacked hipsters sitting on the running board of one. "Is this bus leaving soon?" I asked.

"About ten minutes."

We got to Casablanca that night. There, the Arab quarter or *medina* was on one side and the European sector on the other. Automatically, I chose Arab intrigue, and was drawn into the dark marketplace alleyways layered with scent. Men and women in *galabias*, the floor-length Arabic gowns, swished through the bazaar with the little ones holding on. All the women wore veils. There were tea shops, purply-green in atmosphere, with men on floor cushions passing long-stemmed kef pipes, and sipping from tall glasses of hot sweet tea with mint leaves swaying.

Scouting a cheap hotel wasn't hard since everyone knew some French. I chose a blue one and was given a windowless room for about a penny a day—fringe benefits included moisture, mildew, and a resident British writer-type next door.

Aside from sunshine, I had come to Morocco in search of Frances. We hadn't been in touch at all, but I had now learned about Taghazoute, a little beach community outside Agadir, a resort city in the south. That would be a logical place to look for her. (And take a swim.)

Now Phase Two. This time I'd play the helpless tourist, someone highly unlikely to scam the system, a polar opposite of that so-and-so who cashed the checks in Algeciras yesterday. For this I'd get all dolled up. With the air of a spoiled American, I'd feign *ennui* at the annoyance of having to report stolen Travelers' Checks.

American Express was near my hotel, so I meandered over first thing in the morning. The thick makeup made me a borderline floozy, but I floated through the *medina* ignoring the show-stopping attention I got from the populace. In Amex, I was asked to please take a seat, they'd be with me shortly. I did so as the staffer tended to another young woman before me on line. An American guy sat down beside me. "What are you here for?" he asked.

"I had my Travelers' Checks stolen. What about you?"

"Well," said he, loudly and proudly, "I'm reporting some Travelers' Checks missing, too, but I didn't really lose them. I still have them and after they refund me, I'm going to cash them."

"How much?"

"A hundred bucks."

"Aren't you afraid of getting caught?"

"Yeah, but I'll worry about that if and when it happens."

"Aren't you afraid of getting caught right now by talking so loud?"

"They're not listening."

"Next," called out the person at the desk. As I stood up, the girl who'd been ahead of me turned to leave. It was Frances.

Our jaws simultaneously dropped. "I knew I'd find you!" I said, and we tightly hugged.

"What are you doing here?" she stared in disbelief. "And what are you *wearing*?" Her head tilted sideways as she took in my clingy, floor-length rayon dress (formerly my mother's) that dragged on the ground, suede boots too warm for spring in Morocco, and a shaggy white sheepskin vest I'd bought in Istanbul. My freshly curled hair framed too much mascara and blush.

"I came to Morocco to find you, but I never thought it would be so easy!"

"How'd you know I was in here?" she asked.

"I had no clue. But that's another story.... There's tons to talk about. Want to wait for me then go have a mint tea somewhere?"

"Sure."

Somersaulting over the coincidence, the joy of seeing each other again, plus the exotic Casablancan backdrop, we went for tea and tangled tales about all that had transpired since America. "Okay," said Frances, "now what are you doing here, and why didn't you at least write to tell me you were coming?"

"Cara wrote saying you'd been in Morocco, so I just hoped you still were. I was on my way down to Taghazoute to look for you."

"How'd you know I was down there?"

"Were you?"

"Yeah, I spent the last five months renting a little house on the beach there. But it's really lucky we collided because I left two days ago and I'm on my way to Tangiers. Then I'm getting the fuck out of this fucking country."

"Why?"

"These Arabs are driving me crazy. I got raped twice on the beach down there and I really hate it here now. The only thing I learned to say in Arabic was, 'Get out of here!' The Berbers are nice; they're the ones in the south and they're really good country people; they speak a different language and everything. I really got into them. But I'm having a bad time with the Arab men."

"You're going to Tangiers? When are you going?"

"I was planning to go tomorrow. But now that you're here, maybe we can go somewhere together."

"How were you going to get to Tangiers?"

"I have an old VW. It's beat up, but it runs."

"Well, maybe I'll just go back up to Tangiers with you because I'm supposed to meet this guy, Gilbert, there in about a week."

"Okay, let's go tomorrow."

"But first I have to go back to American Express tomorrow because I'm doing a Travelers' Check number and they're going to finish processing me tomorrow."

Frances knew all about the Travelers' Check routine because it had been her ex-boyfriend who'd originally turned us onto the opportunity two years earlier. "So what are you doing in Casablanca?" I asked.

"Well, I'm doing another kind of scam. Something I started doing in Taghazoute.... There's this big tourist resort town down there called Agadir, and all these businessmen from America come there to exploit the place. They're typical corporate types, always married, who want to have fun while they're away from home. So I let them wine and dine me and think they're cool, then I stay overnight in their hotel room, and in the morning when they go to their meetings and they ask me to stick around and wait for them, I agree to. And then, as soon as they leave, I steal all their money and their cameras and stuff."

"Are you *KIDDING* me?!"

"Well, it's not a personal rip-off because they're all on expense accounts and they have insurance—they get everything back when they go back to the States. Besides I make sure they have a very nice time."

I was speechless.

"I know it sounds pretty bad," Frances admitted.

"You actually *sleep* with them?"

"Well, once you get past the bullshit they're usually pretty nice guys. And they take me to dinner and it's really not too bad."

"Jesus. Don't you think that's getting a bit extreme even for us? Is this a profession or what?"

"No, I'm not going to do it anymore, but I really needed to get some money so I could get out of Morocco, and it was the only thing I could think of besides selling drugs. Everyone does that down there and it's really a bad scene if you get caught, so I didn't do it."

"So, what are you doing in Casablanca? Same thing?"

"Well, I met this guy in Agadir who was coming up here to do some more business, and he asked me to come with him. I told him I'd meet him here and I did yesterday. He's leaving tomorrow, so I'm staying at his hotel till then. It's a free place to stay, plus you don't have to deal with Arabs all the time. I'm not kidding, if you'd been here five months, you'd be ready for some peace, too. And it's nice to have a decent shower, you know."

"So are you going to rip this guy off, too?"

"Might as well. I mean, he's really nice, he's a nice one, but why not? I swear they get everything back as soon as they get home."

"Yeah, but they think they met this real nice girl and they have a great time and then they come back to their room and find out you stole everything. What a drag."

"Well, that's what they get for fucking around and cheating on their wives and all the things they don't even think twice about. It's not that I think it's the greatest thing in the world but, let me tell you, it's not that easy to make money around here, and what I'm doing is probably the least complicated and least dishonest way. Otherwise it's just selling drugs or straight prostitution or going back to the States and working for the phone company. I don't want to go back to Long Island!"

"Well, in the final analysis, it's not too different from what I'm doing...I guess.... It's just a bit personal, that's all."

We arranged to meet at American Express the next morning. I was to bring my baggage so we could leave directly for Tangiers.

Back in my seedy hotel, the British writer invited me to his room to smoke some kef. He seemed harmless and might have some pertinent info, having resided in this grim establishment for something unfathomable like two months. Who would subject themself to this kind of gloom for that kind of time? But after a pipe-ful of his kef, I learned about the capabilities one loses under its influence—three hits and all I could do was bungle myself back to my damp cell and lie on the bed shivering for three hours, lacking the coordination to even get under the covers.

$$

- 19 -

Cheap Hotel

Frances and her VW were there as planned the next morning. But her victim's meeting had been delayed, so she'd have to go back to the hotel one more time. She'd been careful not to let on that she had a car so he couldn't track her down afterwards. Now she'd leave it parked in front of American Express and walk back to the hotel. We agreed to meet there again in three hours.

My own proceedings had gone smoothly so far. Questionnaires had been filled out covering the wheres and whens of the theft, and I would be refunded three hundred dollars now and three hundred later. Explaining that I had to press on, Amex agreed to send my first installment to their Tangiers office.

Took a final stroll around Casablanca, then wended my way back to Frances' car, in which I'd left my belongings. But the car wasn't there. "She even ripped ME off!" I said out loud. Had she taken her hustling beyond even the realms of kinship? Would she blow off an eight-year alliance for a used camera? I didn't really think so, but eight years ago I'd never have dreamed we'd back into each other separately double-dealing in Morocco.

Fifteen minutes passed. Was I unkind distrusting her, or naive waiting for her return?

No, Frances wouldn't do that to me....

At that moment she reappeared, but registered the funny look on my face. "You didn't think I'd rip *you* off, did you?"

"For a minute there, I must admit...."

"Come on, I'd never do that. I just went to get some gas because I got here early and I didn't want to hang around in case the guy came down to American Express or something."

Due to heavy March rains, the roads were flooded as we journeyed north. It was slow going, allowing us time to ponder the immediate future. I'd harbored an East African dream for a long while—supposedly there were beautiful beaches on the coast of Kenya, not to mention all those incredible animals. In Belgium, I'd purchased an elaborate map of the entire African continent, complete with railways, roads, and even caravan trails. I now produced it, asking Frances how she felt about a BIG adventure. But it didn't take long to conclude that neither of us could remotely afford it. So we munched on bread and cheese and settled for smarmy Tangiers. "I have an idea," I ventured after a time, "and you're one of two people I know in the world that might actually go for it."

"Do tell."

"This is a way to avoid having to slum it: We get all spiffed up, we look really great, we go into a nice hotel—one with a pool and a good restaurant. We look like such unaffected rose petals that the gentlemen at the front desk don't even request our passports; they just hand us the cards to fill out. Then we write down phony passport numbers that we've memorized beforehand and phony names."

"What if they insist on seeing our passports?"

"They won't. But if they do, we'll just go to another hotel and try again."

"Right, okay. And...."

"Okay," I continued, "we fill out the cards and they give us room keys. We stay in the hotel—wine, dine, swim, relax, get tan. I'll go to American Express and do my business there. We can do whatever we want. Then when we're ready to leave, we'll just saunter out when no one's looking and never come back."

"This sounds pretty good, but we have to have a story so that if we talk to anybody while we're staying there we don't blow it."

"We can say we're sisters."

"We're sisters and we're rich Americans and we're on the tourist circuit."

"We can say our parents are meeting us somewhere after we leave Tangiers."

"Agadir," suggested Frances.

"That's good. So we have to make up names and stick to them and memorize passport numbers before we go in."

"And we have to get rid of this car," Frances said. "They should never know we have a car. We have to hide it somewhere and never use it while we're staying there. Then when we leave, if they're after us, they won't think of searching for anyone in a car."

"Right," I agreed. "We can just park it somewhere. But also we shouldn't take much of our stuff to the hotel, so that when we leave, even if we're carrying all our things, it won't look like we're leaving for good because we won't have much. But where can we leave the rest of our stuff? In the car?"

"No, it'll get stolen in four seconds. Let's check some bags into the concierge at the bus station. We'll have to pay but at least it won't get stolen. And we can use the bathroom there to get ready and sort out what we'll need."

"Great. This might just work," I said. "There's really no way we can get caught. No one pays their hotel bill day by day, it's always at the end. And at the end, we just won't be there. We just have to make a clean getaway. And while we're there, keep everyone believing we're the sweetest, richest things this side of the Atlas Mountains."

"Okay," said Frances, "I'll be Mary."

"And I'll be Nancy. Think of a good corporate last name."

"Johnson and Johnson?"

"Perfect. Mary and Nancy Johnson."

We memorized passport numbers and birthdays, picked a hometown in New Jersey, invented a history of our travels in Europe, and selected a U.S. college we were attending. We pulled our best clothes from the heap in the back seat and checked our unneeded baggage into the bus station. Then we parked the car on a side street not far from our first targeted hotel. If asked, we'd explain that we had little luggage because this was just a short side trip away from our parents who we'd rejoin in a few days.

We entered the lobby, two unescorted twenty-year-old wasps, a local boy's dream. Was there a room, we asked. Yes, there was; would we be so kind as to fill out a card? With pleasure, we filled in the blanks. No one asked to see our passports. We were given a room overlooking the pool and tiled Moroccan rooftops. Satisfied, tired, and hungry, we showered then sashayed down to the restaurant for a bottle of wine and a lazy four-course meal.

In the days that followed, we made a point of eating only in the hotel since elsewhere we'd have to pay. In no time, we became the pet lodgers. Meanwhile, I collected three hundred from the Tangiers Amex office. However, they needed a forwarding address to send the balance to…in three months.

Three months? Jeez…where-oh-where would I be in three months?

But three hundred bucks was worth having an address, especially after what I'd gone through to earn it. Where-oh-where would I be in three months? I said I'd let them know in a day or so.

Meanwhile Gilbert was due at the Velasquez, conveniently located just blocks from our place. But as April first approached, Gilbert did not. No letters, no telegrams. And something about him seemed entirely capable of brushing off trifles like risqué play-dates in Morocco.

Things were starting to fall apart. Frances and I had each put on five pounds, a stubborn rain was confining us to our free room, money was low, my East African pipe-dream had blown away, and someone had smashed a window of the VW even though there'd been nothing in the car. 'Mary' was angry, and her full-boil venom about the region now bubbled over into a decision to clear out. She was lured to the northeast—apparently she knew someone in Italy…. And she had the car to either drive fast or sell. We both knew that once we bolted, we'd want this episode securely behind us.

Gilbert never showed. For me, Italy and Europe in general were less than enticing after the eight-month winter I'd just spent up there. But I needed an address….

Someone had mentioned a cheap, six-month, round-trip ticket to New York. That could mean spring and summer in East Hampton, earning some money for six months, then returning to Morocco to continue traveling in Africa. This was the best and only plan for me. So I gave American Express my father's address—of all places—deciding to go…*home* the next morning.

Frances had no interest in America, and prepared instead to cross Algeria in her breezy VW. She had no qualms, her French to get by on, her Arabic "Get out of here!" and needed little else, she said, besides gas money—that she had, thanks to American corporations with Moroccan interests.

As planned, we had carried our baskets every day, even empty sometimes, so that when we left that last time we'd appear to be off on just another day-trip. The night before our escape, we told hotel staff we'd be going to the market early next morning for a whole day of shopping. So they wouldn't be surprised to see us leaving at seven a.m., nor assume us missing until well into the night—by which time I'd be in New York and Frances in Algeria. But should our room be entered for some reason, we left behind articles of clothing, toiletries, and paperback books, indicating we'd be back. And just for good measure, Frances henna-ed her hair orange. Without our real names or passport numbers, they would only have our physical descriptions to go on. No one would be looking for one flaming redhead bound for Algeria in a VW, and my flight departed at nine a.m.

Frances drove me to the plane where we said a fond who-knows-where-we'll-meet-again farewell. Then I flew west and she sped east, with my incredible African map as her guide.

PART III ~ USA

- 20 -

Welcome Home

May 1971

East Hampton was beautiful as always. The first thing I did was ask around about Jonah. He'd just left for Ibiza, after asking around about me. Next I asked around about Gilbert. He'd just arrived in New York. "Oh, my daahling," he cooed down the phone, "didn't you get ze telegram I sent you in Morocco? I said I couldn't make it, but I invited you to join me in Paris. I waited there for you."

"Not very long Gilbert, it was only two days ago."

My father, amazed to see me in one piece after being abandoned on day one of the Latin Love Trip, actually donated a room of the now kid-less house to my cause..."but only under the condition that you get a job immediately." By "immediately" I should have known he meant in the parental sense. He started getting antsy when no paychecks came in as I unpacked, and by breakfast the next morning, was pacing and telling me, as if for the first time, how he'd once worked setting up pins in a bowling alley, because "a job's a job and there's always something to learn."

"But Dad, they have machines that do that now. I'd look pretty dumb down at Forty Lanes applying for that."

"You know perfectly well that's not the point. The point is you're going to have to work whether you like it or not."

"Dad, I just came back from Europe *yesterday*. I returned with about four times as much money as I left with. You should have more faith in me. Don't worry, I'll get a job, I'll get a job!"

"Don't start with that attitude or I'll throw you right out of here. You and all your siblings have an inexcusable way of acting like the world owes you a living, well I got news for you…."

I could see my father had had a peaceful, brat-less year with his new wife, and had no secret yearnings for fatherhood revisited. He saw his advanced parent status as that of a wise and distant friend, or preferably a pen-pal out of ink. Reasonable proximity to his flock, he reckoned, was over yonder ridge, meaning the Rockies, and don't call either. But his most successful strategy was in creating an atmosphere so oppressive that to reside under the same roof was to beg for ulcers. The refrigerator was decorated with an invisible padlock, and hours for eating were common household knowledge subject to change only when one was caught following the rules—the closer you got to obeying the system, the more new laws were imposed. It was designed to make you fail; you'd either be cast brutally to the winds of adulthood by him, or abused into the realization that adulthood was the only escape from his tyranny.

Each parent has their own unique way of saying ta-ta for now little freeloader, but my father's method went uncontested since there was no unconditional love of the mother mercifully taking us back in. Nadine worked hard at being 'nice,' as she forayed into step-mothering—and envy was one of several emotions we didn't have for her—but her "my home is your home" manner gave us the willies. And beneath a thin but pious dedication to one big happy family, she'd take a quiet day in the garden any time over somebody else's needy teenagers, relegating poor Dad the enforcer of the new order. "We have decided…." he would begin slow sentences, looking anywhere but into our eyes, "that…" and he'd unveil the latest pro-parent legislation. Like our three dogs were to stay outside from now on while Nadine's standard poodle named Peggy was given keys to even the cars. Questioning anything only invoked Dad's iceberg imitation, that emptied rooms faster than a fire bell.

Nadine was okay, though. She was open-handed with not only advice but boiled onions *au gratin*. Material things, socks and underwear, who needs 'em? Her own two children, however, could live in our house, in our bedrooms, forever—because they were 'in a difficult position.' So they gained a father, meaning they now had three parents, and we lost one, so we now had none.

A house revolves around the ambiance of its kitchen. Our house—once full of kids, laughter, animals, music, and open-minded adults—had always had a good feeling to it. But now just try getting a bite to eat and dark spooky shadows appeared from behind the stove, looked in the windows, and listened to the creaking of the refrigerator door swinging on its haunted hinges. "Guess I'll have an apple," you decide, and close the refrigerator door quietly—apples and peanut butter sandwiches were the only food approved by the twenty-four-hour poltergeists. Crunch, you take a bite of one that's too red and probably mealy but at least not bruised like the rest, and suddenly you feel cold air behind you. You wait for the words...and you don't wait long.

"*What* are you doing?"

"Just eating an apple," you say, but you feel like you're saying, "Just snooping through your wallet, Pop, weeding out the twenties." The air gets colder.

"Don't you KNOW that THOSE apples which you are HELPing yourself to withOUT permission were ordered six months ago by special request from your step-mother's naturopath in Health Valley, Colorado? THOSE apples were transported, by foot, two hundred miles across the Himalayas and had to be ordered years in advance just so you can nonchalantly BITE into one without asking!"

What do you say to that? Obviously the peanuts in the peanut butter had their story too, so you trot down to A&P and buy some Twinkies. Rather than start a house fire by burning the wrapper in the bathroom sink, you toss it into your waste basket.

Fatal. "What were you doing eating junk food in my house?" He's holding the sticky wrapper.

"I was hungry and it was after nine-thirty a.m. and before one o'clock p.m."

"I don't want to hear your tired excuses. If you want to kill yourself, kill yourself somewhere else. I don't want junk food in MY house. If you can't manage to keep the same hours as everyone else living here (who *were* they is what we wanted to know), I suggest you find another place to live." Then he'd soften a bit, "If you get hungry between meals, have an apple or a peanut butter sandwich."

Dad figured if he forced everyone to live the good life, he wouldn't be surrounded by temptation. That's why he spent the better part of each day in the garden. The cabbages were his friends. And when they came into the house, they stayed in the salad bowl where they belonged, they didn't make long distance phone calls. (But in case they got any ideas, the telephone was decorated with a visible padlock.) Dinner was usually broccoli, spinach, and a green vegetable. Collards for dessert. Ever since my mother had died, now two and a half years ago, Dad had sworn off everything but lettuce, parsley, and Johnny Walker Green. He longed to go to the Valley of Eternal Youth where the Happy Hunzas lived, but said it was buried so deeply in the Himalayas that he'd be an old man by the time he got there.

"Who the heck can follow your standards, Dad? You can't!"

"I can't YET. Takes time. They say it takes the body as long to get well as it took to break down…. Gee, that means I'll be dead before I live forever." He dropped three ice cubes into a glass and reached for the cabinet. "Some people have the discipline."

"Who?"

"The Happy Hunzas in Hunzaland."

"Their discipline is basically lack of alternatives—what can they possibly do wrong up there? Know anybody else who has that kind of strength?"

"Oh, there's lots of people, don't kid yourself. Dr. Shelton and his health school in Texas are probably the best example. He calls it a school because people who go there learn about sound living, but it's really a fasting institute. All they can have is distilled water. And when they complete their fasts, Shelton puts them on his regime."

"What does that entail?"

"Well, not much," Dad laughed. "Nothing on his bill of fare would appeal to your polluted palate. He doesn't even use honey. No seasonings, no stimulants, no alcohol, no meat, no cooking— just raw, organic fruits, vegetables, and nuts. You couldn't sustain that diet for half an hour. It's hard to believe but he doesn't even eat grains—no bread, no cereals. And his only beverage is distilled water. Even juice is out; he says we should eat the whole fruit."

"Sounds like the life of the party."

"Let me give you a piece of serious information:" Dad's face became earnest except for that little twinkle in his eye, "Fasting's no picnic." I had to smile. "Shelton's helped a lot of people," he went on. "He actually saves lives all the time. His magazine has mind-boggling stories about the positive effects of fasting."

"Well, who goes there?"

"Anybody who wants. Sick people who've heard about it. Apparently any ill can be improved—and Shelton says healed—by fasting and then following the purification diet. And overweight people go there to lose weight and learn how to eat properly. Some people just go there to clean out and get a fresh start. It's pretty hard to do it by yourself, but at Shelton's you got no choice—all there IS is fruit, vegetables, and nuts. Old Man Shelton's probably so pure by now that one look at a chocolate chip cookie would put him in the grave."

But when we had company, all bets were off. Then it was Twinkies for appetizers, hot-dogs, potato chips, marshmallows, booze, cigarettes, then all pile in the car and go get ice cream. Really weird, but we understood…you could only break the law when Dad broke it. You were guaranteed a swell time when he did, though.

21

Gimme Shelter

When I got back from Europe, the last thing I needed was negativity. It was just a damn shame my hometown happened to be the most expensive place in the U.S. The affordable dives I was accustomed to scoring were glaringly absent. You could rent a one-room shack called a cottage for the same amount you could earn all summer if you got a good job—i.e. you'd break even at the end of the season to face a freezing winter in a dead resort town. Or you could have two jobs and get ahead financially but never get to the beach, so why pay all that money to live near the ocean? It was hard enough for New York doctors and celebrities to find summer houses they could afford, for us impossible. Thus, all the young people lived with their parents. Except us. We ended up living with other people's parents, kind of home-hopping, playing it by fear.

But now that I'd lived in Ibiza without electricity or running water, why should I need these luxuries Stateside? It was summer, I could rough it. Lots of old houses had little sheds and out-buildings on their properties—I'd look for one of those to rent. Nothing fancy, I'd always be working or at the beach anyway. The idea was not to spend money so I could return to Morocco in a few months. For the moment, I had my father's VW (for a rental fee of twenty dollars a week) to scout dwelling possibilities....

Until the VW deal was terminated because three whole weeks passed and I still wasn't a Harvard professor or even a waitress at the diner. But I knew finding work would be a breeze—restaurants would sign you on in a day; *lodging* was the challenge. Limited now to bicycle radius, the search became intense. Then one day over tea,

I broached the subject to my friend, Leo. "Sure wish I had a tool shed. I might have to build a lean-to."

"What about our tool shed?"

"What tool shed?"

"Over there," he pointed out the window to an overgrown bush. "Inside that bush is a little tool shed."

I hurriedly pulled him outside to where we squirmed through the thicket to unearth a Winnie the Pooh hideaway. "Little" was a generous word for it—measuring about fifteen by seventeen—but it was large in charm and privacy. I was totally enchanted and Leo was bored so we made a deal—I'd live there and he'd help me fix it up! Provided Gwen approved....

Gwen and Earl, Leo's parents, had had enough of the "swingles" scene, as it was called, in the Hamptons, and decided to summer on a smaller, hotter, more exotic island. Ours was not to reason why they preferred the Isle of Manhattan to the Isle of Long, but to be blessed by their absence. Their overall property included several dwellings. There was the Big House, relatively new with three or four bedrooms. There was the Studio, smaller with its own bathroom. Nestled in the hedge was the tool shed. And down a dirt trail was the Little Studio, a sky-lit cottage with one bedroom and a loft.

In the Little Studio resided Gwen Marie, Leo's younger sister, and Clark, someone she loved and others didn't. But they were lost in each other, and averted their eyes as Leo began playing MC for a three-ring circus springing up on their land. Not far from the Little Studio was a two bedroom cottage in which resided "Aunt Sarah," last seen seven years ago watering her roses. (It was never revealed whether she was a spirit, a spy for Gwen and Earl, or fiction, but she remained ever a consideration late a night. "Shhh! You'll wake up Aunt Sarah!" someone invariably hissed whenever the volume rose, sending the mob into reverent silence.)

Leo built a wood floor for my new living room (an earthen floor would be pushing it, even for me), then, together, we built a loft bed. At my father's suggestion—he was nice again, I was moving out—I laid a snazzy brick floor in the back room, with beach sand between the bricks. I nailed old windows onto the empty square holes, and hooked a big swinging window where a back door used to be. Leo offered use of the bathroom in the Studio, plus free reign of the Big House in the event of cabin fever.

The first night, when my electricity set at eight p.m., I decided I'd rise with the birds. I'd use my bicycle for transport, and for a living I'd sell organic donuts like the ones on the Island of Formentera.

Gwen Marie's best friend, Jill, was another caretaker of an un-parented house. On Thursdays and Fridays, in exchange for all the donuts she could devour, Jill donated her kitchen so I could prepare for weekend sales. But her father, a shrink named Doc who came out weekends, was not to know his home doubled as a bakery as he sweated in New York. Never was he to suspect that someone called C.U. Round had base operations there for Holesome Donuts. Doc actually enjoyed arriving Friday nights to a plateful of healthy junk food, but couldn't compute that lingering odor of sesame oil. Fortunately, Jill's fourteen dogs, particularly Baked Bean—community heart-throb, named for an uncanny resemblance—shouldered that burden.

One day I was at my father's, probably squaring up some debts, and someone leaked that Gilbert had been calling and my father had been withholding the messages. "Dad," I approached him, "has someone named Gilbert, a guy with a French accent, called here at all?"

"I'm not sure. You might have had a call or two."

"Dad, can't you just write down the name and number if someone calls for me?"

"Look, I know about this guy and I don't like the smell of it."

"What do you mean?"

"Just quit messin' around with married men!"

"I'm not messin' around."

"You heard me! I'm not going to tell you again." He left the room.

But Gilbert and I were smitten. We'd transcended the age differential and hurdled an ocean only to reconvene in the Land of the Free. I could forget such littleness as being stood up in Tangiers, but

I couldn't wait to see his crazy face. Not knowing where his wife figured in our narrative, I expected to find out soon enough.

I told him about the tool shed.

"It sounds just mahvelous," he said, "we must go zere for the weekend together."

"I go there every weekend."

"Oh, my daahling, I must come and see you zere. It must be so perfect for you."

A tool shed was perfect for me?

"Yes," I said, "it's perfect. But it's not perfect for you. I mean, there aren't any restaurants around, and there's not even running water." I could imagine taking him with me to the gas station where I brushed my teeth every morning. "No...I don't think you'd like it that much." I could just see him pulling up in the limousine to a hut half the size with none of the comforts.

"Of course I would, my daahling. I would like anything zat you chose."

"Well, I didn't exactly choose it. There wasn't a selection."

"But it sounds so nice with ze flowers all around...."

"Honeysuckle.... And no telephone." That would do it.

"That would be very peaceful. I would ADORE a weekend without ze phone."

"And no lights."

"I bring some."

"Bring plumbing too."

"We will get all those things for you when I get zere. But is it nice? You are 'appy living zere?"

"Yes, very."

I knew Gilbert wouldn't come. Even if he got the knack of life in a broom closet, he'd never muster the passivity for a weekend at the beach. And his alligator valise contained no bathing trunks. Suppose he did turn up, though, how would I explain him to people? What if my father saw us bumbling down Main Street for coffee on Sunday morning?

22

Gilbert

Manhattan was a better backdrop. Gilbert organized the logistics of where and how we'd sneak away for a snuggle, and often it was at the penthouse of his 'secretary,' Jean-Paul. We'd enter with Gilbert's key, and with a haphazard nod to Jean-Paul, we'd gallivant across the half dozen zebra-skin rugs, up the stairs, and straight to Jean-Paul's tiger-skinned bed, carefully bolting the door. Jean-Paul was a smallish, bi-, fine-featured blond who was annoyingly French and amazingly unconcerned about lending us seclusion.

Or there was Binky Black. One afternoon after lunching with this fellow in a restaurant, Gilbert lackadaisically asked if Binky planned to go directly home afterwards. "No," came the reply.

"Well zen do you mind giving me ze keys to your apart-e-mo?" Without a word, Binky handed them over and we scurried to another penthouse, not unlike Jean-Paul's.

Binky and Jean-Paul were no spring chickens either, and I saw a pattern emerging where these three gents looked seedier and seedier and I more and more like the dumb young fool.

The next time we rendezvoused, it was at The Plaza; a double date this time with Jean-Paul and a sleek young model named Dixie. Gilbert and I went straight to the reserved suite overlooking Central Park where Jean-Paul and Dixie were already stationed. I still hadn't second-guessed Gilbert for a moment, but Jean-Paul's sincerity left *beaucoup* to be desired. This Dixie chick was a little unsettling, as was the ornate decor of the double beds and mirrors. Shortly after the first round of gin and tonics, I gave Gilbert an "I don't like the looks of this" look and he conducted me into the bathroom for a conference. Assuring me the room was just a nice place to have din-din, no one was spending the night, we then un-denimed and continued conferring enthusiastically. Then we languidly re-denimed and strolled back out with flushed faces to where Dixie and Jean-Paul offered us the Academy Award for Indiscretion plus two more gin and tonics. We feigned innocence, but from then I was mollified in knowing that Jean-Paul and Dixie hadn't been enlisted to corrupt me, but possibly the reverse.

Instead of a weekend in the shed, Gilbert opted for a month in Europe. And I was left with the realization that his wife wasn't the only one pregnant. I resigned myself to the heartless hands of a clinic in Queens, and Gilbert, sucking on a spliff in one of Europe's capitols, knew nothing of it. Wondering when he was due back, I phoned our liaison, Jean-Paul.

"I don't ever want to hear zat name mentioned again in my life!" Jean-Paul then slammed down the phone.

Soon, however, Gilbert returned and phoned me himself, desiring another lucid, out-of-body experience. When I told him about Jean-Paul's mysterious comment, he was unfazed, "Oh, he get like zat sometime. He's moody. Do you think I should fire him?"

"You mean you actually pay him to denounce you all over town?"

I never knew what was in store when I made a date with Gilbert. This excursion to his New York revealed, for the first time, the interior of his residence. The coast was clear, he told me, for a three-day weekend. Fine, I thought, half hoping to hear the grueling details of a fight with the wife, or maybe how she'd run off with Binky. Not one for formalities, Gilbert had me uncomfortably planted in their comfortable bed upon arrival. Glancing furtively around the outrageously uninteresting room, I felt the need to know the whereabouts of the family. "Where are your two daughters?" I commenced.

"Oh, zey don't live here. Zey have their own apart-e-mo."

"A two-year-old and a four-year-old have their own place?"

"Oh yes, zey have always lived in zere own place. We think it's better for zem and better for everyone. It's just around the corner, we see zem all the time."

"God, I should hope so. And is the new one going to move right in with them?"

"Yes, after she get used to New York a little."

"Gilbert, that's shocking! How can your tiny little kids live all by themselves?"

"Zey don't live alone, love, zey have their nanny with zem at all times," and he laughed.

"Well, that's a relief…I guess. And where's your…wife?"

"Oh don't worry, she won't be home all weekend. She's in the ze 'ospital having our new daughter."

"She is?? That's HORRIBLE!"

"No, it's *fantastique*! We are very 'appy."

"But I shouldn't be here if your wife's in the hospital having a baby!"

"No, daahling, it's okay. I will see her. I will go and visit her every day. Whether you are here or not. We can't stay in ze Plaza because I have to be here to answer ze phone. Don't worry about her, she is only thinking about ze little baby."

"I'm not worried about her, I'm worried about YOU. You should be only thinking about the little baby."

"I AM thinking about ze baby. In fact I call ze 'ospital right now!" And he did, while I lay nudely wondering which one of them thought maroon, brown, and navy blue were a neat color combo. The whole place had chaotic, teenage overtones, and not a corner was intended to impress anyone. Despite being a lavish brownstone, the home seemed to accommodate nothing more than collapsing on the floor, changing clothes, or guzzling a quick Pepsi. I never did find the kitchen, even when Gilbert left me on my own as he dutifully visited the hospital.

"Well, while we're on the subject," I said when he hung up, "I have some baby news of my own…."

Sunday afternoon his daughter was born and he had to go and be where he should've been all along. "You can stay here if you like. It will only be a couple of hour," he said, reaching into his closet without looking and pulling out one of twenty identical denim jackets. I knew I'd experienced the best of Gilbert. New facets of his personality were definitely detracting from the friend who'd so buoyed me in Brussels. I walked outside with him, more certain than ever that he was from another galaxy—the eyes gave him away. He walked me to the corner as the limo waited in front of his townhouse. We didn't say a word. We stood a foot apart and looked at each other. "I love you," he said.

"I love you, too," I told him, then turned up Lexington and he turned to the shiny black car. I to the beach, the summer, the tool shed, the rest of my life; he to his new baby, his wife, his whirlwind of work, drugs, Jean-Pauls, Amsterdams, foreign beds, and airplanes.

Needless to say, our orbits didn't cross after that. He became a memory, albeit seismic. But one Hollywood night, seven years later, I found myself with a friend at the dinner table of none other than Binky Black, now a West Coaster. Somehow younger, he was now the husband and father of a Swedish tribe of assorted sizes. Gilbert, he said, to my utmost surprise, was still his pal, alive and well. (Gilbert couldn't possibly still exist—that was lifetimes ago. Surely he'd burned out like a comet.)

The following day, Binky held a Christmas Eve party and invited me back. And stepping lightly across this palm tree Noel, suddenly appeared the unchanged figure of Gilbert. The denim jacket was white linen now, but the glass of champaign, Gitanne cigarette burning, and sapphire eyes were all right in place.

"Do you remember me?" I probed his astonished stare. He'd never struck me as someone with a memory.

"Of course!" he gasped at the question. "Of course I remember you, my daahling, I *love* you!"

"Are you sure you remember me?"

He was almost insulted, "Yes! I remember everything. I remember Brussel, I remember you lived in a tool shed. I have even told people zat I know someone who lived in a tool shed—" He stopped. "Do you remember ME??"

I hugged him tightly.

He was over the moon to see me. In fact, you might even say he needed me now. He and his wife were divorced. He had a little car he buzzed around in—balancing coffee cups on the dash-board—but was otherwise penniless. He was sleeping on the floor of his step-son's Santa Monica apartment. Bursting with ideas and humanity-oriented theatrics, he was viewed in glossy Hollywood as a nut.

I had loved just that madness, and respected the universal mind he sold subscriptions to, but he hadn't needed support when I was a free-falling waif in Brussels, when his spirit was the truest thing around. And in New York, he was just plain shifty. Now I'd landed. And I could no longer hold onto the strings of his balloon. After spending a couple of evenings with him, one night I just slipped away. I couldn't really explain that he'd had every chance with me....

And the third daughter, born that unfaithful Sunday, had only lived four years. She was hit by a truck while walking down a country lane with her nanny.

- *23* -

Fenton's Doghouse

Leo's place was getting crowded. He and Thurber (his dog) and Tapioca (his friend) and Marc the Narc (a stranger) were secure occupants. But being less secure didn't divert Jules (another friend) and Cara (my sister) from moving in, too. Red and David pulled up in a van after driving around the country for a year, and Leo said they could spend the summer in the driveway and use the house when they got van fever. Mimi and Lily proposed a tee-pee as a variation, and Leo gave the green light there, too. Then Abe asked if he could pasture a couple of horses for the time being, and the horses enhanced the Indian theme, so that, too, came to pass.

The tee-pee was a work of art. Mimi and Lily were commended for not just its genius construction but their resourcefulness in providing their own accommodations. And this add-on made it possible for all their friends to live in it, as well. (Everyone has wigwam envy on some level.)

The tee-pee was a special place. In the evenings, people would filter in and pass the peace pipe around. They'd talk about how incongruous Clark was, how great the ocean was, how nifty the tool shed was, what was playing in the drive-in, and how awful all the week-enders were, and how awful it was what was happening to the beautiful Hamptons and the rest of the world, and how great Gwen and Earl were, and who was that new guy making eggs this morning, and is there really an Aunt Sarah, and if there isn't who waters her roses, and if there isn't also can we live there, and too bad Sonny got stuck in Nova Scotia with no draft card, and is Marc really a narc, and did Gwen Marie really drive into the drive-in topless so the ticket guy wouldn't look into the back seat where Mimi, Lily,

and I were giggling under a blanket? Then someone would intro-
duce fire water and the spirits would flame up, leading more often
than not to whooping, jumping, and mass migration to a local bar
known as Fenton's Doghouse.

One night in the tee-pee, the mass migrated and I found myself face to face with Jules. I took him by the light of the moon to
see the tool shed and he stayed the rest of the summer. That left a
vacancy in the Big House into which Cara inserted Harry, a *bandi-
to* from Miami. His friend, Randy, came with him and that's who
was making eggs. Gwen and Earl were somewhat taken aback when
they dropped in unannounced for a weekend.

The first big storm took the handsome tee-pee away, leaving a
soggy circle of sleeping bags around a black dent where the camp-
fire had burned. So Mimi and Lily moved over to Doc's to be closer
to Baked Bean and farther from Gwen and Earl who were learning
the sad truths about both summer in the city and unchaperoned
young people as tenants. There was nothing actually *wrong* with the
household, but the turnover of new faces was disconcerting, and
some of the names—"Hi Mom, I'd like you to meet Abe the Car
Thief, Peter the Pervert, and Marc the Narc. That's C. U. Round, she
sells donuts, and that's her boyfriend, Jules, who doesn't work because he has no expenses." (Even other people's parents didn't like
the sound of that.)

"And where does Jules live?"

"In the tool shed, too."

"So that's why there are two bikes there every night—we didn't
know it HELD two people. How many others live in that tool shed?
Is that where the Indians moved to?"

"No…uh, the Indians went back to…uh, India." Sensitive data
had to be withheld from Gwen and Earl, who were tight with Doc.

Jules was an 'other glove' boyfriend, meshing easily into my
no-frills lifestyle. Rustic and comfy in his old jeans and plaid shirts,
his shed-dwelling prowess and cycling stamina bowled me over. We
peddled and body-surfed through the days and tooled around in
the shed at night. Cozy and sexy, outdoorsy and minimal, he was a
country cutie—relaxed, capable, and true.

I could've stayed with him (and Molly, his Border Collie) forever—the balance, the friendship, and the jokes were really all a girl needs. But did I want to settle down, have babies, stay on Long Island? This corner of the globe was definitely home sweet home for Jules, who was turning thirty any minute.

I couldn't even think about it. In theory, I was saving coin to get back to Morocco—I had that plane ticket. (What I'd do in Morocco was fuzzy, but the world was still achingly unexplored.)

After many trials, to the glee of Jill's dogs, the Holesome Donut recipe was perfected. With no sugar or white flour, these treats were now irresistible. In half dozens, they were sold in plastic bags with informative bright pink lettering on labels cut from paper bags.

In 1971, everyone at Pam's Market—a glorified farm stand (health food stores didn't exist)—was in need of a non-toxic donut. So Pam, a lady I'd known since childhood, ordered six dozen—twelve bags full, and pledged to reorder every Friday all summer.

With the cost of ingredients as my only overhead, all my prospects in bicycle radius, and no rent at the tool shed, I was in the black the minute Pam paid for her first batch. A proud entrepreneur now and part of the solution, I was the 'back-to-the-garden' daughter my father had raised. He, the Mediterranean, and even Jonah had taught me what matters and what doesn't. I was now living with no electricity, no car, and had my own healthy business! (Dad and I didn't necessarily concur about mating, but regarding the environment and natural health, I was his firm follower. He'd been organic farming and composting since I was ten, and studying holistic health since Mom died from medical treatment. Now, with my bicycle, donuts, and tool shed, I had the low carbon footprint worthy of the family name.)

So where else to flog my wares?

"What about Eats?" Pam and a few others suggested.

"Eats?"

No one seemed certain what Eats was exactly or its hours of operation, but supposedly some enterprising young woman named Simone was serving nutritious food somewhere.

"Is it a restaurant?"

"Kind of. It's at Fenton's Doghouse."

"How can a restaurant be in another restaurant?"

"She's doing her own thing on the back patio. Just go over there, you'll find her."

Saturday morning I strolled over with my donuts. "EATS IS COOKIN'" announced a sandwich board outside. I crossed the dim, empty bar-room and dance floor, and followed a ray of sunlight to the patio out back. There, under the wisteria, I found a collection of hungry hipsters swilling o.j. and chomping on granola. A James Taylor type was strumming acoustic guitar and singing. Hand-picked flowers adorned not just the tables but the plates.

"Can I help you?" a gracious woman with superb posture stepped toward me as I inhaled the scene.

"Uh, yes, are you Simone?"

"I am," she had a half smile. "Welcome to Eats."

"Thank you. My name's Wendy, aka C. U. Round, and I make and sell these Holesome Donuts." Displaying a bag, I opened it to offer a sample. "Several people suggested I come and meet you because you're also into healthy food. Here, try one."

"Yes, we are absolutely into healthy food—it's not just me, we're a co-op—and I'd love to try a donut." Reading my label first, she then took a studious bite. "Very good," she confirmed. "You make them yourself?"

"Yeah, and I sell them on weekends when the crowds come out."

"We sell our own baked breads, too," she said, steering me to a small table by the entrance, where a basket contained tidy, wrapped loaves of banana bread, zucchini bread, cranberry-oat bread, and more. "We serve slices of these in bread baskets at each table with the meals. People enjoy them for free, then on their way out, they buy loaves to take home. Our prices are extremely reasonable since we do our own baking."

"That's a great idea, to let people sample them for free."

"It works because people haven't had these breads before, but once they taste them they get excited, and they know they won't find them in the grocery store. Come in the kitchen, you can try some."

I trailed her into Fenton's streamlined kitchen. There, a young guy named Greg was flapping jacks as Rachel, a friend of Mimi and Lily, grabbed a couple of omelet platters and headed out to the tables.

The bread was fresh, moist, and delicious. The whole enterprise had a sing-song ambiance obviously orchestrated by this Simone. "Tell you what," she said, "if you'd like to donate one or two packs of donuts to us every weekend, we'll cut them up to offer in our bread baskets. In exchange, you can sell them on our sale table and keep all the money."

"That sounds perfect," I said, "When do you want me to deliver them?"

"You can bring some tomorrow, if you'd like. Then every Saturday morning. We're open nine to three on weekends."

Ka-ching—one more account, this one in walking radius. Business was booming. It's phenomenal how quickly one can get rich with zero overhead.

$$

As Nature Intended

The following weekend, in response to my curiosity about her eatery, Simone invited me to stay after closing for a meal on the house.

This lady was a study in dignity. From her square carriage to her enunciated speech, to her uncanny and unselfish aptitude for business, she was impossible to dislike. Embodying the spirit of the era, she wanted desperately to change things for the better. But where I threw vigor at my challenges, Simone threw serenity. Nothing could rock her gondola. With the reserve and oneness of a Buddha, she was so unpretentious, so not trivial, that she appeared detached. Some who didn't know her considered her stand-offish, even odd. But Simone wasn't a child or party animal; she was nine years older than me and determined to hit thirty from a position of strength. She wasn't even a local, but from Southern California. She'd bucked the trend by going from west to east, and was now applying her Golden State charisma to the East End of Long Island.

As we sat tête-a-tête over omelets, she filled me in, "The eggs are from Iacono's Egg Farm, and I grew the herbs."

"But how did you get the Doghouse to rent the restaurant to you? They must be charging you a fortune."

"No, they let us use the space for free."

"What?!"

"Well, the restaurant's unused in the daytime, so that's kind of a waste," Simone said simply. "Also, if we're serving breakfast and lunch here on weekends, it brings more attention to their place. We use their equipment, but bring all our own food. Our menu's completely different."

"But they let you use their whole kitchen and everything? That's amazing."

"Just the patio. They also get 100 percent of all bar drinks we sell."

"Well that makes sense, it's their booze, right?"

"Yeah. But," she giggled, "I think we've sold maybe two drinks so far. Nobody ever asks about alcohol. They come for our fresh-squeezed orange juice."

"This kind of sounds like a better deal for you than it is for them."

"They're fine with it. They like having their place open more. And they get free food if they come in (but they don't). Plus we leave everything cleaner than it was. It's kind of experimental, no one really knows where it will lead. Of course if this were to continue and thrive, we'd probably re-work the terms."

"Are they part of the co-op?" (Co-ops were a new business model that few had experience with.)

"Let me explain this co-op," said Simone, "because maybe you'd like to be a member.... Co-ops are great because a number of people together can accomplish what an individual cannot. I could never start a restaurant all alone, nor would I want that kind of workload or financial responsibility. But with a few others, it's totally doable."

"I completely agree. So who else is in it? Does everybody pay a monthly fee then all share the profits?"

"No, it's a work co-op. Ownership of the restaurant is shared and all the work is shared."

"So Greg and Rachel are members?"

"Yeah. They have to be in order to work here because we don't 'hire' people, everyone is paid by dividing our proceeds."

"Who else is in it?"

"It started about six weeks ago as a partnership with myself and a man named Stewart. I wanted to get more members, but he had a more traditional partnership in mind, where he would pay, someone else would do the work, and the profit would be shared. But co-ops only work when all members are equal. So once Greg and Rachel came in, I let Stewart out."

The EATS menu consisted of free-range organic omelets, whole-grain pancakes with local honey, homemade granola, homemade yoghurt with fresh-picked local berries, homemade gazpacho, farm-fresh salads, fresh o.j., fresh fruit salads, and maybe a sandwich or two. The clientele was continually transfixed by not just the taste of everything but that someone was making their own yoghurt, granola, and gazpacho, scoring organic veggies from gardens and farms, offering yummy breads (and donuts), and presenting it all on the shady back porch of Fenton's Doghouse. I thought it a cool thing with a savvy sailor charting the course. "So what do I have to do to join?"

"Just start helping with everything that needs to be done," Simone chuckled, then explained how, with no backing (after Stewart left), no borrowing, and no money, she'd built the business on a series of agreements. Locals who grew vegetables would donate a bag of tomatoes or zucchinis in exchange for a free lunch. Berries could be picked in the woods. Granola was homemade with oats, raisins, almonds, coconut, and cinnamon. Yoghurt was a snap to make and inexpensive. Whole-grain pancake ingredients were also minimal. Free-range eggs from Iacono's Farm were discounted since she bought many dozens. Local folksingers wanting audiences were always willing to play a few hours for a good meal. And fresh flowers to decorate with could be plucked from any field. (Gazpacho was labor-intensive but fresh tomatoes were delicious, inexpensive, and easy to come by.)

And where did those bread loaves come from?

Here Simone had struck a deal with the good Pam of the Farmer's Market, who had not only a commercial kitchen for her own bakery and deli, but all the ingredients in her store. Simone had suggested that on Thursday nights, after the Market closed, she use Pam's ovens and giant mix-master to knock out massive batches of five or six different breads. If Pam provided the kitchen and ingredients, Simone would do all the work and give Pam one-third of the loaves, wrapped and labeled, to sell each weekend at fancy prices. The other two-thirds (up to eighty loaves) went to EATS. (And once Simone had me on board, we two could bang out a hundred twenty loaves, label and wrap them, in three or four hours.) Then Friday mornings, Pam would wake to a gleaming kitchen and a mountain of tempting breads that her weekend patrons would snap right up.

Simone and I were just what each other needed. I was holistically eye-to-eye, dug her concept, had restaurant experience up the yin-yang, and brought in my resourcefulness, my friends and family, and my inherited work ethic. Plus I lived five minutes away and Jules had a van. (Simone, too, traveled by bike.) My only caveat in joining was that I keep my donut business going.

So, Monday through Wednesday we'd arrange food acquisition. (Even my father bartered organic produce for occasional breakfasts for himself and Nadine.) Thursdays, we'd write up that week's menu, pick berries in the fields and woods, make fresh yoghurt and granola, and whip up gazpacho. Fridays, we'd gather last minute supplies, plus it was donut day for me. Then Saturday mornings, Jules would pick up the eggs while Simone and I ferried food to the Doghouse in bicycle baskets and backpacks.

After closing on Sundays, we'd sit down for a hearty meal, laugh over mishaps, divvy up the proceeds, and take stock philosophically. We were always in the black, always thrilled that another week had worked so well, and ever eager to do better in the week ahead.

But Simone's original dream of an earthy collective of enlightened beings kept hitting the wall. "I'm finding out that most people just want a job, to go to work, get paid an hourly wage, then go home and forget about it," she said, like a child discovering there's no Santa. Greg and Rachel just didn't share the vision. And my exuberance actually freed them to have the simple summer restaurant jobs they wanted. "But why on Earth would you want to be a waiter or waitress when you can be a co-owner?" Simone beseeched them. "Why would you want an hourly wage when you can have a stake in the business?" It was beyond her beatnik brain.

"Because...." they'd shrug. And we two filled in the blanks after they left us to wash the dishes and sweep the patio—neither of us daunted by brooms or dirty plates, particularly in upbeat company.

"Fine," Simone conceded to them, a few weeks into my membership. "If what you want is to be just another of our expenses, like heads of cabbage, then that you can be. Be waiters and we'll pay you by the hour. When you're done serving, home you go." But thereafter, though Greg and Rachel cheerfully and dutiful performed their roles, Simone demoted them karmically, forever branding them as our 'heads of cabbage.'

And the 'co-op' was again a two-way partnership. Had I not so appreciated Simone's pizazz, ingenuity, and love of hard work, I, too, may have recoiled from being *a restaurant owner*. But her forte for making something out of nothing and leaving everyone thrilled to assist her never ceased to amaze me. And EATS caught on.

From my first day on the job, it was nothing but fun. We were half a mile from the ocean in the lush Long Island summer. We were serving sensational food under excessive praise from all who dined there. We had bikes as transport, no overhead, a modest income, and we each had a great new friend.

On our days off, to escape the swelling crowds, a few of us would walk down the beach about half a mile for the magnificence of just the white sand, grassy dunes, and shimmering waves. Removed from the populace, there was little need for swimsuits—no one could see our 'disgusting' bodies way out there, and the police didn't know about the spot. We named this haven Naky-Nowy, short for "Naked Nowhere," and there we'd rejuvenate, luxuriate, and confabulate.

About ten or twelve regulars frequented the spot, including Simone, me, Jules, Peter the Pervert (of course), and occasionals from Leo's tribe. Just as everyone wants to experience Paradise, everyone at some point wants to skinny-dip and lie on an empty beach naked in the sun. The only rule at Naky Nowy was that you had to be naked. No one could sit around with us in a bathing suit—souls and bodies had to be bared with the rest of us. Yet never was there a sexual moment, implication, or even flirtation; we were just harmoniously there together all summer long.

Word eventually got out about "The Nude Beach." And strangers began wandering into our midst. Our only recourse to their 'curiosity' was to enforce the rule, "You can stay, naked." And they wanted to stay. Who could resist giving nudity a try? Or to at least hang out with unclad females? But countless lives were transformed by a few hours or weeks at Naky-Nowy where the conversations were as novel as the sand against skin. And speaking of organic, speaking of natural, speaking of equality, speaking of open-minded, being naked in the sand with a circle of others is liberating on all counts.

But our secret place was becoming more like beach theater, particularly once the New York mime troupe discovered us and began practicing naked handstands and cartwheels there.

One Friday, as I was manufacturing donuts at Jill's, someone burst through the door proclaiming the police had Simone. Simone, the Cooperative Citizen? She didn't even have a car.

As Simone later recounted, three uniformed cops hiked in behind the dunes, all the way from the Main Beach, for a Naky-Nowy ambush. Completely unnoticed by the non-conformists, suddenly there were six shiny black shoes center-stage. And what followed was right out of the Keystone Cops. With cries of "Pigs!" and "The Man!", bare buns escaped in all directions. Overdressed for the occasion, the cops couldn't give chase. But as they lingered, it was clear they weren't there for the life experience. In moments, they nabbed the only three nudes who hadn't high-tailed it.

Simone, of course, recognized fleeing as admittance of guilt, or cowardice at the very least, and held her ground in all her glory. Along with her, basically frozen in the headlights, were two young newbie nudes from New York. The three were ordered to suit up and march back to civilization where a squad car was waiting.

At the station, they were booked for "lewd and lascivious conduct in public." That's when Simone had issued the S-O-S to whoever had a phone, hoping someone with a vehicle (Jules) would rescue her.

Once located, Jules responded accordingly and was enlisted to calm the terrified tourists, too. But their beach-day-gone-terribly-wrong was just the beginning. One they'd mistaken for a bare beauty draped across a dune was no cowering kewpie doll when it came to questioning authority. "Listen," Simone nudged them about twenty years forward in their thinking, "we're innocent. Our naked bodies are not lewd or lascivious. Those charges are false and we have to fight this in court. But we have to stick together."

Just what Billy and Julie wanted, to stay linked to this incident they wouldn't even dare relay to a their closest friends back in the City. They were speechless. "Give me your phone numbers," said Simone, "and I'll keep you abreast of what happens from here, and let you know when we get our court date." Their mouths were hanging open. They'd be demanding that the State of New York grant them their right to be naked in public? What if Mom finds out? What if we're on the front page of the NY Times? (Naked.) They reticently gave Simone the digits, then accepted a lift with Jules (who had hair past his shoulders) back to their rental car at the Main Beach parking lot.

Simone, whose demeanor never faltered, showed almost no sign that her blood was a-boil. Fueled by the injustice, probable male chauvinism, and Calvinist mores, she simply rose to a new challenge. "'Lewd and lascivious,'" she shook her head.

Simone held firm against the State's charges and, under the auspices of a patriarch named Judge Drood, the case became known around Leo's and the Doghouse as "The Crude Lewd Nude vs. the Prude Rude Drood." Her city-slicker sidekicks soon evaporated, leaving Simone alone to lock horns with the Empire State. A pro bono lawyer materialized at EATS and guided her to trial. But when, upon entering the courthouse, he advised her to wear her birthday suit in the courtroom to emphasize her position, she saw that he was as weird as the case against her. She laughed off his suggestion, but they lost the case.

Without missing a beat, Simone appealed. A female lawyer from the City, also pro bono, now picked up her cause, and this time they won. Fully dressed. And from that day forward, in the State of New York, thanks to dear Simone, clear distinctions were enacted into law between being naked and being lewd or lascivious.

- 25 -

Dropping Out

Fall 1971

Mimi had graduated from the hip little private school in a potato field that she and Lily attended. She got A's in Goat Milking and God is Dead. This school 'de-emphasized' traditional bullshit like reading and writing. Math and the alphabet—except L, S, and D—were snubbed, and the principles of freedom and expression were so encouraged that attendance itself was optional. The kids spent whole weeks in the frozen yoghurt store. All for a modest few grand a year. When I asked Mimi about the multiplication tables, she said she wasn't into carpentry. She was into India, and wanted to sign up for any college program that would get her over there.

"How about the Peace Corps?" my father tried his standard pitch on his most recent high school grad, knowing Peace had been her best subject.

Mimi shrugged, "I'm not into corporations, Dad."

Dad was giving up. "I'm just suggesting you look around. There are all kinds of supervised programs abroad that allow you to be useful while seeing the world. Do yourself a favor."

"How about getting on a bus?" I suggested. "No point in going to India if you're going to be hooked to a bunch of American kids over there. The point of traveling is to get away from all this." My father threw me a disapproving look and returned to the garden. While handing out advice, I included Lily, who was wondering how she could suffer hitching fifteen miles to school and back all winter, not to mention sitting through Intermediate Soy Bean, without Mimi. "Drop out," I recommended.

"Drop out?"

"Yeah. What are you learning that you can't learn on your own? Why don't you hit the streets and learn some spelling?"

"Hey, that's neat, I'd be a high school dropout!"

"You've got the education of a play-school dropout."

"But what will I do? I don't want to go to India." Her knowledge of geography was comprehensive—there was Long Island, India, and Berkeley.

"The world's waiting for you. Where do you want to go?"

"Berkeley I think."

"Well, maybe we'll go together…I was thinking of visiting my friend Kevin in Seattle. I want to see the Oregon coast, and I also want to check out Big Sur."

"Big Who?"

Four days after our conversation, we put our thumbs out in Bridgehampton.

"Where ya headed?" asked our first ride.

"Seattle."

"I can take you as far as Southampton," he chuckled.

Going by way of California—since it was too cold to take the northerly route and since we were mutually intrigued by Oregon (now that I'd explained to Lily it was a state not an herb)—meant our journey would be a mere four thousand miles. By mid-afternoon we were sweet-talking two cops in New Jersey where hitching was illegal, and by midnight were standing in a traffic circle near Columbus, Ohio, wondering where and how to spend the rainy night. But rain is actually a hitch-hiker's ally—people take pity on you, especially if you look as bound to get abducted as we did. A station wagon stopped and suddenly we were set all the way to Kansas City.

Riding north from Denver, we encountered our first if-y character, a woman of about forty with no fixed destination. The power of a glance is fully exploited between hitch-hiking companions; you both get the same funny feeling within minutes. Or sometimes the one in the front is first to notice something, like the inevitable bottle. In this instance the alcohol was hidden from view, but our chauffeur's inability to stay within the white lines was hard to ignore. Being female, we'd given her the straight-forward version of where we were going rather than the cagey rendition we offered the other gender—with them it was best to discern their destination before revealing ours. Now, having divulged that we were headed for Cheyenne, our driver said, "Well maybe I'll just take you all the way up there since I got nothin' else to do." What's a hundred and fifty extra miles on a quiet suicidal afternoon? We were now swerving from side to side.

"Would you like me to help with the driving?" I volunteered.

"No thanks, honey," she was bent over the wheel, "I love to drive."

I waited a few more minutes, while Lily threw 'boy-what-a-nut' looks around the back seat, then I said, "I hate to mention this, but I really have to go to the bathroom."

"Me too," said Lily.

"Any chance of stopping at the next gas station?" I asked.

"If ya gotta go, ya gotta go!" the driver threw both hands in the air. "We'll stop at the next one."

Thank goodness it wasn't far up the road, and there Lily and I pow-wowed in the restroom. Hard-pressed for an effective lie under the circumstances, we opted for the truth. The lady was waiting in the car when we returned. "Um, we've decided," I began, "that we just can't let you drive us all the way to Cheyenne. We appreciate your kindness, but we can surely get another ride with someone who's heading up that way already. We just can't let you do it."

"But I want to," she flung open the door. "Come on. I said I would and I will."

"No, we can't accept your offer. It's so very nice of you, but we can't let you do it." She wasn't pleased with the turn of events, how would she fill her day? But seeing our conviction, she drove off dejectedly with half a smile and half a wave.

The sun was getting low, a bad sign. "What state are we in?" Lily asked, another bad sign.

"You mean have we crossed the border yet?" I gave her the benefit of the doubt.

"What border?"

"The Colorado-Wyoming border."

"Oh...I thought we were going to Cheyenne."

Our next ride wasn't much better but at least they made good time. Speed of light. It was an old Chevy with monstrous wheels setting it four times higher than all else on the road. Despite the screaming aura of reckless youth, the late hour meant we had to climb on up. The two couples on board, local juvenile delinquents passing beer cans to and fro like a juggling team, welcomed us along. Though uneasy about the alcohol, we'd now observed that most everyone on those long roads was equipped with liquid refreshment, so we just settled back and prayed. And soon, again, we were roadside in the middle of Wyoming as the souped-up Chevy shot off north, blowing the horn in abandon.

Now the sky was deep salmon, low mountains black against the horizon. Standing there shivering, we listened into the distance for an approaching vehicle. Nothing came. And when it did, it passed us. "We're never going to get a ride," I moaned.

"You always say that and we always get a ride," said my sidekick with a prophetic smile.

"True, but this time is different. This time we really aren't going to get a ride." The population was about two square people per mile, including hitch-hikers.

"Then you always say 'this time is different,' and we still get a ride."

Always travel with a cheerful optimist, I decided there and then, and we got a ride. All the way to Salt Lake City. Jetting along, the nocturnal hours passed, hinting of eternal desert on all eighty sides. It was clear we shouldn't continue past Salt Lake without daylight.

Around midnight, we were deposited on a cloverleaf outside the city. We stood on the chilly off-ramp like space travelers looking for signs of life. Ten long minutes passed, forcing us to review our options: we could wait there perhaps till morning and freeze, we could burrow into our sleeping bags by the side of the road but we only had one, or we could walk into the city—nowhere to be seen—and hunt for a room. Choosing the latter, we ambled slowly along the road, hoping the town would materialize. We then heard a car coming. As it approached, we jumped up and down waving our arms.

It stopped. A yellow taxi with two passengers in the back. The driver had the world's nicest face. "Going into town?" asked the world's nicest voice. "Hop in," he looked back to his two passengers for approval. They nodded and we clambered into the front. "I gather you two aren't from Salt Lake City," the driver smiled, pulling onto the black, empty highway.

"No."

"Come to visit?"

"No, just passing through."

"Have you got folks here to stay with?"

"No, we're hoping to find a room for the night."

"Where're you from, if you don't mind my asking?"

"New York."

"So are we!" chimed the chumps in back. "We're just coming from the airport. Here on business for a few days." They beamed happily at the coincidence, unaware that a population of sixteen million meant there was more chance anywhere of running into a New Yorker than not running into one. "You know," said one, "we're going to the Holiday Inn, and, uh, you could stay in our room if you wanted. There'll be space on the floor, or, uh, whatever.... I mean, you know, you might not find anything else."

The cab driver was obviously a peach, but these two? "Well thanks," I said, "but we'll look around. There's bound to be something."

The driver gave us a paternal wink. "I have an idea," he whispered.

We arrived at the Holiday Inn. "You sure you don't want to stay with us?" needled one of the New Yorkers. "Might be fun."

"We're real sure."

"You know where we are if you get stuck."

"We're not going to get stuck."

"Creeps," muttered the driver as the door slammed. About thirty, lean, and avuncular, he'd won our hearts. "Listen," he started, "this is going to sound off the wall, and if you don't like the idea, I'll help you find a hotel, but your best bet would be to stay at my place....

162

There's a double bed, you can both sleep there, have a bath, a cup of tea, whatever you feel like. You're probably exhausted and it's quiet there. I'll be driving my cab all night. I just started and don't get off till seven in the morning, so you'd have the place to yourselves. Don't feel funny about it, I'm a traveler, too, and I've been in a lot of strange places at two a.m. I've been helped out many times by strangers, also, just when I thought my luck was down, and I'd like to help you out." Lily and I looked at each other, both wasted. "Anyway, you think about it for a minute because I have to pick up another fare. Then I'll take you wherever you want to go."

Where to stay was momentarily forgotten as we rode through the generic back streets of Salt Lake City. Our friend's name was Jim. Saying he was a traveler was an understatement—he'd spent at least two weeks in every state including Alaska and Hawaii, and more often months or years. He'd been in Salt Lake about a year now and was thinking of moving to Montana next to do some ranching. Half Cherokee and half Mormon, the West was his native home, and his ultimate destination was wide open space.

We now pulled up to a neighborhood bar and two rowdy hillbillies climbed drunkenly into the back seat. "I do believe this is one fine town y'all got here," one of them slurred as he slumped into the seat. "What's the name o' this here fine town?"

"It's Salt Lake City, you half-wit," bellowed the other, falling against the first.

"Salt Lake City…well I'll be goddamned!"

They wanted to be taken to their truck and were going to sleep in the bed in its cabin. Aha…Lily and I were thinking alike. "Where're you going in the truck tomorrow?" I asked them.

"Sacramen-no," they drawled in unison.

In keeping with his saintliness, Jim interceded, "You fellas heading out first thing in the morning or you got business in town or somewhere along the way?"

"Well, uh, we gotta unload in the mornin', but after that, why, we're on our merry way! Sacramen-no, here we come!"

Jim looked at us. We gave a nod. He proceeded, "These two girls here are looking for a ride to Sacramento. You got room?"

"Lord, Lord, landlord, two girls? Always got room for two girls. Got room for ten girls!" And they had a belly laugh over that.

"Well these girls are in a hurry and they're not interested in any funny stuff. If you want to give them a lift, they can meet you tomorrow morning at your truck. Otherwise, they'll find another way to get where they're going."

"Hey, sure, we'll give 'em a lift. We'll take 'em out there to California. It'll be a pleasure to do so, doggone it."

"What time?"

"I'd say about eight o'clock. Yep, that'll do it, eight bells and we're rollin."

We'd reached their truck, an enormous semi. "Okay," Jim confirmed, "tomorrow morning, eight o'clock, these two ladies will meet you here. Agreed?"

"You bet."

As we headed for Jim's house, we wondered about our impending ride. "On the positive side though," Lily pointed out, "it could mean one fast ride straight to California." We decided that if they were sober and sane tomorrow, we'd go. And Jim insisted on personally delivering us to the truck.

At his cozy house, he served us tea, put extra blankets on the bed, then had to get back to work. "I'll wake you up when I get back at seven so you have time for a hearty breakfast. I'll take you for steak and eggs so you're fortified." We'd probably need more than fortification, maybe stun guns, but his good will was a Godsend. We snuggled into the sturdy bed and suddenly there was Jim, looking none the worse for a night of cab-driving, standing in the sun-flooded room saying, "Let's get breakfast."

♥

- 26 -

Keep on Truckin'

The Alabama boys were off-loading great slabs of meat from the huge semi when we arrived at eight. Jim wanted to actually see us off, but we implored him to go home to bed since it could be a while and the trucking operation appeared to be legit. He made us promise to send a post card from Seattle, and told us to call if things didn't work out with these dudes, or if we ever returned to Salt Lake.

Around nine-thirty, the guys finally finished their work and climbed into the cab of the truck where we'd been waiting. Lily and I were relieved, but only briefly. Our companions drove directly to the service station of a truck stop and instructed us to hide in the back bunk while the truck underwent some repairs. "You can't let anybody see y'all in the truck because it's ee-legal to carry riders. If the mechanics see you, they'll make you git out."

"Well, how long will it be?"

"Won't be but a minute." And they hopped out.

"Where're you going??" I whispered out the window.

"Shh-hh!"

It was dark in the garage, and pitch black in the bunk, with the curtains drawn that separated it from the front. And it was also broiling hot. We waited. Nothing happened and not a sound was heard. "Maybe they're real quiet mechanics," I whispered, trying to paint a brighter picture for my little sister.

"I don't like these two," she shook her head. "I think something fishy's going on. Maybe they're going to kidnap us."

"They can't kidnap us here, we can just scream. There are people all over the place." Half an hour passed. One of the drivers came back momentarily to get something, but hurriedly slipped away again.

Having been stashed in the bunk before arriving at the garage, we had no certainty what our actual surroundings were. With the understanding that this hive was swarming with mechanics, our discretion, apparently, would be our ride to Sacramento. "They said we were in a garage," Lily whispered, "but we don't know if there's really anybody else around or not because we're afraid to look out. I think we should open this little vent here and peek out."

"Okay."

Opening the vent, Lily spied out, then turned back to me with wide eyes. "The drivers are right over there and they're talking to two other guys, other truck drivers it looks like, and they're motioning to the truck. They're talking about us, I think. It looks like they're talking about who's going to GET us."

"GET us?"

"Yeah."

But being unduly suspicious could cost us a good, long ride. Overnighting in Salt Lake had slowed us down considerably. (When hitching, you just want to get there; and, unfortunately, a little risk comes with the territory.) So we gave our escorts the benefit of the fourth doubt and remained in the shadowy cabin as it grew warmer.

But soon the ride wasn't worth the unrest. We climbed out angrily, anticipating seizure and removal from the premises.

But there wasn't a soul around. We tiptoed to the door, then out into blinding daylight, seeing then that the place was a bustling gas station attached to a truckers' restaurant. Semis from far and near were fueling up and rolling out. We didn't see our perpetrators anywhere, but figured we'd station ourselves in the restaurant for a while. They'd find us. First we retrieved our bags from the truck, just in case they took off without us.

We drank coffee and weighed our few options as another half hour passed. In theory, we had a ride all the way to the west coast, but in fact it was after one p.m. and we were all of two miles from Salt Lake City. But if we hitched from here, the best deal we'd get was probably worse than the bum deal we already had.

We then spotted the two bimbos strolling in for coffee. They weren't at all surprised that we'd come out of seclusion. "After a quick coffee," they said, "we'll be ready to leave this joint."

"Whew," I sighed. "It's so late though, it looks like we'll be traveling all night." Hardly a night to look forward to, crossing the desert with this southern sideshow.

"Nawh…too late to set out now. We done booked ourselves a room for the night, back in Salt Lake. The four of us'll just stay the night there, have us a good ol' time, and get goin' at the crack o' dawn. We got some beer, too." Lily and I stared at them. "Now don't you go worryin' about payin' for the room," said one, "we'll take care of it."

"We're going to the ladies room," I said. "Take your time with your coffee and we'll meet you in the truck in fifteen minutes." We took our baggage with us.

Knowing they were inside bent over coffee cups, we rushed out to the gas pumps, dropped our baggage, and stood waiting as one semi after another rumbled in to fill up. Despite many trucks going west, we were now feeling more selective.

"Hey, you girls want a ride?" What sounded like another come-on was from the window of a mammoth truck just lumbering in. We looked up into an eager young face—another hungry highway man, no doubt. No one could be trusted anymore.

"Yeah, we want a ride," I bristled, "but that's all we want. We don't want SEX if that's what you mean."

"Oh, excuse me, Miss," and he rolled up the window.

Lily grabbed my arm, "He's not the one we're mad at. He might've been perfectly innocent!" I looked toward the truck. The guy turned away with embarrassment. "He seemed kind of nice," Lily said.

"They all seem kind of nice at first. Look, we gotta put everything on the table from now on. If he was perfectly innocent, he's not anymore. We can't afford to get trapped in semi bunks, wasting time and getting nervous. I'm sick of this nonsense."

Another guy jumped out of the same truck and walked over to us. "I'm sorry if my buddy offended you," he apologized. "He really didn't mean any harm. He's perfectly innocent. He just thought you might need a ride, that's all."

"Well," Lily atoned for me, "we've been hassled by a few truck drivers lately, so we're a little wary."

"Are you trying to get somewhere?"

"Trying," I said.

"Sacramento or Seattle," Lily told him.

"Me and my buddy are on our way to San Francisco by way of Sacramento."

"When?" I asked coolly.

"Right now."

"Where're you going to spend the night?"

"We're driving all night, we gotta make time. We're stopping briefly in Reno and that's it." No Alabama accent, no beer cans, just clear eyes and a friendly face—this guy seemed fine. "If you're going that way," he said, "we wouldn't mind some fresh company; it's a seventeen hour drive. I always pick up riders; I like to talk to people while I drive—passes the time. And my partner and I," he looked over his shoulder, "well, we don't have much to say to each other." He laughed. "In fact, I can't believe you were afraid of him… he's a virgin. He almost cried when you snapped at him that way."

We all had to laugh. "But won't you get too tired to keep driving all that time?" I pictured the truck sliding dreamily down a canyon wall.

"There's a bed. We take turns sleeping."

"But is there room for you to sleep with two more people squeezed in the truck?"

"There's room for the Last Supper. Come and look. Three can fit in the front and one in the back, easy. Even four in the front will work with featherweights like you two."

Lily looked to me for affirmation. I nodded. "One thing though," said this guardian angel, "don't tell Billy I told you he's a virgin. He'd kill me."

We put a few fast miles between ourselves and our anti-heroes. "Lord, Lord, landlord," Lily mopped her brow, "that was one dog-gone mornin' we done spent in that there truck."

"That's okay, you half-wit, we done survived. Sacramen-no, here we come!"

This monstrous rig showed us how comfortable and pleasant the trucking life can be. The visibility and views were stupendous, the bed behind the seats was long and wide, and both the drivers loved being on the road. They entirely welcomed our unexpected and light-hearted (now) company. With Frank happily married, Billy a virgin, and us having stated our terms up front, there was no innuendo or agenda, freeing all four of us to have a lovely cruise together. We got the gist of Frank and Billy's clash early on, told them it was a bore, and lured them into the telling of their life stories instead—we had seventeen hours. So, after the desert showed us colors we'd never seen, we coiled into a velvet night of mesmerizing tales and the dark endless highway.

As promised, there was a stop in Reno. Frank and Billy always allowed themselves a couple of hours' gambling in the state of Nevada. "Just enjoy yourselves in there as long as you want," we told them. "We'll be right here whenever you come out."

It would be fun to check out the casino, and I was twenty-one, but Lily had just turned sixteen. Knowing it might be a long wait, we wondered if we could stroll into the casino unobserved.... From the response we'd been getting from the general public though, apparently we looked *young*.

But I then had an idea, and Lily agreed we had nothing to lose.

We combed our hair, put on lipstick and mascara, and walked up to the door Frank and Billy had disappeared into. There, a not-too-intimidating gentleman told us the age was twenty-one and he'd need to see identification.

"We're old enough," I told him, "but we don't have any ID on us."

"I'm really sorry, but I can't let anyone in without it."

"We really are old enough," I said, and Lily nodded.

"I'm sorry," he said. "I really am."

"Well, let's look through our bags," I said to Lily. "You never know, maybe we'll find something...." We both dug into our bags and rummaged around.

"Oh!" I suddenly exclaimed, "Great! Here's my driver's license." I handed my valid New York license to the guy, who carefully studied it, then smiled in approval.

"So that should be fine," I said, "you've got ID for me, and my sister's older than me."

Lily smiled.

"Oh," the guy paused for half a second. "Okay, go on in."

Billy and Frank were more than surprised when we strolled up to the table where they were gambling. But they weren't interested in losing much money or time, so we were all soon climbing back into the big rig.

Though we'd be driving all night, Lily and I felt completely safe hunkering into that great machine—so alien to us, so familiar to Frank and Billy—then barreling into the deep, black, Nevada nothingness, across the cold desert floor toward the faraway coast. These guys were the real deal, and the truck was the latest and the greatest. There was something poignant about that long ride we four took together, the two men appreciating us as much as we did them. With just the hum of the paternal engine, the gentle voices of our drivers, the warmth of the cab, aglow by the instrument panel, it was a fairytale about two little waifs rescued by kindly strangers, and being fully reassured that the world is good, people are good, and happy endings do happen.

It got late. Nevada grew deeper still. We were all getting sleepy. "Listen," said Frank, "it's a big bed back there, two people can easily fit. Me and Billy do it all the time, and we sure as hell wouldn't if the bed was smaller. Let's not make a big deal about it, let's just say whoever's tired should get in and go to sleep and not worry about whoever else might be sleeping at the same time. I think we've established enough trust, and we'll all sleep better in the bed." For the remainder of Nevada and into the green rocky hills of northern California, there were nearly always two bodies snoozing side by side in the bed, with two alert ones talking and driving up front. The only arrangement that didn't occur was Frank and Billy in the bed with me and Lily driving the truck.

Then…another cloverleaf…and the jet-engine truck regained momentum with an arm waving out each window. It was hard saying goodbye to those two.

27

Berkeley

After a fine stay with Ibiza Kevin in Seattle—now making leather bags and belts, claiming to be done with the road (and donating his sleeping bag to me as proof)—we headed down toward Berkeley, Lily's promised land and drop-out Mecca of the Western Hemisphere.

Choosing the scenic route, we went west from Seattle, and were picked up by a small procession comprised of a recycled school bus and a recycled U.S. Mail truck towing a VW bug. Inside the hand-painted vehicles was a posse of unlikely companions, who'd been cruising together for months. They welcomed us and whatever we could contribute for gas. Securing both lodging and transport was great fortune, as was their leisurely pace in which to worship Oregon's rugged shoreline. Leaving no scenic overlook overlooked, our caravan crawled down the coast for five full days. In Eureka, California, we finally parted company, as they went east and we south. But I then discovered my back-up cash stash of $250 had gone with them.

Though the universe was merely evening the score with me, the theft vexed my traveling plans. My New York bank account might still reflect the summer's hard work, but sending for funds would take a week or two. With a dubious winter already on the way, stalling felt all wrong.

Lily, meanwhile, satiated with Geography, was ready for her next course, and sensed a simpatico demographic on Telegraph Ave. Here she could learn Social Studies by simple osmosis and do grapefruit fasts under the supervision of experts.

The Berkeley scene was too reminiscent of Amsterdam and Ibiza for me, so after delivering Lily to her friend's dorm at UC Berkeley, I continued hitching south to see Big Who.

Lily was a Californian by the time I got back—it only takes twenty-four hours to forget everything east of the San Andreas fault. (Or do it in six with organic mescaline.) In just three days, Lily had taken up residence with the One World Family in its large "Family" house consisting exclusively of curtains, carpets, candles, and posters of mandalas. I was ushered through a maze of orange drape-doors to Lily's room. She wasn't in it, but another girl, wrapped in a sari, told me Lily was in the restaurant working. With directions, I located the One World Family Restaurant on Telegraph Avenue, and there was Lily, in her sari, dishing out tofu behind the counter. "What on Earth are you doing?"

"I joined the One World Family."

"So I see…."

"You wanna join?"

"No. Who are they?"

"They're the people who own this restaurant and the house I'm living in…. I'm them. I own it as much as anyone as long as I live and work with them."

"What religion are you now?"

"It's not a religion, it's a commune."

"Well, there's something pretty cult-y going on back at the ranch."

"Well there's this leader guy who's kind of like…the leader, but he's real nice and he even works at the restaurant."

"Do you have to pray to him?"

"No."

"What do you have to do?"

"You just have to work so many hours a day, and you get free room and board in return."

"Be careful."

"Free room and board. Don't worry."

Worry about Lily? No flies on that kid, she just knew a good deal when she thumbed into one, plus she loved brown rice. Lifting a forkful to her mouth with chopsticks, she giggled, "Free. All I can eat," and she was wasting no time discerning her capacity. Her brothers and sisters shuffled past us serving tweedy mounds of One World Food to stragglers from the Unrelated Masses who drifted in off the crowded street. The Halfwit would be alright. (And the nickname endures to this day.)

We'd been on the road about a month now, and, without money, I kind of had to head home. Plus, I missed Jules. But I lacked the fortitude for another three thousand miles of freeway. Hitching by private planes was the only solution. I boogied out to San Francisco Airport and was pleased to learn about a small private terminal right next door.

At the Butler Aviation information desk, a man said the best strategy would be to wait for the pilots to pass by as they checked in before departure.

It was a long day. The pilots were amenable enough, but mostly going north or south to places like LA or Portland. Mid afternoon, I met an oil mogul off to Texas, but he just snapped, "Wear a skirt next time and you'll have more luck." Then, to make things bleaker, two more hitchers turned up.

These two gals had no set destination and were short on clean clothes to boot. They had their sites on Lake Tahoe but, learning I was trying for New York broadened their outlook and they elected to just do whatever I did and go wherever I went. My most overt body language couldn't discourage them. So, rather than one innocent pilgrim appealing for a lift, we were now three mangy hippies wanting a free ride. And what we got instead were predictable lectures about values, social mores, and the benefits of a college education.

Evening arrived and it appeared we might spend the night there. I had to re-route these babes or it would be many nights. Lake Tahoe sure sounded nice, I mused aloud, maybe I'd mosey up there myself, maybe forget about New York, winter coming on and all that. Hm, picturesque Lake Tahoe or grimy New York? The waffling wayfarers realized they weren't really that keen on New York either, they did not need that headache—what had they been thinking?

As for me, alas, people there were expecting me at this point—but as soon as I could break away from that hell-hole, I'd head straight back to idyllic Lake Tahoe.

Meanwhile, I still had one undeveloped scheme for which a couple of helpers wouldn't hurt. I'd once met a guy who'd traveled from Los Angeles to Denver in the pet compartment of a plane, dressed as a dog. A friend with a legitimate ticket had pretended to be his owner and gotten him securely into his cage and onto the plane. Then, in Denver, once unloaded from the pet compartment, the 'dog' had leapt out of his cage right on the landing strip, and fled the scene (on two legs).

For this undertaking, allies would be welcome. So I pitched it to my new chums, envisioning the three of us sealed into jet-black isolation thirty thousand feet above the Rockies, disguised as Dalmatians, sharing the close air of other critters in the cargo hold.

For more data, I made an inquiring call to TWA (Trans-World Airlines) feigning concern about the well-being of my Great Dane I was shipping to New York, "Is the pet compartment really safe? How close to each other are the animals? Oh, one on top of another…. But it must be terribly unpleasant for them…. Oh, you drug them. Is that absolutely necessary?"

"It's absolutely necessary," the official voice replied. "It would be a terrifying experience for them otherwise. And it's chilly."

Under sedation, it would be difficult to bounce out of one's cage upon arrival. Plus we had yet to secure costumes…. At this point the durable duo bowed out, but would willingly assist if I persevered.

I didn't.

It was eight p.m. now and pouring rain. Butler hadn't closed down for the night so we could camp on the carpeted floor of the lounge if necessary. My pals were having a merry, unconcerned time of it—not getting there was half the fun. Plus they lived in San Francisco and could just go home! Well, woof-woof, I lived in New York (sort of) and had exactly twenty bucks.

Tired and restless, I decided to wend my way over to the big terminal and maybe cozy up with the Presidential leer jet or something. I left the girls watching TV, saying I might see them later and I might not.

Damp and dreary, I arrived at a ticket counter of the sleepy San Francisco Airport. I approached a sympathetic-looking ground host, "What are the possibilities of flying without a ticket?"

He smiled.

"I'm serious," I said. "I don't have enough money and I'm determined to get to New York."

"You could hitch-hike."

"That's how I got here and I can't face the road again so soon." (Cara was the only one I knew with the stamina for round-tripping by thumb.)

"You could try hitching from Butler Aviation on a small plane." This guy was alright.

"I've been trying all day, it's not as easy as I thought. There must be another way I don't know about.... What about cargo planes—where do they fly from?" Maybe I could travel as a parcel rather than a pet.

"They fly from a freight terminal about a mile away called Flying Tigers, but they don't take passengers."

"Can't you stow away on them?"

"No, they're very strict. Not long ago, a young guy stowed away in the freight compartment of one of those planes and was found D.O.A. He froze to death. Those freight compartments aren't pressurized, so don't you dare get on one of those."

"But don't they have any seats at all?"

"Yes, some of them have a few seats up front to take deadheads back."

"Deadheads, D.O.A.'s…yikes. What are deadheads?"

"Deadheads are just stewardesses and pilots who have flown in from somewhere and don't have a scheduled flight back, so they take a cargo plane home."

"Do these planes go to New York often?"

"Yeah, all the time. If they'd let you go, you'd surely get a flight to New York tonight."

"Well, how do I get to Flying Tigers? It's worth a try, isn't it?"

"Sure, why not?" he smiled encouragingly. "Flying Tigers is down a long narrow road that leads from the back of this terminal. It has a big red neon sign on top, you can't miss it."

"Thanks!" I was off.

"Good luck!" he called after me.

I found the back door of the airport. There was nothing out there but rain, planes, and ground crew. Dodging 707's, I found the unlit little road and started walking toward a neon glow. Exclusively for airport vehicles, the traffic was slight, but I hailed a baggage wagon, climbed aboard, and in moments was composing myself before the Flying Tigers entrance. Everything about the dark drizzly building exuded a behind-the-scenes air, not open to the general public. (Like going in the stage door during a Broadway show.)

Having semi-pulled myself together before coming out into the rain, I looked a bit misplaced nonetheless. Still, I didn't imagine stewardii got dressed up for a midnight freight flight, so I'd blend in okay. Squaring my shoulders, I marched through the swinging doors. Inside was a broad open room that felt toasty compared to the mess outside. At its far end, a window framed a friendly-looking man at a desk. An adjoining locker room could also be observed with a few people bustling around—stewardii probably or possible D.O.A.'s. Walking up to the man at the desk like I was old hat around here, I said, "Miserable night out there." Then I paused for him to feed me a cue, leaving my smile where it was.

"Are you flying tonight?" he asked.

"Yeah. I'm a deadhead." I tried to sound casual but had a feeling deadheads didn't call themselves deadheads (like jerks calling themselves jerks). I nodded my head toward the locker room, "In there?"

"That's right," he said. I let out half my breath as I crossed to the other room. There, I acknowledged a pleasant-seeming lady who might be on my flight, and I opened my locker. I hadn't asked *where* this plane was going—I'd broach the destination issue later—now all my energy was on credibility. I could feel the scrutiny of the man in the window, so I assumed a routine air...ho-hum, off to New York. "Miss," he called out.

I played deaf.

"Miss...." he called louder. Everyone heard. I had to acknowledge him.

He beckoned me over.

"Yes?" I replied, re-approaching his window.

"What's your number?"

"Oh, my number," I laughed. "Two sixty-eight."

"Two sixty-eight?"

"Yeah."

He looked at me sideways. "Can I see your card?"

"I don't have it with me.... What's wrong with two sixty-eight?"

"Nothing wrong with two sixty-eight, it's a fine number. But there's only seven seats on the plane."

We both started laughing. "Well, you got me there," I said. "No, I'm not really a deadhead, but I take these cargo flights all the time. I'm in a special category."

"Oh you are?" he nodded slowly. "What special category might you be in?"

"Well..." I tried to sound modest about it, "my father owns this company."

"Your father *owns* this company?"

I nodded.

"What's your father's name?"

Oooh, tough one. And I better answer quickly—one's father's name doesn't require ponderous thought. "Flying Tiger," I said.

I got a chuckle but not a flight. Back out into the rain. I went back to Butler to watch TV.

28

Wingin' It

The two girls, cocooned into sleeping bags, were out cold in front of an old Sinatra movie that depressed me further. It was only eleven p.m., too early to give up. Hearing a stir of activity in the waiting room just outside our lounge, I wandered in to see what was brewing. Several freaky-looking freaks had milled in and were settling on benches. They were amiable so I sat down beside a young man clad in a homemade coat patched in a hundred places with souvenir badges. He carried a leather suitcase so gummed with travel stickers it looked like a large cube of fruit Jello. More razzle-dazzle types were still filtering in, complete with children, guitars, and feather hats. "Where are you going?" I asked the guy.

"Puerto Rico," he replied.

"On a small plane?"

"No, we have a charter. A DC 10."

"Oh. You're all going to Puerto Rico?" The terminal was now almost full of these fantasy folk.

"Yeah, you wanna come?"

"Can I?"

"If there're any empty seats when we're ready to go, I'm sure you can come."

"Why are you all going to Puerto Rico?"

"We're going to set up for a rock concert that'll be held down there next month. We have to put the whole thing together, build the stages and get everything organized."

"Do you all know each other?"

"More or less. We do this a lot, in different places. You should come along, it's gonna be great. How much time you got?"

"I got my whole life. But I was in the middle of trying to get to New York and now here's you…. Could I work with all of you? I've only got twenty dollars."

"Yeah, I'm sure there'd be something to do. Listen, see that guy over there?"

"Robin Hood?"

"Yeah. He's the one with the stand-by list—lovers and whatnot. Sign up."

"Really? You think they'll let me?"

"Sure, why not? Tell him how much you want to go."

The West Indies were the last thing on my mind. Twenty dollars would last about two days. Still, how often does a bojangle band whirl you onto a plane and fly you three thousand miles to the Caribbean?

"Do you have a stand-by list?" I asked the man in green tights.

"Yeah, right here."

"Can you put my name on it?"

"Who are you?"

"I'm not part of this group…but I can play a mean recorder."

"And you wanna come to Puerto Rico?"

"It all sounds ideal to me."

"Then I'll sign you up."

"That looks like a pretty long list, you think I'll get to go?"

He winked, "You'll go."

"Thanks," I said. "I like your elf boots." He shook his foot and bells jingled.

I went back to sit with the patchwork fellow, relieved that my sleepy TV friends were oblivious to this sudden change in itinerary. Forty-five minutes later, a DC 10 pulled in and the whole show picked up their gear and moved toward the exit. I would have to wait till everyone had a seat to see how many standbys could go.

Suddenly the dozy duet stumbled in rubbing their eyes, certain this was a dream. I briefed them on recent events, omitting my own participation. But they could see I'd made a couple of friends and they didn't like the looks of this—they close their eyes for ten minutes and I sneak off to the hot tropics. "You're going too, aren't you?" they accused.

"Yes, it's grounds for divorce, I'm walking out on you." Then I suggested they go sign up, too, (suspecting it was probably too late), and they did.

"Why didn't you wake us up?" they dug in.

"I didn't know you wanted to go to Puerto Rico," I said.

The man with the patches passed me on his way out to the transport bus. "See you on the plane," he whispered. "I know you'll get to come."

"There's only a few extra seats," Robin then announced to the eager group, "and we have to be quick about this, so if I call your name, get directly onto the bus. And if I don't call your name, don't come and try to talk me into it." He read out five names, paused a moment, then called mine. There were quite a few sad wanna-go's now remaining in the vicinity so I contained my excitement.

"Oh well," sighed the two land-lubbers, "have a good time."

I boarded the bus and we chugged off toward the plane. On the bus was a tearful young lady, who shouldn't have been on the bus at all, clinging like a wet cat to her boyfriend's arm. He was going, she wasn't. Despite Robin's warning, she was imploring him to let her go along. "No more seats," Robin said simply.

"Are you going?" she turned to me.

"Looks that way," I nodded.

"Are you part of the group?"

"No."

"How'd you get to go?" the corners of her mouth pouted at the injustice. Just what I needed, more guilt.

"I signed up and my name was called. Why are you so miserable?"

"Because HE's going," and she hugged him harder, "and I want to be with him. I can't BEAR to have him go away for so long."

"Only a month," I shrugged, "and it's a job not a war." But she seemed certain she'd never see him again if he flew away without her tonight.

I looked at him to see whether he was apt to survive without this weight dangling from his elbow. He looked fairly self-sufficient. As her chin dropped morosely to her chest in a final heave of woe, he turned to me and said quietly, "She's just being dramatic."

"Do you wish she could go with you?" I asked him in a low tone as she wept.

"I don't really care," he said. I pretended not to register his flirtatious look, but then felt sorry for her, remembering too well what it was like to be left behind.

"You really want to go, don't you?" I said to her.

"I really want to go," she said with drum-roll conviction and a fresh flood.

"You can have my seat."

"What?"

"You can have my seat," I repeated. "It's more important to you than it is to me." I would live without a trip to Puerto Rico, but the same might not be true for her. I hated telling Robin I'd be returning to the terminal. Sending this little sniveler in my place was hardly an exchange of the favor, but my lucky excursion was leaving a wake of ill feelings from a host of pathetic strangers, and I took it all as a portent not to get side-tracked from the side-track I was already on. The lovelorn lady showered me with thanks, gave her honey a happy hug and off they flew. (This one's for you, Jonah.)

29

Traveling East

I fully redeemed myself with the drowsy damsels back at the fort, but turning down a free trip to the Caribbean convinced them I was nuts. Nuts or not, there was a lot to do before I collapsed or got eaten by a squirrel. I trundled back over to the commercial terminal to see what was shakin'.

"Thought maybe you made it on Flying Tigers when you didn't come back," said my friend at the ticket counter.

"Almost. Then I almost got on a charter to Puerto Rico, but I'm still kickin' around. Got any new ideas?"

"I wish there was some way I could help you, but they keep tight controls around here. I can't think of anything."

"Couldn't I be your wife? Your sister?"

"Yeah, but you have to arrange that stuff in advance."

"Oh well…I'll just go sit on a bench and mope."

A few minutes into my moping, an elegant blonde took a seat beside me. "Where're you trying to get to?" she suddenly asked me. "I was standing behind you at the ticket counter and heard your conversation."

"Hope you're not an authority…. I'm trying to get to New York."

"No, I'm not an authority," she smiled, "I'm a stewardess. Why don't you sneak on a plane?"

Were my ears deceiving me? An airline employee suggesting this? "Last time I tried that they turned the plane around on the runway and dropped me off back at the airport," I confessed.

"Well, you probably didn't know everything you need to know to pull it off smoothly. How much baggage have you got?"

"Just these two," I indicated my small carry-ons.

"Good." She then proceeded to open a brand new vista. "It's easy. You see, if a plane is about to make a long flight, like from here to New York, they always start out with a fresh pilot and crew. So if you got on a plane from here, in the morning, that was going straight to New York, you couldn't sneak on. But if you bought a ticket from here to LA on a plane that was *continuing on* to New York, you could just stay on. Here's why: after a long flight, the stewardesses are supposed to stay on the aircraft till the new crew comes aboard and then tell the new stewardesses the passenger count. But usually, in fact almost always, the stewardesses are too tired and just want to get off the plane and get to bed. So they don't wait for the fresh crew, they just split.

"So when the new stewardesses get on, they have no idea how many passengers were already on the plane and just stopping over. If you were supposed to get off in LA but stayed on instead, the new stewardesses would just assume you had a ticket. And unless the plane was absolutely full and a new passenger was booked for your seat, you'd never get caught. Of course you couldn't check any luggage or you'd lose it in LA They usually start fresh crews around seven or eight in the morning, so try to find a flight that leaves for the long part of the trip around that time."

Digesting the material, I repeated back the key points, "So the plane should be coming in from a long flight, and it should start out on another long flight at my stop-over city."

"Right. And don't worry about someone being booked into your seat after the stop-over because there's almost always some extra seats and you can just move if you have to. But usually passengers don't much care which seat they're in. Take a middle seat—people are only fussy about window and aisle seats."

"Why are you telling me all this?" I had to ask. "You're not acting like a normal stewardess."

"Because I completely sympathize with the horrible problem of getting from place to place without much money. I used to scam around all over the place, sneaking on boats or trains and getting where I wanted to any way I could. I hated to travel so slow but I couldn't figure out how to sneak on a plane. I was always praying someone would come along and help me do it. Finally I solved the whole problem by becoming a stewardess. And when I became one, I promised myself that if I could ever help someone else sneak on, I would. Especially a woman. So I'm glad I had this opportunity to tell you how to do it. I wish I was going to be on the flight, I'd cover for you."

"You're incredible. Even if I don't make it, it was worth it to know there are stewardesses like you."

"Most stewardesses go into this because they love to travel and can't find a better way of doing it."

"So you like being a stewardess?"

"Yeah, it's great. After you do it for a few years, at least with Pan Am, which is who I fly for, you get to pick your cities, and you can pick different ones every month. It's perfect for me because I can travel all over the world plus have a good job. Also, if you're smart, you can make lots of extra money by importing things."

"What kinds of things?"

"Well, stewardesses and pilots hardly ever get checked in customs, and if they do, it's never thorough, so you can have all sorts of things stashed on your body. Like diamonds. Or...well, you know. Working for the airlines can be very lucrative if you take advantage of it. And I sure do. All the smart airline people choose their cities with a mind for business."

We were both exhausted. She gave me the name of her hotel in case I wanted to freshen up or catch a few hours' sleep before my launch, but I had to research flights for an appropriate one and buy a ticket to a nearby city. We sincerely wished each other well. "Whoever would've guessed?" I thought, as she walked away across the terminal like something off a page of Vogue. "Life is really okay."

There was a flight to LA, then on to New York, departing at seven a.m. A little sleuthing revealed that it was coming in from New York before landing in San Francisco. I hoped that the fresh crew would board in LA for the trip back to New York, not in San Francisco. I had to wager that eight-thirty was the more likely hour for the day shift to commence than seven. To my cordial ticket agent, I gave sixteen dollars, one way fare to Los Angeles, along with a cheesy explanation that I was going to continue the private plane effort from down there. He thought it a fine idea.

Down to one flimsy ticket and four flimsier dollar bills, this investment HAD to bear fruit. At dawn, I made quasi flight preparations in the ladies' room. As always, I was equipped with the accoutrements for a female impersonation. It wasn't overly glamorous this time—but neither was the era, or San Francisco. I was striving for a portrait of innocence, even virginity. I was going to 'fall asleep' during the LA stopover, and if my slumber looked convincing enough, maybe no one would have the heart to wake me if I was in their seat.

Boarding the aircraft, I automatically felt sneaky and had to remind myself that I was actually legal as far as Los Angeles. Regardless, I refused all in-flight services to keep a low profile. As the plane began the descent to LA, though, a rush went through me— the courageous portion of the program was nigh. Installed in my middle seat, I would now fall into a cavernous sleep to make Rip Van Winkle an insomniac, and not budge till my popping ears announced we were again on the ascent. Dropping my head to one shoulder, I exhibited a smile out of Bethlehem and relied exclusively on my hearing. The plane landed. A voice announced we'd be on the ground for half an hour. People on all sides got up and deplaned. (Was I now performing this pantomime for a hundred fifty empty blue seats?) But soon conversation resumed in the cabin, and, not looking forward to another twenty-five minutes of fake slumber, I had no choice.

Fifteen uneventful minutes passed, then the seats began refilling.

Now the scary part.... I curled up the corners of my mouth slightly. Around me, new passengers freed themselves of hand luggage and settled into assigned seats. Pressing in on all sides—I could hear humanity's hot breathing, the coins jingling in its pockets. Would it claim my chair? More Homo sapiens clumped up the aisle in my direction, but I chanced not a peek.

How full was the plane? These latest arrivals hesitated in my section, mumbling. How many were they? And what were my odds of retaining the middle seat if a pair of love-birds took the other two? The mumbling ended in an uneasy silence...my pounding heart the only sound.

As I was wondering whether the fetid air in this fuselage would suffocate us before the "no smoking" sign went on, I heard someone softly say, "Oh-h, don't wake her up." Someone then took the aisle seat to my right. It must be half of a pair, I reasoned, with the other half now maybe across the aisle. Nobody took the window seat to my left—so the plane wasn't full. In that respect I was SO lucky.

Now a ready-to-go hum pervaded the sound waves. Seat-belts clicked and discreet prayers were muttered to the God of Planecrash. Time-wise at least, my trial was nearing completion. Any counting of heads that had taken place was not done by a math whiz because we were now rolling down the runway, and the only thing differentiating this self-smuggle from the Fort Lauderdale attempt was that Bernardo wasn't on hand to blow my cover.

Then, lo and behold, we took off. "Our flight time will be three hours and ninety-eight minutes," announced the peculiar pilot.

I played possum until even if I got caught they'd never turn back. A stewardess was serving morning coffee when I groggily came to. The man on my right smiled, "Boy, you were really out cold. Have a good sleep?"

"Yeah."

"Hope you weren't getting off in LA because you missed it."

"Really? We've been to LA already?" I chuckled, "No, thank goodness I didn't have to get off there." Nice as my neighbor was (not to mention his companion sitting across the aisle), I dared not fraternize, and was saved from it in the nick of time by a mild skirmish in the aisle. Seems another passenger had stolen forty dollars from the stewardess' coffee trolley and got caught. By this time I was shielded by a paperback. And from there we went directly on to meals, movies, and general airline protocol. In no time at all, the pilot's voice said, "We're preparing to land in Philadelphia."

Philadelphia?

Where'd Philadelphia come from? Philadelphia was the one thing I didn't need right now. What was going on? Were we crashing?

"Are we crashing?" I asked the gent beside me.

"I hope not," he answered, implying that Philly was no surprise to him. I didn't dare ask anyone else where the hell Philadelphia came from. Maybe I made a wrong turn back at the gate in San Francisco. Oh well, could've been worse; at least I got across the Mississippi. I listened for an update from the cockpit, but only when we were on the ground, did it finally come. "We'll be stopping in Philadelphia for thirty minutes before resuming the flight to our final destination, New York."

By then I'd resolved that if Philadelphia was good enough for Ben Franklin, it was good enough for me. It would be lunacy to risk another stopover just for the luxury of flying the last hundred miles. Bolstering up a final bit of pluck, I plucked my bags from the overhead compartment. The boogie man could still be lurking by the exit, or a platoon of uniformed ones could bar my path in the corridor; I wasn't home free yet.

My breathing was fairly regular as I marched the miles of hallway that promised an eventual Philly. I felt even sociable. A dapper business man was matching my pace. "Looks like a nice day," he volunteered.

"Yeah, looks great," I almost sang.

"That was some flight, eh?" he had a misgiving gleam in his eye. This airlines could be slicker than I thought—did they actually have 'plane'-clothes men sprinkled amongst the passengers?

"What do you mean?" I asked lightly.

"Well," he said, "several strange things happened. Didn't you notice? You don't usually see any law-breaking on a plane, and if you do, it's usually just one incident."

"Oh, you mean that guy who stole the money from the stewardess?" I veered him toward the other felon.

"Yeah, he was one. And there was that other thing."

This indirect detection was amazingly low-key, why didn't he just whip out the handcuffs? "What other thing?" I asked breezily.

"The thing with the coat."

"What coat?" My skimpy sweater could never pass for a coat.

"Didn't you hear about it? It was up in the front section and everybody up there saw the whole thing."

"What was it?"

"Well, some stewardesses went over to this lady in a fur coat and asked to examine the coat. The lady refused, and finally they insisted, saying it was their legal obligation to protect other passengers from possible illicit activity on the plane. They took the coat, and later we found out it had packets of heroine sewn inside the entire lining. So she's being arrested when they land in New York."

"Dear me. I guess that just shows how much illegal stuff is going on all the time." We'd reached baggage claim and were about to part company.

"Yeah," he said, "if two got caught, I wonder how many didn't."

"At least one, I'm sure," I laughed. "Bye!"

30

Nobody Home

I'd have preferred a steamy bath, a downy bed, and an Aunt Jemima mountain range, but instead I had the chore of hitching four hours to the end of Long Island in winter.

November in East Hampton, what was I doing here? Jules was at work painting rich people's houses when I finally rolled in, so I waited under the covers where it was warm. I wasn't alone though. An unusual couple had rushed me at the door, the larger trampling the smaller. Molly and Bellringer, a border collie and a kitten respectively, rivals for Jules' affection, were chagrined to find me, not him, at the door. Bellringer wasn't someone I recognized, but any friend of Molly's was a friend of mine, so the three of us snuggled into bed for a snooze.

Jules soon joined us, adding turpentine fumes to the sweet scent of kitten, and we all stayed there for about a month. "The kitten's Molly's," said Jules, "but she might give it to you for a home-coming present. If you want."

"Okay." So I had a pet. "Why'd you name her Bellringer?"

"Cuz I met a guy named Rick Bellringer who convinced me that my life was missing a cat, then happened to have a spare."

"Does he deserve having anyone named after him?"

"Well, Bellringer's a good name for a cat, don't you think?"

"No. Unless she could ring a bell."

"That would be a plus."

"I'll teach her."

"How?"

"Pavlov."

I hung a little bell just above the kitten's empty food dish, and we chimed it religiously before feeding her. In a matter of days, tin-tinnabulation delivered a smiling cat to the food plate. Then we withheld both the ringing and the food. Bellringer was hungry, but there was no music, no tuna. Molly, meanwhile, had the usual bowlful. Giving us the benefit of the doubt, the darling kitty waited patiently in the feeding corner.

We felt sorry for her but knew she'd figure out what to do. She pondered her options: she could starve—taking about a day when you weigh twenty-two ounces; she could wedge in beside Molly's chomping jowls and gnaw on globby hunks of Gainesburger while Molly mistook her head for one; or she could ring that bell and see what happened. Feigning oblivion to her plight, Jules and I busied ourselves with preparations of our own dinner. "Meow," Bellringer suggested humbly, "I'm still over here by the empty plate."

"Did you hear something?" I asked Jules.

"Nope."

"Meow. It's me. Over HERE." She then edged toward Molly's bowl and lifted a paw. Molly growled.

"Maybe they need a little affection," the kitten decided then, and did the chain-step in and out of our four feet for a while. To no avail. "Meow," she whimpered again, then retired to a tragic little posture by her plate.

Playing into the moment, Jules began conversing about sea-food. "Lobster will always be my favorite food," I joined in.

"Hippies shouldn't have expensive palates," Jules swerved the dialogue back to his recurring theme.

"I'm not a hippie, I'm a nostalgic vegetarian."

"What's the difference?"

"The difference is that this is 1971 and the Hippie Movement's been here and gone. Vegetarianism is a personal conviction unrelated to trends."

"It's a personal conviction for hippies, because it's a luxury they can afford."

"What do you mean, it's cheaper than eating meat."

"The luxury of choice is a bourgeois phenomenon. Vegetarianism is an admittance of money in the banks of rich relatives."

"Ding-a-ling!"

We both whirled around to Bellringer's corner. "Ding-a-ling," she bumped her little head against the bell again.

"Bellringer! You did it!" I scooped up the tiny thing in my arms as Jules cracked open a can of reward.

Once stunt-cat mastered the dinner bell, I thought she should learn a few more fundamentals. Like traveling. The notion of a pet bore unwieldy preconceptions of domesticity that, together, she and I would have to rise above. I started her with local jaunts in Jules' van. She was too inexperienced to know the standard cat strategy of inserting herself between the floor and the brake pedal, and was so young that in just two or three van rides, she accepted vehicular confinement as part of life. In fact, she preferred it to walking on the beach, a family activity she found bewildering and pointless (though her sister, Molly, was ecstatic at the shore, intoxicated by mere whispers of the b-word).

Bellringer preferred hitch-hiking to beach-combing, and when Jules wasn't using the truck, often accompanied me on local hops. And, once accustomed to it all—especially since Molly was so road-worthy—the little one actually preferred travel to staying home alone.

After the initial rush of being off the road, I soon found myself back in the web of what to do. Jules offered me some overalls, a paintbrush, and a starting wage, but that profession seemed to only enhance my frustration. Simone, who'd moved to a loft in the City, invited me to join her in packaging granola at the health food company she now worked for. "It's good honest work," was her platform. And my father (certain I'd traded Lily for pelts in the Northwest) handed me the latest issue of 'The American Guide to Colleges and Universities,' while knowingly spending my would-be tuition on an out-of-character purchase: tickets to Spain, Italy, and Greece for himself and his honey. (Seemed he heeded my advice more than I did his—while telling me to settle down, he was flying the coop. They'd even traded in Nadine's Ford for a VW camper.)

Meanwhile, lording over the manor in Dad and Nadine's place would be Step-Granny.

All Nadine-related people and things, including this Step-Granny, evoked purple pessimism in my father's off-spring. But Dad sternly forbade any overriding of her authority. Though everyone viewed this as a risky experiment, the kids could "in no way be trusted alone," and dear Oma in New York had gone out with the last dynasty. At eighty-one, though, I couldn't help expecting Step-Granny to be a pushover, and looked forward to visiting the ancestral halls without that parental stopwatch timing my stay.

Returning from a journey can afford one surprising peace of mind. A fresh perspective can nourish the psyche for a good two weeks. November was a delectable month, one of cycling along the now empty wooded lanes as the leaves upstaged everything. The ocean remained warm enough to swim once or twice, and after Californian contrivances, the un-peopled simplicity of this weathery place was pure. But the onset of winter threatened both me and my attire. Toying with the fantasy that desolate sands and wavescapes are inspirational, I wondered if waging a war against the thermometer for six months would deliver me to spring with a manuscript. I found a leaky pen, scribbled a weak verse, then decided to project onto someone else. "You know, Jules, I'm worried about you."

"Oh, thank God someone's finally worrying about me."

"I don't know what I'm gonna do about you."

"Become my benefactor."

"You've got a grave misconception about my assets, and a one-track mind."

"Well, you don't seem to worry about not working."

"You sound exactly like Dad."

"I mean you're perfectly at liberty to help me paint, but you don't. So you must have something salted away."

"I don't paint because it's not part of my progression. It's not the concept of work I object to, it's the fumes."

"Anyway, I'm *not* worried about you," he said.

"Good. Don't be. Even when I up and leave you because you're IN A RUT."

"We've had this rap before and I told you the only way out of my rut is to drive out in a Mercedes. So I'll paint houses till I'm rich. Or till my sister's rich boyfriend feels so sorry for me that he donates one of his Porsches."

"Well, if you're waiting for pity, take mine. You're not going to paint yourself out of your rut because you don't start work till mid-afternoon, and that's only two days a week. If it takes you three months to paint a bathroom door, maybe painting's not your bag either."

"I work slow because I do a damn good job."

"You do a better job drinking coffee and talking real estate with the attention-starved housewives who hire you."

"Well I'd go nuts if I just had to paint!"

"If you want to paint your way out of this rut, which you insist is financial, then you have to do nothing but paint. Since you're not capable of that, you'll have to get out some other way. I think you should blow this joint, Jules. You've been here for thirty years. You're too caught up in the hierarchy of land-ownership. If you can't leave here for your own benefit, do it for me."

"Well, there are a coupla places I want to go," he admitted. "I promised myself years ago that I'd go to Big Sur and meet Henry Miller. I really have to do that. Soon. He's getting old."

"Well, there you go, that's a good plan."

"You wanna come with me?"

"I just got back."

"Good, then you know the way."

"No, I can't. I have to suffer. And it's something I have to do by myself. You have to pack up and leave. Just to prove to yourself that you can do it. It's a good trick to have up your sleeve."

"I'm not trying to subtract myself, I'm trying to multiply. And I don't have a backer to finance the trip."

"Back yourself. Paint faster. You're the one who always says it's a lucrative racket."

"You're not completely off the wall. I'll think about it. I'm pretty fed up with the kiss-ass mentality around here."

So Jules now had a semi-sense of direction. And his I'm-really-an-artist-not-a-housepainter method of coloring walls gave way to the determined stroke of a worker with an aim.

With both a boyfriend and a nuclear family within two miles, it was odd to rent a one-room cottage and move in with my cat. Overbearingly color-coordinated, and microscopic by all standards, it still lent seclusion to my notion of forcing myself through a Bohemian winter—sprouting mung beans and dissecting social patterns with fellow unemployed restaurant personnel—culminating in some form of the written word. Lao Tzu, I discovered, was the only one with a real grasp on solitude; maybe the direction for me was East. I perused the shelves of Rizzoli in New York and purchased a copy of 'Teach Yourself Chinese.'

"You shouldn't waste time like this," Jules warned, "because Chinese menus always have English translations."

"Jules, this isn't a quest for luck-fuck-foo soup, it's philosophical."

"Well good fuck-foo-luck, 'cause you're gonna need more than Chinese philosophy to outlast the winter in your cottage."

That was what I needed to find out....

Back on the ranch, Step-Granny was running the most benevolent regime to date. She had expected KP duty and modest managerial detail, but other than a lengthy list of names, knew nothing of the family her daughter had married into. Aside from Nadine's two boys, though, twelve-year-old Dale was the last hold-out of our original clan. Mimi had joined Lily in Berkeley, Cara was making a demo tape in New York, draft-dodger Sonny was hiding in the Canadian woods, and I was in my cottage. Now—maybe she was lonely—Step-Granny made it plain that All was Forgiven, Come on Home. So I'd drink tea at the wintry kitchen table with this crackly sprite with a comic bent, finding her the most congenial faux-relative thus far.

But no sooner had she settled in with her needlepoint when, one afternoon, a cloaked and mysterious bearded man stomped snow from his boots and entered through the back door without knocking. Beneath the heavy gear was our own long-lost Sonny, mildly disconcerted to be greeted by a fake grandmother alone in our house. With the ID of a friend of similar description, he'd slipped across the border for a brief return to the homeland.

So Step-Granny's first task was to shelter an illegal immigrant. And her next, just days later, was to tell an untruth to two FBI gents who came trick-or-treating complete with photo of Sonny. Alone when they appeared, Step-Granny really outdid herself. Having never been briefed on wartime tactics, her instincts were nonetheless superb as she calmly declared that she'd never met the young man in question. And, yes, he used to live here but moved to Canada months and months ago, and no one knew exactly where, or even if, he was living.

The incident put a damper on Sonny's homecoming, though, and he hightailed it back across the 49th Parallel. So, one was not apprehended, but....

Scarcely had Step-Granny bungled Sonny out the door with a bag of sandwiches when a phone call from San Francisco informed this busy house-sitter that Mimi and Lily had been picked up shoplifting on Telegraph Avenue. The booty consisted of Tigers Milk bars, and the punishment consisted of jail bars. They'd stay there, it was mandated, until at least one of their parents WENT to the institution and signed their release. Step-Granny had told the prison authority, who wanted definite arrangements made about these convicts real soon, to call us back tomorrow.

'*Mañana*'— again the superb instincts.

Perhaps Dad and Nadine had seen enough Renaissance remains and plaster half-torsos by now to appreciate some contemporary architecture. But no one would be tickled fuchsia to swap out the Sistine Chapel and the Acropolis for the Oakland County Detention Center for Juvenile Criminals.

Step-Granny sent me smoke signals on this occasion, and we brewed tea and reviewed the situation. On the emotional side, we hadn't the hearts to annihilate the glory of Dad and Nadine's Mediterranean bliss-trip. On the practical side, we hadn't their address. And Step-Granny's awareness here that the coupling of under-aged jail-birds and middle-aged love-birds could be disastrous won her more kudos. Meanwhile, we both reckoned a sober spell in the poker wouldn't harm the rascals and might even awaken them to the ways of the world.

Mañana arrived too soon. As the wall phone ominously rang, Step-Granny and I looked at each other like Pooh and Piglet stuck in a tree. Finally I answered it.

"This is the Oakland County Detention Center for Juvenile Criminals calling in reference to two of our inmates, Mimi and Lily Raebeck. Are you the person I spoke to yesterday?"

"No, but I'm their sister."

"Well, we are trying to contact their parents or legal guardian. We can only release them into the custody of their lawful guardian."

"We can't reach their parents at this time," I said. "They're out of the country."

"Well, if the parents can't come to sign their release, what can we do?"

"I don't know. What can you do?"

"The two girls would have to stay here, and it's not our policy to keep petty larcenists for extended periods of time."

"What do you mean?"

"The degree of infraction is moderate by our standards."

"You mean they're not bad enough?"

"We house a more seasoned convict."

"Oh, they're not good enough."

"Our facilities are not equipped to accommodate minor felons like your two sisters, Madame. Sorry."

"Well, gee, we hate to inconvenience you like this, why don't you just let 'em go?" Step-Granny gave an approving nod.

"We certainly can't do that."

"Well, seeing that their parents are not in the U.S., I believe that, as their older sister, I am their legal guardian at this time. But I can't possibly come to California right now."

"How soon COULD you get here, bearing in mind that our facilities are already over-crowded?"

"Bearing in mind the short notice, I don't think I can get there at all." No one could reimburse me for the airfare if I flew out there… and if I went by land, Mimi and Lily would surely have used their wits to free themselves by then. "But perhaps a short sentence would be beneficial to my sisters," I ventured, knowing this was not what the voice wanted to hear.

There was a silence. The voice was thinking things over. So was I.

"I'm afraid we're not talking about a short confinement, Madame. Unless a legal guardian releases them, they will remain either here or in another house of correction indefinitely."

"Well, the only thing I can do then is send a telegram that authorizes their release. How about that?"

"That's not our customary procedure, and it would not suffice in freeing them altogether. However, with that temporary authorization, I could release them from here and they could be moved to the Runaway Center."

"What's the Runaway Center?"

"The Runaway Center is an institution for homeless minors. They will be kept there until we can find foster homes for them... which may take many months."

I pictured my sisters in girl scout uniforms with violin cases. "Just a moment," the Detention Center voice said. "One of your sisters would like to have a brief word with you."

"Wendy??" gasped a hushed, breathless voice.

"Boy, you two really did it this time—"

"Listen," Mimi's emphatic whisper was in the mono-drone of someone intentionally not moving her lips, "Send-a-telegram-releasing-us-to-the-Runaway-Center-and-when-we-get-there-we'll-run-away."

"How?"

"Do-it. It-will-work."

"Okay. Is everything alright?"

"Can't-talk-gotta-go."

"Hello?" it was the detention lady again.

"Hello," I said. "I think the Runaway Center will be okay for the time being. I'll send a telegram today, releasing them. Then, as soon as I can, I'll come and collect them from the Runaway Center. That's best for all concerned."

With Step-Granny's blessings, I cabled the release-gram. "Do you think they'll really escape from the Runaway Center?" she asked me, concerned.

"Mimi sounded pretty sure it would work out. Somebody must've tipped them off. Anyway, I guess we've done all we can for now."

Dad and Nadine were due back soon, probably the reason we never received another communique from the hip hoodlums. For all we knew, they were now attending parochial school in Mill Valley.

31

Bye-bye Lao Tzu

With my hounding, December's precipitation, and his parents' Yuletide arrival to their home that he'd been 'caretaking,' Jules discovered an untapped talent: saving money. And his general paranoia was redirected into a plan to drive across country. Then one day, he packed his drop-cloth, ladder, bicycle, and dog into his van…and left.

Santa and Mrs. Claus made it back from Europe, but otherwise my own little world was pretty scant for Christmas. Bellringer and I hung up our lonely stockings and got coal. All in all, things were dull, and it didn't take many days of staring at the orange-flowered curtains of my cell to realize that, without Jules, solitude was impossible. Throwing hexagrams and studying the Tao te Ching convinced me of a sympathetic universe, but the local indicators were dismal. Alcohol was the communal solution—full tilt, every night. But it wasn't my substance. Carob Häagen-Dazs wasn't cutting it either. For a twenty-one-year-old dropout, it was basically hang out in bars, leave that place, or perish.

These woolly, gray days forced reflection about my blemished history with Jonah. Why did feelings remain? Why had I believed him when he said he loved me?

Maybe because he'd been my life-raft in those first months of losing my mother. He'd flown at me in a romantic hurricane, and my heart had then clung to him. Even though I was finally free of school and all the prerequisites for adulthood, a bird finally out of its cage, now my soul mocked that freedom, coiling instead around this first love that young women wait for.

Okay, I happened to get a crazy person, but that's who I got—it was still new and commanded my life. I thought I was learning the man-woman thing and believed that because we 'loved' each other that we'd attain the heights. Okay, he was crazy, but kind of crazy-wonderful.

And weren't these *lasting feelings* proof of true love? I never viewed them in practical terms, like, "If it doesn't work out, I'll find somebody else." First love is *lasting* love; 'somebody else' is unthinkable.

I was young, alone, and stridently affiliated with the hippie doctrines of ideal 'love' and sex without consequence. Through our sheer numbers, and the undying forgiveness of parents, our generation dumped cultural norms in a few short years. For better or worse, there was no stopping us. We could earn our own money, leap onto planes or highways, and we always had each other— all over the globe and fully in sync. Nothing held us back. Not parents, not mores, not better judgment, certainly not religion, certainly not tradition or status quo, and certainly not fear. The world of possibility, fresh love, novelty, and adventure sparked our every decision. (Not to mention the drugs.) Only those with tight parental controls or tight parental bonds resisted the call to madcap freedom.

By the early 1970s, wildness was literally the norm. And even parents were getting groovy, growing their hair, smoking pot, divorcing, and lettin' it all hang out..)

But, in the midst of it all, I knew nothing of the difference between men and women. I was just a girl, not a woman. Regarding Jonah, I didn't assess the 'relationship' or dissect anyone's neurosis. None of this crossed my mind. I never considered how maybe I hurt him, in being outspoken, distant, or too independent. I knew nothing of his own fears and insecurities; I believed he knew what he was doing. I bought his ruse of being in control, and viewed myself as the tattered ragamuffin on the receiving end. I was just a believer afloat on the mythological river of love. Its magic had to be bigger than our weakness, bigger than writing on the wall. I simply expected, and later just hoped, that we'd get closer, stay together, do fantastic things. True love doesn't end.

Plus, Jonah wasn't someone I had kissed good-bye under the Eiffel Tower, but someone from my hometown, who'd continue to cross my path. So, emotionally, I held on. And on and on. But did he miss me, did he think of me? Never a word....

Finally...I knew I had to get over him. But, in those 20 x 20 square feet of winter, I encountered depths of disillusion, relentless sadness, and cruel heartbreak I'd never known. My mother was gone. My family was shrapnel. Must I let go of this last fading smoke ring? The very last piece of my heart.... Couldn't I please just keep one hazy mirage, one remaining trace of sweetness and purity?

And what did the vast world out there hold for me? Where would I go? Where would I ever belong?

♥

Thank God for Jules, rut or no rut. He wasn't cagey or duplicitous, complicated or mean. He was my cute, comfortable friend and lover, the other glove. He was transparent and wholesome, reliable and devoted. And when he phoned from North Carolina, all I could say was, "Wait for me—I'll be there tomorrow."

Knowing the truth about pet compartments on planes, I couldn't subject my cat to something I myself had chickened out of. And I was already checking in my bicycle, so Bellringer would have to ride with me. Discreetly. "How about putting her in that?" came a random suggestion from Dale, nodding at a Styrofoam cooler in a corner of the kitchen.

Bellringer started getting suspicious when we hit the airport. But she could handle it—the flight to Greensboro would only be ninety minutes. I saved the Styrofoam surprise till the last moment, then popped her in and boarded the plane.

I found a pair of empty seats in the last row. Things were going smoothly back there, but even before take-off, when I peeked under the Styrofoam lid to reassure my little buddy, I realized she was not only furious but in short supply of oxygen.

Then another very bad thing happened. At take-off, three stewardesses unfolded some heretofore invisible seats directly behind us. So I'd have to ignore the Styrofoam box till they got back to work.

But the Styrofoam box wasn't ignoring me. For an inanimate object it was pretty lively. It seemed to be upset, not at peace with itself. At first it only squirmed, but soon it was actually jumping around in its seat. (Fortunately no one could see.) Finally we were airborne, the box now mewing in low distress. As soon as the crew got busy again, I yanked off the lid to check the captive. Thank God I hadn't waited longer—Bellringer was nearly suffocating! (Any cretin would've assessed that the box was airtight.) So much for ingenious solutions from younger brothers.

I could hardly expect Bellringer to stay in there now. So while the stewardesses were out of our vicinity, I stuffed her inside my jacket. Momentarily appeased—no longer dying—she was still disgusted with the afternoon in general. Throwing me a miserable look, she meowed loudly. Nearby heads turned but I just looked around as well.

Whenever the serving trolley passed through our section, I'd briefly force the feline back into the box, but by the close of the first hour, I was sweating and out of ideas for cat pacification. She was a worse traveling companion than even Jonah. So I held her up to the window—maybe she'd appreciate the thrill of it all. She wailed instead, and everyone on the plane turned around. I just smiled oafishly, pressing the guilty party down against the seat, and acted like I had meowed. For a joke, ha ha, next I'm gonna do a rooster. Anyway, folks, even if there is an animal on board, it's just a harmless little kitty cat, I wouldn't spring a rattlesnake on ya.

Finally, FINALLY, I felt a descent, and informed my fluffy date that the worst was over, she could relax now and take it easy. "We'll be seeing Molly soon," I whispered.

She scratched me.

The change in altitude was not perceived as positive. I couldn't contain the militant upriser; if she didn't yelp, she clawed. Finally, she made a kamikaze leap into the aisle. In my lunge to grab her vanishing tail, I almost fell on the floor as it slipped through my bleeding hand. The three stewardesses were secured behind me again, and as the cat strolled up the aisle toward the front, I turned to face them with my foolish grin. To my tremendous relief, they were absorbed in conversation and hadn't noticed. Plenty of passengers had, though. Several reached down to stroke her as Bellringer swished past. Because everyone was strapped in, the incident remained low-keyed, but the cat remained at large till we finally came to a stop.

I, of course, was first out of my seat and up the aisle. Clutching the Styrofoam box and disregarding the odd comment, I snatched the cat from the floor on my rush for the door. Safely in North Carolina now, I doubted they'd ship us back to New York, so I just carried her outright. "Where'd *that* come from?" asked a wide-eyed stewardess at the exit door, not believing the unlawful critter had been overlooked.

"Oh, she's been with me the whole time," I said lightly.

"From New York? You can't take cats on planes!"

"You can't??"

"No!"

"I just did."

"They have to go in the pet compartment!"

"They do?"

"Yes!"

"Oh."

We looked at each other as I edged out the door.

"Don't do it again."

"I won't."

"No, don't."

Jules was there to meet the plane, but that annoyed Bellringer further. Entirely off people by this stage, she insisted on making her way to the parking lot solo. Whatever her plans, they didn't include us. She walked bravely on ahead through the terminal building. But I knew Molly and the van outside would reassure her.

32

Deep South

Getting a whiff of the warm southern air, seeing Jules, and setting out on another journey cured my blues. I cured Jules', and Molly cured Bellringer's. (Molly didn't have any.) So after a night in Greensboro, our comprehensive unit set forth. We were equipped for just about everything—the back of the van contained two bikes, Jules' ladder, drop-cloth, and painting supplies, our baggage, and my sleeping bag. Molly stationed herself on the panel between the two front seats and Bellringer dreamed in the sun on the dashboard. Though chaotic, we weren't uncomfortable.

Hating major highways, I labored to convince Jules that extra time and mileage should not be debated—this was an opportunity to really see the country. Having originally come from the South, I longed to submerge in its lushness, rickety towns, and warm, lazy ways. And I wanted Jules to know its sweetness. But he had "Easy Rider" phobias and saw a leisurely drive through Alabama and Mississippi as a suicide mission. "Let's just do sleeping pills instead," he suggested. He lacked confidence in the vehicle, too, and pictured our quirky quartet trying to thumb or cycle our way back to civilization after getting stranded and/or lynched.

Already in the South—we'd at least agreed on a southerly route—Jules believed a straight line from North Carolina to perhaps Albuquerque was the rational course, while I fancied a picturesque cruise along the Gulf of Mexico to include New Orleans, then Galveston, Texas. From there, we could amble across the Texas plains, maybe take a peek at Dr. Shelton's fasting institute in San Antonio, then scoot on up through New Mexico to perhaps Albuquerque. "Jules," I lobbied, "rather than being alone, you now have lots of company, my contribution for half the gas, plus a stand-in driver. 'Two roads diverged upon a wood, and I, I chose the one less traveled by....'"

"This isn't Walden Pond in 1846, it's a two-tone Civil War zone in 1972."

I did not favor the tedium of endless green freeway signs directing us to truck stops, big cities, and other freeways. I believed that the actual road you choose is destiny itself. Jules saw that we could be miserable on the wrong road or (potentially) content on the right one. "Which is the right one?" he threw in the sponge and threw the map into my lap.

"The smallest."

Those quiet rambling roads told the truth of the deep south, and the people we spoke to were only pleasant and helpful. We felt no racial unrest as we moved through, and enjoyed harmonious moments with whites and blacks everywhere.

Being skill-less itinerants with no possibilities on a vacillating horizon, I voted for frugality. If it took us four or five days to get to Albuquerque, four or five motel bills might be crippling. Jules asserted we'd be ridiculous to make the journey any rougher than it already was; yes, we had a van, but so what, there was no room to sleep in it, and no blankets. Meanwhile, the van started overheating in a remote stretch of Backroads Nowheresville.

I should've realized that Jules was an old man, thirty, and that one shouldn't add hardship to what was already a strenuous undertaking for him. But at twenty-one (though Eddie Sherman constantly reminded me I was past it), I generally took my stamina to the limit. "We can drive all night, taking turns sleeping," I proposed. "We can clear a little place next to the bikes where one person can sleep in the sleeping bag." This was the last thing Jules wanted to think about in the poverty-stricken outskirts of Mobile, Alabama. "We can always park somewhere if we both get tired," I concluded.

"Then what?"

"We can take a snooze."

"Where?"

"In the space we make by the bikes."

"Both of us?"

"The other one can curl up on one of front seats."

"Without a blanket?"

"Well, it's not cold—and the animals can keep us warm."

"What do you think this is, a chapter out of 'White Fang?' I give up. You're crazy, but I refuse to hassle anymore. We can try it your way, but I'm telling you in no uncertain terms, if I get tired and can't sleep comfortably, I'm checking into the next motel I find. Even if it's a hundred dollars a night."

"Okay, but don't worry, everything will be hunky-dory."

But the only thing that was hunky-dory was America. She was beautiful…at every turn in the road…as always. We drove all night the first night, taking turns dozing but not too cozily. That lent grumpiness to the following day. And when we reached New Orleans the second night, Jules fulfilled his vow by turning into the first motel he spotted.

Another battle ensued when he caught sight of the "No Pets" sign in the office window. "They stay in the car," he said, "because I'll be damned if I'm gonna search the Mississippi Delta for a place that accommodates fauna."

The poor four-leggeds—they'd been so good, and had endured as much strain as we. "The motel people don't need to know we have fauna in our room," I said.

"They saw them in the van when we drove in. If they're not there later, they'll knock on our door, see them, and throw us out."

"You're so paranoid! Maybe they didn't see them."

"Then they're blind."

"Some hotel proprietors are blind," I spoke from experience. "Even if they saw them when we pulled in, they'll just assume they're sleeping in the back of the van."

"I'm not arguing about it…but they're not coming in and that's that." He opened the motel room, lay down on one of the beds, closed his eyes, and ceased communion.

Molly and Bellringer looked anxiously out through the windshield. Dying to stretch their legs, they were hungry too, and altogether insecure in light of recent developments. "Jules, I'm not traveling another centimeter with you," I announced. "You and Molly can go out west alone, and me and Bellringer will just make our roots in New Orleans."

"Fine," muttered the cadaver.

I then went into the bathroom, locked the door, sat on the floor of the shower stall and loudly wept. But Jules had fallen into an impenetrable slumber, and when the weeping wore me down, I skulked out of the bathroom and collapsed on the other bed.

Jules woke in a more negotiable frame of mind and said dinner was the first order and we'd consider the quadrupeds later. Returning to the motel afterwards, we ushered our depleted pets into the room and all made somnambulist history.

Next morning, it was clear that exhaustion had been responsible for the rows, and we set out more jovially. A warm sun beamed across the Gulf and the magnificent day would be fully exalted as our course hugged the waterline all the way to Galveston. With bathing suits handy, we synchronized lunchtime with a pretty stretch of beach.

But, although we'd almost tapped out the pet theme, there was a little more conflict left to mine. Whenever we stopped—for gas, food, or a breather—Molly automatically hopped out with us because she spoke English and would get back in the van when asked. Not so for Bellringer, who tended to meander off. Jules decided she was stupid and immature and didn't deserve privileges. "You don't understand cats," I said. "They like to explore places."

"I didn't come here to understand cats. If I wanted to study cats, I'd go to Africa not the Big Easy. We're gonna lose her, you know. I can't believe you let her walk off wherever she wants."

"What can possibly happen to her? She'll be back. She's not far away, and perfectly aware that we're her meal ticket and her ride to Albuquerque."

"Exactly, we're her ride to Albuquerque. And why the fuck would she want a ride to Albuquerque? Think about it. She's sick of this trip. The minute we stop, she leaps out the door and splits."

"Jules, all we have to do is call her when we're ready to go, then give her enough time to realize what's going on and come back."

"Yeah, half a day."

"No, we just have to allow her cat-time, about twice as long as Molly."

Jules then located Bellringer sniffing around an old tire behind the gas station, and tried to seize her. Claws and all, she resisted. "Okay, we're leaving," stated Jules. "I'm not looking for her again. She's vicious. And uncooperative. If she's so intrigued with fields of tall grass and litter, she can see how she likes spending her life in it." He slammed the door and started the engine.

"Look Jules," I said, "let's give her the benefit of the doubt just this once. If we sit here and wait a few minutes, let's just see if she comes." I loudly called her name. Surely she'd heard the engine starting up.

"We're leaving," Jules released the emergency brake. "And from now on, whenever anyone asks you if you have a cat, the answer will be no. And if they ask you if you have a boyfriend named Jules, you can give the same answer."

I didn't close the door on my side and continued to lean out, watching for the little one. Suddenly she came bounding across the pavement and leaped into the van. I flashed Jules a winning smile, Molly licked Bellringer's head, and Bellringer looked around pleasantly. "Okay," Jules began, in a way that promised this was no joke, "that's IT for the leisure club. From now on we're concentrating on getting there." He paused momentarily, realizing that we hadn't yet decided where there was.... "I am going to repress ALL my aggression and direct my FULL attention into DRIVING; now that my leadership has been undermined by a cat. You and Bellringer can sit there and preen over the effectiveness of your coup. And since I'm just a HUMAN, just a MAN," he was shouting now, "I'll kowtow to the intellectual omnipotence of the CAT! But don't forget, *any of you*," and his eyes pierced each of us, including Molly, "that it's MY van you're all riding in."

No one made a sound. For a long time.

Then Jules spoke again, "And I don't want anyone to make a sound. For a long time."

Later, as the sun sank and I discouraged another motel stop, Jules said for the twelfth time, "We're not equipped to camp."

"True, we don't have a tent or rifles, but this isn't the Amazon jungle. Don't be such a softy, Jules. What do we need that we don't have?"

"Shelter."

"We have a van, a sleeping bag, sweaters, a guard dog…we'll be alright. We can use our shoulder blades for knives."

"The van is crammed with bicycles, painting equipment, cats, dogs…. And I'm not putting my valuable stuff outside overnight."

"We'll sleep outside. We'll find a good spot."

My careful navigation tonight had conducted us into completely undiscovered regions of the Louisiana Purchase. We motored on along a deserted strip of slim pavement dissecting a hundred square miles of swamp. I figured we'd make it through to wherever we ended up…but that's what Jules feared. He was certain we'd break down and be eaten in the night by unanthropologized marsh-men. The morass was endless, and if kismet spared us a breakdown, we'd surely run out of gas. I felt the risk was better than going back miles and miles to the last hamlet.

We made it unscathed through the quagmire, but the other side didn't yield any burgs big enough to afford lodging, or any burgs at all. Now it was three a.m. Exhausted and utterly disenchanted with each other, all we could do was pull onto a dry patch of shoulder and try to sleep. Tossing the sleeping bag, the animals, and all extra clothing on the ground, we then tried to burrow ourselves into the heap. That's when it started raining. So we all rolled under the van.

Sleeping under a truck is unsettling—with black, greasy machinery closing in around your cheeks and hipbones, added to the concern that the vehicle might change gears and flatten you in the night. Despite the negatives, we may have still nodded off had the mosquitoes not chosen that very stowage for their regional convention. Seconds after we four kissed goodnight, they buzzed around in zillions, vying all night for exposed flesh.

Thus morning commenced at five a.m., our bedraggled band less than gung ho to resume the road. I was never to hear the end of our "camping" experience, and Jules was made to feel old and "straight" for not wanting to chance routes that weren't on the map.

33

Driving West

Now we were nearly halfway "there." But where? Time for a new line of disagreement. We'd focused on Albuquerque as a first stop because my friend Red had moved out there and extended an open invitation. It would be good to see her, so we'd sent a post card saying we might pass through. But where would we pass through to? Jules knew a veterinarian in Tucson, but that was the extent of our contacts. We'd have to just see how we felt about the southwest as we journeyed through. It was warm at least.

If Glen Campbell's dreamy version of Galveston was accurate, then there were two Galvestons. The one in Texas was a sprawling, waterfront oil refinery, with a forest of diseased Eiffel Towers for a skyline. If life existed at all at this space station, it was underground or inside the thousandfold oil drums comprising the "town." (Or, quite likely, we were somewhere else altogether.)

From there, we turned inland. It was late in the day, but we wanted to make San Antonio. Exhausted again, temperaments were rough. For a change. Jules was struggling to contain a huge load of blame, and, indeed, the fatigue was entirely my fault. But some existential side of my soul believed that willingly facing one's destiny at every bend in the road may involve some suffering. A little discomfort didn't seem a high price for a decent adventure.

The only road to San Antonio was a highway, so I had to permit it this once. And we were cheered when hints of human life gradually replaced the plains on either side. And eventually signs began advertising three-dollar motels: "20 miles to go"…"10 miles to go"…"2 miles to go"…"next exit"… Then "Thanks for Enjoying San Antonio."

Oops.

At the next exit, we did a cloverleaf u-turn, and headed back. The three-dollar motel signs were in full force from this direction also. "2 miles to go," then "next exit." We'd get off there and find our way into town.

But the road at that exit gave no indication which direction went to San Antonio, and there were no buildings at all in any direction. So we chose north. We drove and drove. After three miles of literally nothing, we turned around and headed back. Passing the highway again, we now went south. For five miles. This road touched upon civilization nowhere. There was no trace of a city. A flat horizon offered no clues.

Confused, irritated, exhausted, lost, gringos, hungry, filthy, car-crazed, and nearly psychotic, we were not amused by San Antonio's little games. Jules naturally assumed this was yet another twist in the universal plot to eighty-six him from the face of the Earth.

"Maybe I should take the wheel," I suggested. "'They' won't realize you're in the car, and then the city will turn up somewhere. Or do they know your license plates?"

"I have a better idea," he replied, "which you'll reject because it will take the 'fun' out of this—how about stopping to get a map?"

"Where are we going to find a map? We haven't even seen a gas station. Let's look for someone to ask if San Antonio's anywhere near here, and if they don't know, we can ask for a gas station."

There was no one to ask—no houses, no gas stations. So we turned around and went back to the highway. We went east again one more exit—were thanked again for enjoying San Antonio— and got off there. Ah-ha, a gas station.

"Get back on the highway, and go west (again) two exits.... Watch the signs," instructed the attendant.

"But the sign before the second exit says 'Thanks for enjoying San Antonio,'" we told him.

"Way-ell," he drawled, "that means 'thank y'all for enjoying San Antonio in advay-ance.'"

"Oh." Thank you in advance, highway logic. "Do we turn north or south when we get off the highway?"

"Either way."

"That's not fair," said Jules, eyeing the guy suspiciously. This might be the perpetrator of the whole movement right here.

"What do you mean 'either way'?" I asked the guy.

"All roads lead to San Antone," he sang merrily.

"Bullshit," said Jules, "no roads lead to San Antone. In fact, if there was anywhere else to go within two hundred miles, we'd go there instead, just to get away from this place."

I took Jules' arm in friendly fashion and tried to make light of his insinuation that Texas was lacking something, like one of its major cities. "Does San Antonio really exist?" I laughed, "or is it just hear-say?"

"Oh, it exists," the Texan nodded his head slowly. "Look, there it is," he pointed in a southwesterly direction. Sure enough, for the first time we saw a hazy Emerald City.

Well, that was incentive! Armed now with a map, we climbed back into the Sherman Tank and barreled back onto the highway. Obediently, we continued west for two more exits, ignoring the 'thank you' sign, and got off.

San Antonio, a town with personality, was having a lively afternoon. In the southwesterly spot it had occupied on the horizon, there was now a vacancy. Since we had our choice of directions on this new road, we'd expected the city skyline to make the choosing easier. "There it is!" cried Jules, who had pulled the van over and gotten out for a three hundred sixty degree scan. The metropolis had re-miraged due east—typical San Antonio-type thing to do now that we were on a north-south road. "No wonder that guy said 'either way,'" Jules moaned, getting back behind the wheel. "Either way you miss…. Let's try north first."

Though the road looked arrow-straight—meaning that something visible to the east should really stay to the east—San Antonio ice-skated along the horizon as though this was a game of tag and the van was 'it.' There were no right turns that might potentially lead us closer, and we couldn't work out where we were on the map.

Jules was losing it. The worst thing was that we didn't give a darn about this city to begin with, but with the sun going down, it would be more chancy and time-consuming to look for another one than to find San Antone.

We turned around and went south on this same road. Reaching the highway again, we crossed it and continued south. This is when we decided to forget about Crazyville and go absolutely anywhere as long as we got there. Before we flipped out. Jules had a way of looking like he was about to pop, and was quietly doing that—dilating his pupils, pumping his neck arteries, projecting waves of rippling static. It had something to do with his early childhood. "Next road, any direction, we take it," he hissed. The distant skyline, last seen directly behind us, had vanished again. And at this point, anything would suffice for housing—a hollow log, an overturned wheelbarrow. We came to a small road to our left, certainly leading nowhere. We checked the map under a lighted match and the road was marked "small road leading nowhere." We turned onto it and drove a couple of miles—at least we knew where this one went. We came to a few little houses and kept going. A few more and a gas station. Some signs ("hope you enjoyed nothing"), and a traffic light. We saw a few Mexicans. We kept going and wherever we were continued being there…more houses, some cross streets, more traffic lights, a few stores. This might even be a teeny town. We stopped to ask where, if anywhere, we were.

"San Antonio," piped a Mexican accent.

Gosh.

The eventual explanation we got for the sleight-of-land was that the highway complex around San Antonio was a newly designed "belt" system, not yet on any existing maps. Encircling the city, the belt was HUGE, way outside even the residential areas. Since the belt was so wide, when you were driving on it, the road appeared straight so you never sensed you were driving in a gigantic circle. And, of course, the city skyline was always in a different spot.

Anyway, we made it. And because we were long overdue for luck, we happened to be on the road with the three-dollar motels. They proved to be Americo-Mex bacterial breeding centers, and without vaccines we'd never survive a night in one. Further up the road, however, we found a slew of five-dollar stables where the pest-to-guest ratios were lower. Here, instead of objection to cats and dogs, there was disappointment that we had so few.

The next day, we cruised downtown San Antone—after the ordeal of finding the joint, we were kind of hesitant to leave. Plus we should at least check it out because we would NEVER be coming back here.

So with a few pints of Chock Full of Mud, we washed down stacks of pancakes soaked in Log Cabin Poison. I then suggested a recon mission to Dr. Shelton's.

"I'm not gonna pay money to starve to death," Jules missed the point.

"Of course we can't enlist on a fast here and now—what would we do with the animals—but let's just take a look-see. Come on, our route goes right past it. We only have to stay a minute. I'd just like to see if it looks legit, so I can report back to Dad. He asked me to check it out."

Twelve miles north of the city, the little 'health school' was perched on a modest hill, commanding a modest view. Inside, the people couldn't walk, they crept. After a few of these empty night-gowns wafted past us, we saw that the common denominator wasn't old age, it was nothing, abstention, restraint, conservation.

We didn't stay long because the only thing to do there was fast, and, heck, we could do that anywhere. Till lunchtime. But even though we fasted the whole fifteen minutes, we were clearly "eaters," the out-crowd. The quiet eyes of the fasters discerned those putrefying pancakes right through our stomach linings, not to mention the enchiladas from last night polluting our intestines.

So we left the fast fast and moved west again; but not without reflection. People fasted up to sixty days there. Illness could be arrested by this process, and most people were cured. The patients themselves were testimonials. But the primary function of the institute was to provide an environment conducive to restriction, rest, and education. (A seed was sewn. Two years later, I went back and fasted—only eight days. And four years after me, Dad and Nadine drove there and heroically fasted on water thirty days each.)

- 34 -

Albakerky

Driving across the range was refreshing. Seldom was heard a discouraging word and the skies were not cloudy all day. We took a l-o-n-g slim road to El Paso and sent our eyes out to the quintessential edge of the parched plain. Texas is a sure cure for nearsightedness. Here the land seemed all-important—not unused like desert or over-used like agricultural land, just evenly used by contented cattle. The trees were cypress green, the sky an easy blue, and the hills soft and sunny like a lion's coat. Texas was generous today, its warmth good to our skin.

Though still hundreds of miles from Albuquerque, it was only one state away. And we agreed, actually agreed, not to stop again till we got to Red's house. This would mean another all-night drive, but the combination of endless Texas and our funky recent history made us hell-bent to put this trip out of its misery. We'd take turns at the wheel and rest up in Albuquerque.

We'd seen the country, as I'd demanded we must—getting our kicks OFF Route 66—but we'd done it all wrong and the doleful hours (that Jules had foreseen) had been numerous. We were both sorry. But this being the last leg, we were in better spirits. And the expansive power of the southwestern landscape makes all else trivial. Plus we were pleased with ourselves for having dodged a Long Island winter.

New Mexican earth must have some secret additive—easily and unconsciously we switched gears and slowed down. The land was so much wider and simpler than anywhere else. Though sixty miles an hour here felt like thirty, it was still too fast to take it all in. "Nothing" takes on all new meaning when it comes to deserts. But knowing we had real time now and no set plans, it wasn't a matter of just looking at the desert, now we could find out how it lives and changes. Where our lack of a destination had been, gladness now filled in, questions as to where we'd end up were being answered by this majestic terrain.

We phoned Red from the southeast corner of the state. "We're planning to hit Albuquerque by evening," I surmised.

"Great," she said, "we've been expecting you. Have a good trip?"

"Pretty crazy."

"Well, get ready for some more craziness. Guess who else is hitting Albuquerque tonight...."

"Oh God...who?"

"Mimi and Lily. They just called an hour ago. They're hitching in from Tucson."

"Jesus, you can't possibly handle all of us at once."

"No problem. We've got a great big old house. I wasn't sure if and when you and Jules were coming so I didn't mention it to the girls. It'll be a surprise."

"Sure will. See you later then!"

In his fragile mental state and advanced age, Jules wasn't sure he could survive a triple dose of my family. "Poor me," was all he could muster.

New Mexico was Red's Shangri-La—she'd found her place and was settling down. The ideal hostess, she transmitted constant enthusiasm about the Southwest while making us fully welcome.

And Red was more than just a friend and co-inhabitant of Leo's summer commune. Her parents had been long-standing pals of my parents, our mothers both painters in an established Hamptons art group. Red, too, deeply missed our mother. And, witnessing our father's new life, she knew first hand that our 'new order' was a tall order. As an only child herself, Red had a sisterhood with us, especially now. And we cherished her.

"Why don't you stay in Albuquerque?" she asked me moments after we'd moored in her driveway.

"Albuquerque? Me? How would I explain it to people? I mean, isn't Albuquerque a little weird? You go to school here, that's your excuse, what would I do?"

"Go to school, too. The University of New Mexico is fabulous—they teach everything on Earth."

We drank Dos Equis and waited for the fateful knock of the jailbait. We didn't wait long. They soon appeared, complete with 'Donna,' another hipster they'd acquired in Tucson who they treasured as a mediator. At complete odds with their futures, the weary minors were in need of elderly support and misguidance. But first, "What happened after the Detention Center?" we all wanted to know.

"As soon as the telegram came through," Mimi began, "they called a cop to pick us up and take us to the Runaway Center. We had all our stuff with us and sat in the back of the police car. The cop was pretty friendly—you know, kind of California dumb—and we were super friendly and humble with him. And when we got there, he just dropped us off in front of the building, saying 'Go on in,' and drove away."

Everyone chuckled.

"So we stood there half a second then ran away. Guess that's why they call it the Runaway Center."

"You fled? Didn't anyone see you? Where'd you go?"

"No, no one was waiting for us. Not outside anyway. We were expected to walk in and commit ourselves, but who would be that stupid? Even Lily isn't that stupid. So we casually strolled down the block, and once we got around a corner, we just beat feet. We hitched to the freeway and then to San Diego. We had to spend a night in somebody's yard, but otherwise it was cool."

"I might be stupid," said Lily, "but who got busted for stealing the stupid candy to begin with? I can't believe we went to JAIL for two Tiger's Milk bars." A debate followed about who had the hottest hooks and who had the paranoid looks. I'd seen them in action back home and believed both their styles left room for improvement. (The Half-wit's method included detectable hesitancy and moral compromise reflected in her expression, but her angelic persona convinced onlookers they'd imagined merchandise disappearing around her. Mimi was a natural, unencumbered with guilt, but so outrageously blasé that her busy charade drew all eyes to the performance.) Had they pooled their acumen—Mimi's confidence behind Lily as a decoy—they could've managed the Golden Gate Bridge.

Like Jules and me, Mimi and Lily had covered more ground

quarreling than traveling, but here in Albuquerque, under this coincidental constellation, all four of us were now allotted time to contemplate the circumstances. And where a normal person would've fled from this crowd, dear Red produced a hearty dinner—not at all reticent about housing quasi-orphaned drifters, their differences, their lovers, their referees, their pets, and their dearth of plans.

"I wanna go to Mexico," said Lily next morning at breakfast, "and learn how to carve flutes."

"I have to get back to Tucson," said Donna.

"I don't know what I want to do," said Mimi. "I'm so sick of traveling. It's too cold to go back to Sonny's log cabin in Nova Scotia, I can't go to Mexico because Lily's going, and no one wants to come to India with me...."

"Stay here," said Red. "You and Wendy can go to the University of New Mexico. You'll love it." She was stuck on this idea.

"Oh God, another parent," Mimi dropped her head to the table.

"You're not serious?" I looked at Red. "College?"

"It's just fun," she said earnestly. "And cheap."

"Since when are you the scholar?" asked Jules. "You were the queen of the dropouts back in the good old days four months ago."

"I accidentally dropped back in 'cause I came to U.N.M. It's just different here. It's fun. I'll show you a list of courses. We're about to start a new semester," and she sprinted upstairs.

"I'm going to Tucson," Jules decided. "In about half an hour. When people start talking about college, that's my exit cue. I'll take my dog and anyone else who wants a lift."

"I'll take a lift," said Donna. Who was this Donna?

"I'll take a lift, too," said Lily, "because I left my stuff at Donna's in Tucson, and it's on the way to Mexico. Hey Jules, wanna go to Mexico?"

"I doubt it," said Jules. "I did that ten years ago. I'm too serious now. But maybe."

Red wasn't wrong; there was a happy-go-lucky roster of subjects at U.N.M. They even had Chinese. "I'm staying here," I decided.

"You are?" Mimi silently weighed the pros and cons of teaming up with a new sibling. "Okay, I will too."

So Lily, Jules, Molly, and Donna boarded the van for points southwest. Mimi, Bellringer, and I stayed at Red's breakfast table for another cup of coffee, and checked off the courses we'd take. For Mimi, the spontaneous switching of partners was old hat, and for the rest of us, welcome relief.

The whole college thing seemed wacky to me. I mean you file yourself into some would-be promise of a profession you don't want and, for a tidy sum, your parents get reassurance that it wasn't a total mistake having you in the first place. Two and a half years away from Ohio Wesleyan University, I was surer than ever that I didn't conform to the collegiate mold. Nor could I relate to students—they were like 'orange people,' sects, secretaries, EST graduates, or any other flock. They were trying to be good dogs. I was a bad dog.

What a waste, though, of all those facilities—huge libraries, gymnasiums, pools, tennis courts, acres of greenery, languages, information, craft workshops, theaters, music—all in one place! But the students haven't sought this environment, they've been moved there by the conveyor belt of the white collar factory.

Then I had a brilliant idea: auditing! I didn't need college credit, didn't need anyone to verify whether I'd learned or not. Auditing was free, and a new semester was about to commence. With Red's course list, I chose my classes: Chinese, Chinese Philosophy, Chinese and Japanese Art Appreciation, Spanish I, French II, Ceramics, and Recorder-Playing. School was starting in four days. Mimi and I just had to find somewhere to live and then we could audit every class we wanted.

I got my textbooks second-hand (and sold them back later), and from there it was just a matter of...*learning*. Being excused from exams and term papers, college was pure pleasure. Pressure off, I proved a marvelous student, totally removed from tequila binges, reckless Mexican weekends, and checks from home. Brimming with enthusiasm, I even became teacher's pet in some classes. If Jesus could only see me now.

Considered elsewhere as the armpit of the state, Albuquerque was actually one cool town. Nobody gave a good goddamn about anything fancy. There was plenty of room for everyone to have a fine time and that's what they did. Albuquerque thrived with neither an upper nor upper middle class. Those types flocked to Santa Fe to get away from like individuals back east who also flocked to Santa Fe. (Once an intimate pueblo, it was now a sprawling imitation adobe shopping center where tourists and merchants touched down for art and turquoise jewelry.) But ol' Albuquerque had no pretensions. It knew its funkiness preserved its funkiness, and who wants to live in a place that's impossible to spell? Route 66 pierced it through the heart, pumping in droves of travelers who contributed at best eight bucks for a tank of gas, and more often five cents for a pack of Juicy Fruit gum or a postcard of the Old Town.

Albuquerque was casual, man. There were Chicanos and there were students, there were pick-up trucks and motels, there were coffee shops and gas stations. And that's all. The easiest place in the world to hitch-hike—you'd be nuts to own a car. Mimi and I would stand in front of our little rented house on school mornings, just thinking about a ride, and get picked up. We spent two-thirds of our time in the back of pick-ups, usually with friendly Chicanos, their dogs, and their kids. They adored taking us well out of their way.

But Mimi didn't take to auditing as I did. Being on the swim team was her passion, but using another student's name became self-defeating. She didn't dare win at the meets because what if the owner of her name read about it in the student news? So she grew antsy, and finally caught a ride to Boston, then hitched back to Nova Scotia where she could prod Sonny into making that trek to India.

I had to get a new roommate.

- 35 -

Can't Win 'em All

Anna was the perfect house-mate. She was making the most of New Mexico, traveling and exploring everything, as she'd no doubt done every place she'd been. She, too, was a drop out, but now she was saving money to go to nursing school in San Francisco. So she waitressed in a coffee shop. Too sharp for the propaganda that transforms beautiful women into commodities, like models or arm-candy for men, she was doing what she pleased. She wasn't afraid of waitressing, hitch-hiking, or being alone. She knew she wouldn't always have the time to enjoy deserts, sunsets, and amazing places.

Anna's California non-speediness seemed to relax my East Coast urgency. Both free on weekends, we'd set out on Saturday mornings in any old direction. In New Mexico, you didn't have to go far to find extraordinary wonder. We'd hitch north or west or south, then just meander off the road into the rocks or the forest or the desert. We found canyons, Indian habitats, buttes, and mesas.

The Santa Fe Chief was a fast train that whistled steamily into Albuquerque from Denver and back. Still hooked on trains, I'd had my eye on this one for a while. Supposedly its route through the Rockies was breathtaking. Riding the freights, I thought, would make a man of me. And Anna was game. One Saturday morning we decided the day had come. We bundled up, though the March weather was mild, and thumbed out to the rail-yard.

It was a bit confusing, with freight trains all over the place. "Let's look for some bums," I suggested. "They'll have the beat." Jack Kerouac or somebody had led me to believe that rail-yards were bursting with unshaven hobos who played guitars and knew the freight schedules by heart. But we didn't see anybody, just shiny tracks everywhere and segments of directionless trains. We were only interested in The Chief—riding with new Oldsmobiles to Los Angeles had no appeal—but didn't know where to surreptitiously await its awesome arrival. It was bound to come soon, though.

"You look lost," said a voice behind us then. It was a uniformed person.

"We are."

"Whatcha lookin' for?" he was friendly enough.

"The Chief," I said. Didn't want to sound new to the game.

"The Santa Fe Chief?"

"Yeah," said Anna.

"It's comin' through in about fifteen minutes...." he eyed us with interest. "Doesn't take passengers, you know."

The woolly hats were the culprits. "Yeah, we know," we replied politely, then looked at each other.... We needed to know what track to wait beside. We really had to be in a good spot to position ourselves for quick and discreet embarkation.

"Uh," I hesitated...this guy seemed nice enough.... "what track is it coming in on? Just out of curiosity."

"Aaah, knights of the road. That's what I thought. You're thinking of goin' for a ride, aren't you?"

We nodded sneakily.

"Wouldn't recommend it."

"Why not?" Anna asked.

"Ever ridden the freights before?" Judging by his tone, he didn't take us for old hands at this. Shoulda brought a banjo. "You know jumpin' freights is pretty dangerous."

"It is?"

"Yeah. People don't realize it. They think you can just hop aboard and have a free ride. I'll tell you, all the cars on The Chief are locked; you can't get inside. That means you have to ride between the cars. Now that in itself is real dangerous—the engineer doesn't know you're there. He can stop short for any reason and you won't expect it. So you have to hang on tight the whole trip. That's eight hours. That might not be too bad on a different train, but this one goes through the Rockies. So, not only do you have to hold on like the devil, but you freeze. You're blazin' along at sixty, seventy miles an hour, with the wind blastin' in your face, maybe it's snowing, and you have to cling to the cold metal for dear life. Now if you still think it sounds like fun, I better tell you that when you realize that you've bitten off more than you can chew and decide to bail out fast, you can't. Because The Chief doesn't stop once between here and Denver. That's why we call it The Chief, it's a serious train. Still wanna go for a ride?"

We looked at each other.

"I didn't think so," the man said. "People do it for kicks and end up dead. Now what you two ladies want is a nice slow train crossing some flat prairie land. Start out on a train like that."

It was still early, and the weekend by no means lost. We hitched north beyond Santa Fe to a wooded national park, and followed a stream to the top of a mountain. We saw no other people at all. Feeding the stream at the mountaintop was a huge waterfall. We peeled off and let it drench our bare bodies. Then we lay on the smooth bronzed stones next to it and sunbathed, not speaking for hours. The air was empty, clean, and thin, the water a whisper, the sky divine, the sun a kiss. That was the southwest Anna and I got to know.

♥

- 36 -

Waitressing

Anna's waitress job was lousy. The degradation wasn't worth the pittance they called a salary. Plus, Albuquerque was pathetic about tipping. She had to find a better job or leave town. But the only waitress jobs that paid at all, supposedly, were at the strip joints. The many strip joints.

Being a waitress is bad enough, but a stint in the Pussycat Lounge would soil even a pro's resume.... However, after two and a half months of auditing classes, I was low on money, too. So we discreetly inquired, and learned that some of these seedy clubs hired regular waitresses aside from the strippers. "Listen Anna," I said over morning Pero, "I know you're a clean liver, but wouldn't it make more sense to work in one of these places for a month and make real money than to work in Howard Johnson's and go crazy for nothing?"

"I don't know," she searched my face for the line between compromise and sleaze.

"Well, I couldn't handle Howard Johnson's," I said, "ever. But if I was guaranteed that I'd just wait on tables in one of those dives, and that I'd make twice or three times as much, I think I'd do it. But not alone."

"I don't know."

"It would be more interesting. I've never even been inside one of those joints. We could get the inside story."

"I don't want the inside story." She squinted ponderously out the window for a few moments. "But I do want the money. Otherwise I'll have to leave. And I love Albuquerque."

"Look, why don't we go check it out first-hand, talk to whoever does the hiring, and then decide?"

"Okay.... It might not be too-too bad if we're both doing it."

"Yeah, it'll be an experience."

"A bad experience."

Anna was a California girl, born and raised—Albuquerque was her idea of the wildly exotic. West coasters don't like bad experiences. West thinks bad drains you and saps your strength. East Coasters consider bad experiences good material. East thinks confronting and knowing bad gives you more strength. One believes in staying clean, the other believes in getting dirty.

"Bottoms Up" would be the place we'd try first. Supposedly, waitresses were off-limits to clientele there and performed only their prescribed function. We made an appointment by phone to meet the boss, then hitched out there.

This little joint was well out of town, on some obscure highway that probably connected the city dump to a nuclear power plant. There it was, a square white isolated box out in the desert. A blinking sign depicting a martini glass beside a bare derrière identified it. "I'm not going in there," said Anna like a five-year-old in front of the spook house.

"It could be worse." I said. "We came all the way out here, we have to go through with this."

"I don't," she reminded me.

"Wouldn't you rather be humiliated here for a month than slinging burgers on Route 66 for three?"

"I don't want to be humiliated at all."

"Then you're in the wrong walk of life."

"Don't remind me." She was near tears, as I would've been if her trepidation hadn't demanded I be the bigger one.

"Listen, I'm going in. Your company would be much appreciated." I pivoted toward a pink sign saying "ENTRANCE." Anna followed.

It was pitch dark inside and dead still. A waist-high platform centered the black-painted room, and tables and empty chairs spilled in all directions. A fat slob appeared from the shadows, acknowledging us by raising his chin an eighth of an inch. Then he tipped his head half an inch to one side, indicating a small door marked "office" that we sheepishly followed him into.

Whether or not we'd accept employment there was not to be decided by us. "I'm the boss. You can call me Jock," said Jock, foisting two satin, tasseled skirts at us in a manner that compelled us to grab them before they fell on the floor. "When can you start work?"

"What are these?" Anna regarded the garment in her hand with horror. It was sunshine yellow, mine was shamrock green; both were fringed with black bonbons. I tried to pass an encouraging smile in Anna's direction without Jock seeing it, but Anna was the one who didn't see it.

"That's your waitress uniform," said Jock, with the humor of an obituary columnist who'd just been fired.

"Where's the rest of it?" Anna couldn't conceal her annoyance.

"Shoes you have to provide for yourself," he stated.

"But where's the top?" I asked quickly before Anna could whack him across the head.

"That's the top," Jock pointed at the skirt in my hand.

"But it's a skirt," Anna said, while I said, "Then where's the bottom?"

"You wear it over one shoulder," Jock explained, "with one arm sticking out."

"Where's the other arm supposed to go?" Anna wanted to know.

"Under the skirt," now Jock was getting annoyed.

"How can we work with one arm trapped inside our uniform?" Anna nearly shouted. "I don't think I want to wear this uniform," she looked at Jock accusingly.

Clearly the go-between, I asked Jock if he could leave the office for a minute while we tried the outfits on. Rolling his eyes, he departed. Quickly undressing, we climbed into the tulip suits. Imagine wearing a skirt around your neck, tilted at an angle, with one arm out the waistband with your head, and the other arm under the skirt with your body. "These are disgusting," Anna's notion of all the world being like Santa Barbara was in its final hour. She was now scrutinizing me with overt suspicion.

"Anna, stop looking at me as if I'm right in my element. I told you that this is hands-down the worst job I've ever applied for, but I'm prepared to go through with it.... I just won't let it get to me."

Jock knocked on the door then entered a little too eagerly. "Oh!" he was genuinely pleased at the sight of us, even altered his facial expression slightly. "You both look fine. Just fine."

"What do we wear underneath?" Anna loudly asked the ceiling.

"Just normal underwear," Jock answered amiably. "Bikini pants."

"Oh, God," Anna sighed.

"What about shoes?" Jock asked, suddenly Yves St. Laurent with a pencil in his mouth. Was he going to design some?

"Sneakers," said Anna, like a member of the Third Reich.

"No," said Jock, like Hitler.

"But something comfortable," I pushed.

"Wear whatever you want," he decided with a generous flick of the wrist. "Nobody'll notice—you both got great legs. But no sneakers. When do you wanna start?"

"Tomorrow," I said courageously while Anna vomited in a corner.

"Okay, tomorrow for you. Six o'clock. And you?" he looked to Anna. "You don't wanna start at all, do you?"

"No."

"Come on, give it a try. The guys won't bother ya if ya don't let 'em. Come back tomorrow, with your friend here, at six."

"I'll think about it," said Anna.

Outside, the blast of the desert sun welcomed us back from the underworld. "Every time we lift our arms, everybody's going to see right up those go-go outfits," said Anna miserably, as we walked to the roadside to wait for a garbage truck.

"I know. Guess we'll have to work with one hand."

"How do you hold a tray full of drinks and get one onto the table with one hand?"

"Well, maybe this is the one part of the job where you get to use your intelligence."

"Yeah sure."

Jock had also discussed money with us and supposedly—though waitress employers tend to exaggerate about potential earnings—the prospects were as good as we'd hoped. For five nights' work, we'd be making more than we could at any other job we were qualified for in Albuquerque.

We spent the first few nights on the job learning the routine and trying to perform it one-handed. Impossible. So we had to accept the sordid truth that the bug eyes of strange and horny men were prying up our swaying skirts and thinking horrible thoughts about our matching undies. The only thing to do was concentrate on serving drinks and refusing the myriad offers for extra-curricular activities. "When are *you* gonna dance?" was the recurring question. Meanwhile, fortunately, the action on the central platform diverted attention. Three strippers were employed at "Bottoms Up" and each night they took turns performing. They'd probably known or planned on better days, but they were professional, gave a good show, and made a buck.

Oddly enough, once you got used to it, which Anna didn't, the atmosphere wasn't really so slimy. It appeared slimy, but in a funny way things proved to be on the up and up. The jukebox thumped out Neil Diamond tunes, the girls gyrated in their glitter-bikinis, and the men taunted and visually consumed them. Energy mounted, costumes slipped to the floor piece by piece, quarters were balanced on nipples for extra tips, whistles and hoots accompanying these stunts, leading to close-up shimmying for dollar bills. Standard strip-tease. It never got out of hand. One sensed the controlling presence of Jock and a few regulars who oversaw the operation, silently protecting the dancers and obviously pulling in a bundle. The girls prospered too, and actually seemed to enjoy themselves. When their dances ended, they'd walk off the platform and straight back to reality, like any performer. After work, we watched them step into their blue-jeans, get in their cars, and drive home. In fact, I couldn't even connect their off-stage personalities to those tantalizers on the dance floor.

Anna and I, milling around the tables as the only waitresses, were more accessible than the strippers. So, of course the men were going to nudge the envelope with us. But, although predictable and persistent, they actually remained respectful and even polite.

What clinched it for Anna, after several days' work, occurred during a customary half-hour break between performances. The men were sitting around waiting and the jukebox was suggesting something more exciting than another Sloe Gin Fizz. Jock appeared from a crack in the wall and gave Anna a light shove toward the platform, "Get up there and dance."

"What!" she turned crimson.

"You heard me, get up there and dance. The customers are restless. We don't want 'em walkin' out, do we?" Anna stood frozen. "Don't worry," said Jock, "you don't have to take anything off. Just dance one song so the people have something to watch while they wait. Go on." Anna looked desperately over at me. "Don't look at her," said Jock, "she can't help you. Anyway, she's up right after you. Go on, anyone can dance. Just go."

Anna's dancing was not what you'd call inspired. On the platform, she looked like she'd swallowed a plate of worms. I was particularly sympathetic as my own debut drew nearer. So much fresher and prettier than the strippers, the men were lavishing her with encouragement and jungle noises—maybe a little positive feedback might remove the buttercup tutu. They were all leaning in with their elbows on the dance floor. But Anna had to move as little as possible, since her attire was so short and she was above eye level. Her solemn performance consisted of hand and feet movement only. As the jukebox finished "Yellow River," Anna extracted herself from the limelight. I waited for her at the foot of the four little stairs.

"Could you see up my skirt?" she urgently whispered.

"No. Good thing you didn't spin tough. Oh boy, my turn... How was it? Unbearable?"

"Unbelievably unbearable. I'm never doing that again."

I wasn't about to leap up there voluntarily. I'd wait till Jock Strip came and gave me a push. Maybe one of the real dancers would show up first. Fat chance—Jock was walking toward me. Not pleased. "What're you waiting for, a personal invitation?" With a hasty "Very nice" to Anna, he pointed me toward the stage. "Cracklin' Rosie" was erupting from the box and the whole house bent forward in readiness for my premiere. We'd had no idea we held such a special place in everyone's hearts. But aside from being the only non-strippers, Anna and I were also the only waitresses, (who'd served drinks before we were hired was not known), so getting us onto the dance floor was regarded by all as a step in a brilliant direction.

I did my bit to music, an Anna-esque routine since even breathing deeply in that rig was chancy. The only good thing about my act was that it made Anna laugh, for the first time that week. And the last—she quit that night.

On the Road Again

How could I abide the Scrounge Lounge without my bo-som-buddy? Plus I'd have to hitch all the way out there and back by myself. The bartender had been giving us rides, but I didn't fancy those moonlight drives with no third wheel. In light of this ordeal, or in the darkness of it, something solid was needed to balance that scuzzy world.

Jules.

I had three free days till I was due back at work. So I hitched twelve hours, through desert and canyons, to Tucson. My little sweetheart was living with his friend the vet, and helping out in the animal hospital. We'd been in contact since he left and had buried the hatchet. He was pleased to see me and confessed that his term in Tucson could be winding down. "Come back to Albuquerque with me," I invited. "You can share my room. It'll be nice. And I'd love a ride back."

"Okay," he said, just like that. And next morning, Jules, Molly, and I took off in the van, taking just one three-hundred-mile de-tour to the Grand Canyon since Jules had never been there. Happily together again, and with a destination this time, the excursion was harmonious.

"Hey, Jules, whatever happened to your Henry Miller plan?"

"Oh, him...."

"What happened?"

"Well, after I'd been in Tucson for a few weeks, I asked myself what the fuck I was doing in Tucson, Arizona, and flashed again on Henry Miller. I decided I better go see him like I'd planned. So I got in the van and headed toward California. I reached Route 66 and was moving along, moving along, making good time…. I'd been driving about six hours…and then I just….." he trailed off.

"Just what?"

"Just…sort of stopped."

"Why?"

"It just seemed…"

"Weird?"

"Yeah. I mean I thought to myself, 'What if I don't find him? What if I go all the way to Big Sur and I don't see Henry?' The only reason to go to California would be to see him, otherwise I wouldn't be caught dead on the West Coast—I mean Arizona's bad enough. So if I didn't find Henry Miller, I'd just waste all that time and money on a pointless trip to California. So I stopped and talked it over with Molly and we decided to turn around and go back to Tucson."

I looked at him compassionately. It was kind of like my grape story. "Why didn't you go to the Grand Canyon that day?"

"Because I was in a hurry to see Henry Miller when I passed it the first time, and I was in a hurry to get back to Tucson when I passed it on the way back."

Anna got a respectable waitress job on Route 66 and began to enjoy life less and less. For the next two weeks, Jules would pick me up at "Bottoms Up," then he and I would have long talks through the wee hours about what to do next. Albuquerque was by no means a last stop. He was ready to pack it in as a westerner, and begged permission to go home. "It's been three months," he offered as proof. "Count 'em: January, February, March. You don't want to stay here, do you?"

I had to confess, "I'm thinking about Europe, Jules."

"You're always thinking about Europe."

"Well, I've been back in the States eleven months now and *nothing* has happened."

"What d'you mean *nothing* has happened?"

"I mean I work in a strip joint in Albuquerque." We both had to laugh. "My ladder to success is sinking in quick-sand."

"What would you do in Europe, look for Jonah?"

"Jonah who?"

Maybe Jules was right, maybe that was part of Europe's pull... I thought it was Paradise I was searching for, but that hadn't turned up either. "Maybe I'll go to Nova Scotia and check out Mimi and Sonny," I said. "Why don't we both go to Nova Scotia?"

"Because I hate hippies."

"Oh spare me, Jules."

"And there's no work there for me. At least in East Hampton I'm guaranteed work. Look, drive with me as far as Long Island, then if you still can't handle it there, hitch up to Nova Scotia and send me a report. If it's really great, you can maybe talk me into joining you."

"If it's really great, I'll probably forget you."

"Anyway, I'll only come if I can work."

During the third and last week of my employment, the hippie-hater got the van ready for another cross-country cruise. In no mood for Part II of The Pilgrimage From Hell, he would ward off catastrophe this time through painstaking preparations. His efforts weren't for naught—by the time I threw in my skirt at Jock's, Jules had solved the bicycle/ladder problem by attaching a roof rack, and had constructed a comfy double bed plus cabinets into the space in back. So...*adios* Land of Enchantment.

Thus we had a sublime drive back east. In our snug mobile motel, we wove along the curly roads through American springtime. We didn't see a highway. We bought provisions in little stores en route and picnicked beside streams or on flowering hillsides.

In New York, I disembarked at Oma's Manhattan flat. With a serious block against the South Fork of Long Island and alleged parents, I would bypass that headache. After two days in the City, I hitched out to the North Fork instead. From there I'd catch the ferry to Rhode Island then boogie up to Nova Scotia.

Nova Scotia, though the two words formed an enticing sound, wasn't the lure it might've been were it situated closer to Bali. Traveling north is hard any time, but more so in spring. However, I'd recently tried south and west; and my old favorite, east, was regarded as "escapist" by everyone but Lao Tzu.

Freezing to death on April Fool's Day, because Long Island spring falls on a Thursday in late June, I ambled through Greenport, looking around for the Rhode Island ferry. I'd been in town about fifteen minutes and was sauntering down Main Street when a familiar-looking VW camper motored past. It was the eternal honeymooners, Dad and Nadine, out for a weekend drive and sitting so close together you couldn't tell who was driving. They hadn't seen me, but I thought a greeting might be fair to them since they thought I was in Albuquerque. They had turned down a side street that led to the other ferry, to the South Fork. I raced through the avenues, inventing shortcuts like a thief, since that ferry leaves every ten minutes.

Dragging myself breathlessly to the pier where the camper was creeping along in the ferry line, I knocked lightly on the driver's side window, totally shocking Bogart and Bacall. "Well I never," Dad chuckled, rolling down the window.

"What are you two doing here?" I leaned in and kissed them.

"What are *you* doing here? We thought you were in New Mexico," Nadine wondered if family factoids were being withheld from her.

"I was. Now I'm on my way to Nova Scotia."

"Going to see Mimi and Sonny?" Dad asked.

"Yeah."

"Better come with us," he said then, and nodded to the shotgun seat Nadine wasn't in. "There's something at home that you should see before you head up there."

Oh God, probably some court order from American Express.... "What is it?" I tried to sound matter-of-fact.

"Mimi and Sonny," said Dad. "They came home yesterday."

Oops. I jumped in and we rolled onto the ferry. (My guardian angel always on its toes.)

The parental limo dropped me off at Jules' parents' house where the van sat out front. Jules, not displeased at this twist of fate, would now have to accommodate Sonny and Mimi in his safe haven, too, till they got settled somewhere.

But the Hamptons scene was still too recent for me, and too predictable. Summer was ready to pounce, prices doubling. All local discourse revolved around restaurant jobs and rentals, and home-owners were literally lining bedrooms with bunk-beds in which to stock Manhattanites.

Definitely time to boogaloo—but where to? Paradise hadn't turned up anywhere yet, so scrap that dream. Phoebe had kept me posted. She'd briefly returned home to Chicago, but was now living in London....

I grew quiet and let my mind spin like a globe for ten days. I cut off all my hair and considered the world's cities in alphabetical order. This was going to be a sensible and calculated move.

PART IV ~ DESTINY

- *38* -

London

April 1972

April twentieth I left for London. It seemed the only link to the rest of my life and almost too perfect for someone who no longer believed in Paradise. A one-way ticket was suitable, I was going forever. I'd worked it all out: I could speak English more or less; could probably get a job; Britain was on the beaten trail so when I never came back my friends could swing a visit; Phoebe was there (I hoped); and I'd never lived in England before.

My only contact in the United Kingdom was, in fact, Phoebe. But though I wished to make up for the lost time in our friendship, I was primed to go it alone. Whatever she was doing in London, surely she was steeped in it. I'd get in touch soon but couldn't land on her doorstep. Thus, I arrived at Heathrow Airport.

Two other young hipsters I met on the flight told me of a youth hostel in the center of town, so I hung my bowler hat there. But student residences are under-heated reminders of one's footloose status. My hostel mates could spout off the fares to Amsterdam, Istanbul, or Kathmandu, but all they knew about London was that it was too rainy and bleak—they were clearing out. Determined to like the place, I walked around my new neighborhood, nearly eliminating myself at intersections by double-decker buses on the wrong side of the road. I focused on Big Ben, the Thames, Westminster Abbey, fish, and chips. That took a day. Then I researched tea-drinking, duck-feeding, and wearing all my clothes at once. Another day.

I then bought three pairs of socks, did not eat beans on toast, and considered Paris, Brussels, Ibiza, and China.

By the fourth day, I'd discovered McVities Home Wheat cookies—to a sugar addict what Atlantis would be to Jacques Cousteau. But consuming them alone was depressing. Especially with Phoebe possibly just a subway ride away.

A confirmed Londoner now, day four, it was high time to call on old friends. I found Phoebe's address in London's "A to Z" street guide. Pressing the doorbell of 48 Belsize Gardens, I was buzzed in. Slowly climbing the stairs, a door was heard opening on a floor above. "Hello?" a male voice called down.

"Hello," I reached the third floor. A familiar-looking man filled the doorway. "Hi," I said. "Does Phoebe live here?"

"Yeah, come on in. What's your name? I'll tell her you're here." He was American.

"Wendy. But don't tell her. It's a surprise."

"Okay," he smiled, and disappeared around a corner, leaving me to a spacious, sky-lit entryway with a balcony just above, on the second floor of this two-tiered apartment.

In moments, Phoebe appeared up there in a huge men's t-shirt. "Wendy!" her face lit up and she ran down the stairs. "God, it's great to see you!" We hugged.

"It's great to see YOU," and I meant it.

"What are you doing in London?"

"I moved here."

"Where's all your stuff then?"

"Back at the hostel where I'm staying."

"You moved to a hostel??"

"Temporarily."

"Why didn't you just come here? How long have you been in town anyway?" she looked offended.

"About four days."

"You've been here four days and you haven't called me?"

I explained that being a greenhorn I hadn't wanted to lean on her. "Go get your stuff," was her reply. "You're staying here. We like greenhorns. And we have an extra room. God, am I glad you're here."

In Phoebe's kitchen as she brewed tea, I was briefed on who was who. Peter, a filmmaker who rented half of the conjoined duplex, was Phoebe's lover. Back in Paris, she had auditioned for and gotten the lead in a film he'd planned to shoot in Spain that summer. A month after the audition, as a side effect of her communal lifestyle, Phoebe found herself in the family way. Abortions were illegal in France, but not in England, so a trip north was in order. As was some money. She'd phoned her future employer, Peter, for an advance against the film work she'd do in Spain. Sensitive to her (not uncommon) plight, he agreed, and also offered her lodging in London for her ordeal. The film never fleshed out, but a relationship did, and Phoebe never returned to Paris.

I remembered Peter from his auditions at the Artists' Centre.

These days Phoebe was feeling guiltier than ever because Peter had supported her from day one. Despite producing sumptuous nightly buffets for everyone, she felt generally compromised. Being consoled by Peter was no help because his generosity was part of the problem. So, as she hit thirty, she wasn't enamored with herself. She was reaching panic stations—what about dancing? What about her social worker instincts? Something had to give real soon.

To everybody else though, she was still wonderful Phoebe—a darling dervish, humble and giving, bright and beautiful.

I checked out of the hostel and into 48 Belsize Gardens, a flat not without Chelsea Hotel undertones. In the other half of the hive lived Roger, a wily art professor who lived and breathed kinetic sculpture. Wiry, wizened, poetic, and about fifteen years older than his flatmates, he kind of home-schooled everybody by mere proximity. With him lived Clare, a slender, black-haired study in grace. Flawless and deliberate, she spoke carefully and almost without sound. She was like the moon. It was impossible to tell whether those two were in heavenly accord or at drastic odds. Her English reserve kept it a secret, but one did detect something in the air, like the occasional frying pan.

Daniel VanBuren was another slice of the Belsize Gardens pie. He kept a room there as an adjunct to his studio a few blocks away. An artist from South Africa who was enjoying accolades at an exciting time, Daniel, also older, thrived on the collaboration of other creatives. Well-traveled, witty, and ambitious, he wasn't a-political, just wanted little to do with brown rice, hitch-hikers, and detours off the track to wealth and recognition.

In a matter of days, I, too, acquired a roommate—another filmmaker called Kip, a friend of everybody's from Oxford. And the following week, we both said hello to a third occupant, James, a film editor from New York who had come to work with Peter. Equipped as usual with Kevin's sleeping bag, I was prepared for the floor. And our sleepy threesome would talk all night, then sleep half the day, prompting curiosity as to what went on behind our door.

Because it was a good, if fluctuating, household—where everyone shared costs and chores—Phoebe never batted an eye about tripling her cooking and shopping. I was anxious to help, and knowing nothing of London, enjoyed going along on market rounds. Since Peter was not a street urchin like us, Phoebe had graduated from chintzy chocolate to whole meals. "Come on, Phoebe, help me demolish these," I opened a pack of Smarties outside the first market we visited.

"No, save your appetite, I'm making fettuccine tonight." I wasn't sold on this new Phoebe. She had on gold earrings (a matching pair), and her hair was blonder than before. "Don't mind me," she said, reading my thoughts, "I'm sort of wife-ish these days."

"Yeah. I didn't know you had it in you."

"I don't. It's driving me nuts. But Peter pays for everything, and he really bailed me out of a mess. The least I can do is cook and keep the house together."

"You mean if you had your choice you wouldn't be here?"

"I don't know. I mean, I really like everybody at 48. It's just..." I waited for her to finish. "...well, you know. You remember what I was doing in Paris. I mean, I'm not even dancing anymore. I haven't taken a class in six months. I'm not doing ANYTHING."

"Can't you take classes?"

"I just can't ask Peter for any more money. He'd give it to me, but I'd just feel more ingratiated. And besides," she assumed her default everything's-gonna-be-fine mode, "I'm really too busy right now. Dancing's a full-time thing. It'll be okay. Let's buy some cheesecake for dessert."

"But what will you do?"

"I gotta get my own money and go back to the States. I've been in Europe almost three years now. I want to go to college and get a degree in dance therapy."

"What about Peter?"

"Well, he has to go back to New York next year. So maybe we'll go together. I don't know if we're a forever thing, though. He's got that whole bullshit film scene that I'm not into at all. We just don't operate the same way. He's not supporting the real me, he's just supporting the me that's his girlfriend. He wants me to stay around, but not because he believes in what I want to do. Oh well, no such thing as a free lunch."

"I know, I've been told. But maybe there's still free candy," I re-offered the Smarties and Phoebe held out a palm.

"Yeah," she agreed. "Free dental work here, too. I'll give you the name of my dentist and you can make an appointment."

"I should marry one. But I gotta give up sugar pretty soon because my father says at the rate I'm going I'll be diabetic by thirty-five."

"Free medical here, too."

Meanwhile, what was I going to do? The move back to Europe and the excitement of a new country, albeit a gray one, was, for the moment, a rush—but I needed a job!

In Phoebe's kitchen, one damp afternoon, I was having a tea-making lesson. "A spoonful for each person and one for the pot. Let it sit four or five minutes...."

"Hey Phoebe, let's go somewhere. It's spring. I'd love to see the English countryside." I knew I'd be getting a job shortly and this was my only chance to hit the road.

She gave me a look. "You don't have to stir it but you can if you want."

"Just a little jaunt. What d'ya say?"

"I can't."

"Why?"

"It might make me feel better."

"Well then let's go away and have a miserable time."

"Wales is supposed to be incredible," she said, then clamped a hand over her mouth. We studied each other, then Phoebe said, "God, I'd love to get out of this city. Even for half an hour."

"Let's leave tomorrow."

"I have to ask Peter...."

"He won't mind."

"...and I couldn't go for long."

"Me neither. Just a couple of days."

From Phoebe's kitchen, we could see across the entryway to Roger and Clare's, where Clare was chatting with an animated character in a pink t-shirt and aqua jeans. "Who is that guy?" I asked.

"That's Zeke," said Phoebe. "He's a friend of everybody's, comes over a lot. He works for Daniel." She called out to him and waved. He smiled back through the rooms. "You know where we really should go...." Phoebe's eyes had their daring spark.

I waited.

"To a medium I heard about."

"I've never been to a medium, but I'd like to go. To a good one, that is."

"This lady, Sylvia, is amazing. But it costs ten pounds."

"Phoebe, ten pounds would be a minimal investment in futures as foggy as ours."

Zeke entered the kitchen then, his smile like an equator across his face. "Hello, Phoebe, my little crumpet. Why, pray tell, haven't you introduced me to your American friend?" Both fists were on his hips. "Clare says she's been here a week."

Along with the giant smile, this pastel person had black mischievous eyes, curly black hair, and strong square shoulders. He was like confetti—the kind of harmless rascal who had weird things in his pockets, like a crumpled snapshot of corn growing in Yugoslavia. "Any friend of Phoebe," he said, "automatically becomes a friend of Zekie."

"Oh dear," I said to Phoebe after he left.

After four hours on the road, we could tell we'd reached Wales because the names of the villages started to look like linguine—Llyllewyln and Lnleglwothlnn. We almost had to stop hitching because we couldn't pronounce the places we were trying to get to. L's are the ambulance of the Welsh alphabet, given total right of way. And no one agrees from one hamlet to the next how three L's in a row should sound. Some say they're all silent, some say the first one's pronounced like a guttural Arabic H, the second like a C, and the third like a scream in the night. Y's and N's are fire engines and police cars. Then you travel fourteen feet down the road and it's insisted that L's are really W's, W's are vowels, and vowels don't exist. And there are at least fifteen letters the Welsh don't bother with at all. Correct pronunciation there feels like talking around a whole banana stuffed in your mouth. These people are completely hooked on syllables ('syllables' has to be a Welsh word)—they positively frown on a word with less than five. And should you, by some chance, master a Welsh word, the only person who'll understand you is the individual who painstakingly taught it to you back in the last village.

Another indicator that we'd arrived was that the roads grew narrow, becoming tiny tunnels through hedges. More like paved footpaths. If two cars met face to face, one had to back up two miles to the last intersection. A Chevrolet would wreak havoc here. Behind the hedges, when you caught a glimpse, were endless green-carpeted rectangles beneath cotton-ball sheep chomping like lawnmowers. And relentlessly herding them, were two or three Mollys per flock.

Wales was the sweetest damn place Phoebe and I had ever seen. We didn't have a program or raincoats, so there was a good deal of drenched, aimless meandering, but the diminutive proportions and commanding greenness were bucolic bliss for sheep and sheepdogs. Even out in the elements, where we spent the entire trip, it was somehow snug. We tooled around the Lilliputian lanes, putting out our thumbs whenever the rain got the better of us. And, aside from the world's worst cuisine (Welsh recipes are more constricted than their alphabet), the hospitality was unsurpassed. Toward the close of each day, as we roved through town and country, inevitably someone giving us a lift would extend an invitation to share dinner and spend the night. If we so much as mentioned looking for a pension or Bed and Breakfast, next thing we knew we were handcuffed to the driver's kitchen table, plied with fried eggs and chips while his wife prepared the couch with fresh linens. And in the morning, we were stuffed with more eggs and fried bread, to send us off fortified. And after three days, we started to feel guilty admitting we had no lodgings because the open handed response was so automatic. Still, each family begged us to stay longer, forever if possible.

We didn't grow tired of Wales—there was plenty more to see—but after five days we were grubby, saturated, and chilled. And more fried eggs couldn't satisfy that particular yearning for one's own fried eggs and one's own bed (even if it was just someone else's sleeping bag on a floor).

39

New Friends

Having stuck to my oath, I hadn't seen Jonah in a year and a half. If time was the only cure, I wondered what the dosage was. Distance wasn't proving remedial either. No matter where I went, I still thought about him. And since he was the type you might miss by three minutes in any airport, I never knew for sure how many miles, if any, were between us. But I'd made my point, that I could live without him—not skillfully, but still....

Casting my vow to the wind now, I wrote him a note and mailed it to Ibiza.

But in the real world, it was time to find work. Phoebe handed me the current issue of "Time Out" to peruse the ads.

"*The LIQUID THEATRE. After successful runs in LA and NYC is opening a London Company. Looking for forty energetic young people who can act, sing, and dance. Enthusiasm more important than professional experience.*" Had my name all over it.

Meanwhile there was this Zeke buzzing in and out of the flat, now in pink jeans and a lavender t-shirt. "I don't know what to do about him," I confided to Phoebe.

"Fuck him."

"I can't."

"Why not?"

"I can't be casual. Besides I think he has a girlfriend."

"I don't think so. I've never seen him with one. What makes you think he has a girlfriend?"

"Because he never comes on to me. I mean, I'm obviously alone."

"Maybe he thinks you're getting it on with Kip or James. Or both. Are you getting it on with Kip or James, by the way? Everyone wonders what you guys do all night and all morning in that room."

"We just talk till dawn. Believe me, you'd be the first to know if I had a lover. And don't forget, this mixed bedfellows was your arrangement. I'm sure Zeke has a girlfriend and is perfectly content being pals with me. Have you noticed, he's never around at night?"

"Well, I'll tell you one thing," Phoebe said, "he never used to hang around here as much as he does now."

"This is the first audition," said the young female director to the eager but nervous group of would-be actors sitting on the floor. "From the questionnaires, we've narrowed it down from twelve hundred to one hundred. So congratulations so far. Now we need to find out what kind of energy you have and what you can do with it. After today, we'll narrow it down again, to sixty. Then, next week, we'll pare it down to forty, and that will be the London Liquid Theatre."

It was clear that everyone there could do six back handsprings quicker than I could do a shallow knee bend. Half of them were, at that moment, contorting their leotarded torsos into sickening positions, while yours truly, in men's pajama pants, was hugging my knees and staring at the floor. Picture Ozzie of "Ozzie and Harriet" at a Miss Universe pageant.

For the next two hours, we played children's games. Word games, ball games, body games. Best party I'd been to in ages. At the same time, we were wickedly scrutinized. After that trial, to my astonishment, I remained in the running. And the final audition, they said, would be as much fun as this one.

Ha-ha—the final audition was no fun at all. We played the games again, but now in smaller groups. Intently observant, the judges even took notes. We then did some acting exercises, but all sixty of us knew twenty would be axed. And I couldn't spot one candidate less eligible than me.

Back at 48, I was now summoning naughty ideas about Zeke. He was so present, attentive, and light. But he'd pop in, chat amiably over tea, and leave again with no mention of even a walk in the park. So far, I had dissuaded Phoebe from choreographing the hand of fate, but she was hard to contain. And when she announced that

Zeke was coming to dinner, I knew the dear hadn't invited him just to polish off the paella.

"Is your mother in the spirit form?" Sylvia asked as I stepped across the room to take a seat. I sat down, swallowed, and nodded. There was my ten pounds' worth in ten seconds.

"I thought so," said Sylvia. "I can see her standing just behind you to your left."

I looked over my shoulder.

"Yes," she said, "right there. I'll be communicating with you through your mother. She wants me to, that's why she's here. And that's why you've come to me. So I won't be looking at you, I'll be looking to your left, at her. Let's not waste any time." And she seemed to depart somehow.

"Your mother tells me that today is the very first time she's come back in the form of a spirit. And she's telling me to tell you that now that she's returned, she's going to be around a lot. You've been missing her badly since she died, but now you don't have to feel so sad because she will be near you and you will feel her presence. She says it's very, very important that you realize this. She wants you to be happy."

Sylvia studied the space to my left again. "Your mother's holding up three fingers. She's showing me the number three. Does the number three mean anything to you?"

"Well, I was born on a three...."

Sylvia nodded, and looked at my mother again. "It's funny, she's still holding up three fingers. Is there any other reason she might be showing me the number three?"

I thought about it for a moment. "Well, she died three years ago," I said. "Almost exactly three years ago.... Wait a minute, what's today's date?"

"May fifteenth," said Sylvia.

I couldn't speak at all.

"What is it?" Sylvia asked.

"My mother died on May fifteenth."

"Then that's why she chose this day to be here. Your mother has a lot more to say to you, so I'll just convey to you everything she indicates to me, and you'll probably understand most of the references.

And some things may seem vague, but those things might make more sense when you think about them later on. She looked off to my left. "Cheesecake. Your mother is saying, 'Don't eat cheesecake.' That's a funny thing to say. Do you eat a lot of cheesecake?"

You gotta get up early to sneak one past a ghost. "There's a piece of cheesecake right in my basket," I admitted, glancing at it beside my feet. "I couldn't resist it in the bakery across the street."

"Well your mother doesn't want you to eat it. She says you shouldn't eat sweets. Do you eat a lot of sweets?"

"Yeah, I'm a sugar addict and she knows it."

"Well, your mother's here to help you. She's very well, you know. She's much healthier now and looks marvelous. She's very happy now, too. It was hard for her at the end, but she's well now. You mustn't ever feel sad about her death because she is really well where she is now. By the way, she has a big black and white dog with her. Do you recognize this dog? He might be a German Shepherd."

"Oh! That must be Freud! Mom's with Freud? Oh—we all loved him so much. My parents got him before they had any kids, and he was always with us when we were little. He died when I was seven."

The hour with Sylvia was life-changing. There's no way she alone came up with the name of a pet rabbit I'd had. (Osborne.) Or descriptions of two of our dogs. Considering the details she derived from thin air, I was riveted by her forecast for the future.

"You'll be going to a small island...in the Mediterranean."

"Ibiza?" I asked.

"I don't know the name of the island," she said.

"Have I been there before?"

"I don't think so. Your experiences there will be very meaningful. You'll go in the relatively near future."

"And I see a dark-haired man, with dark eyes. Your mother likes him. She's putting him beside you. Maybe you will marry this man."

There was another of her pauses; she checked in with Mom again. "And you're going to get a letter. Soon. A letter of importance to you."

Before completing our session, Sylvia conveyed that my mother loved me and missed me and my brothers and sisters. But she felt we were all going to be alright—she was watching over us. She missed my father, too, and felt bad about leaving him the way she did, but she believed that he was healing now, and in some ways even doing better than when she was living.

The insight into the spirit world that Sylvia provided me, by recruiting in seconds flat my honest-to-God mother—with my mother's humor and my mother's concern for me—was a gift I'd keep the rest of my life. Few times after that day did I feel I'd really lost my mother. Through Sylvia, she had come back to me. "Your mother is a beautiful woman," said Sylvia, "a loving and complete woman. You were very, very lucky. She made you aware of beauty too. And because of her, you remain lucky."

The evening of the Zeke dinner was a celebration for me, also—I now had a job! Hard to believe I'd be getting paid to perform with the Liquid Theatre. After dinner, I happened to pass Zeke on the upstairs balcony, and we ended up sitting side by side on the floor, above the music and conversation below. Having been acquainted two weeks now, we exchanged abridged versions of our personal histories. He had grown up in Africa—Egypt, Ethiopia, and Ghana. His mother was a Greek from Alexandria, his father a Scot in the English army. So Zeke had been a colonial boy in the dark continent from babyhood, and had only lived in England since age fifteen.

"I've been thinking about East Africa for a long time," I said, "but I can't seem to get there. One of these days I'm going, though."

"I'd love to go back," said Zeke. "I miss Africa...the music and the smells and the incredible space. When do you think you'll go?"

"September would be nice," I mused.

"Who would you go with?"

"Myself. And anyone I could stand who felt like coming."

"I'll come with you. I could be ready by September."

I looked at him. Traveling through Africa together was no minor undertaking. "What about your girlfriend?" (Time to get things straight.)

"Which girlfriend?"

"All of them."

"Don't have any."

So we made a secret plan. We wouldn't tell anyone, well maybe Phoebe, and would just keep it in the hopper.

A few nights later, at a party, Zeke asked me to dance. The music was slow, so physical contact was imminent. When he put his arms around me it felt like home. "Let's get out of here," he said after the dance. "Want to come over for a cup of tea?" Brits get a lot of mileage out of the proverbial teapot.

In a studio in Covent Garden, the Liquid Theatre ensemble rehearsed daily. In appearance, this troupe wasn't unlike a certain wild bunch I'd sung, danced, and groveled on the floor with in Brussels. But, aside from three other Americans, this collection was wholly British, thus tame and well-behaved. The performance would be a series of sensitivity exercises culminating in a primordial pantomime-slash-dance illustrating the birth of mankind. The audience would be transported through a maze of smell, color, sound, and touch, and our audition games were now played with them. Full-body participation and touchy-feely fun relaxed the audience completely.

Yoga was intrinsic to our training, and throughout the run of the show, a quiet hour of asanas and meditation was our daily warm-up.

Like "HAIR," the Liquid Theatre was a well-designed concept that achieved its psycho-social aim night after night. We touched people, took away their shoes and ties, massaged and stroked them. It was effective in its time and place, but I wished I'd been around for its origins in Los Angeles or even the New York follow-up because, for me—with an Educational Psychologist father, a dog named Freud as a wet-nurse, not to mention five siblings I'd been playing 'theatre games' with for twenty years—the touchy-feelies of the Liquid Theatre weren't the great awakener they might've been (had I pursued my career as a Foto-mate). It was nice turning people on, but I didn't have Phoebe's charitable aptitude for strangers. As a job though, not to mention a seamless entrance into English life, the Liquid Theatre was more than a blessing.

40

Cold Summer

A chaotic air pervaded 48 Belsize Gardens as halves of relationships attempted to include other halves in summer travels. One moment the place was like a Pan Am computer humming with come and go jive (forcing Phoebe to bolt herself into her bedroom and me to bow out and rent the spare room of a fellow Liquid trouper), and a month later, the place was virtually abandoned.

Pleasantly living out my Liquid life a few tube stops north, in Golders Green of all bizarre terminals, I received a tea invitation from the cordial Peter. "Peter," I answered, "one more cup of tea will be my demise."

"A glass of wine then, we'll make it an American rendezvous."

"Everyone's leaving," he said when I got there. "I knew everyone was going somewhere but I didn't realize EVERYONE was going somewhere."

"Well, I know Phoebe's off to New York, but what about the rest?"

"Roger and Clare are driving a van to Mexico, for the whole summer. Kip's moving to Toronto. James has already gone back to New York. And I'm going to Amsterdam next week for two months. So the place is going to be empty. Which isn't too smart. So why don't you move back in, live here for free, and collect everybody's mail? Just be a presence, basically." It made sense. I'd definitely be around all summer because my job was just warming up.

Even Zeke had one foot in the stirrup. "How can you leave me?" I implored. "I'm passionately in love with you!" (Much of our time together was spent gasping for breath.)

"I'm passionately in love with you, too, but I've been in this city for two years straight without a break. Come with me, you fool." He was going down to the Dordogne in France then driving on to Greece. He, too, would be away all summer. "Greece is unbelievable," he exclaimed. "You're an idiot to stay in London when you could be with ME. In GREECE!"

"Well, I guess it's my turn to stay behind this time. I gotta work. I was lucky to get this job and I'm sticking with it. I'll just stay here and hold down the fort."

So I moved back to 48, concurrently bidding adieu to all my new friends. I worked by night and by day explored London.

Two weeks of that and I was already restless. Then came a letter from Cara. "Guess who I saw last night at Fenton's Doghouse," she began. "Jonah. I asked him what he'd been doing and stuff, but all he wanted to talk about was you—how you were, what you were doing. He wanted to hear everything about you, I couldn't tell him enough. Wendy, he still cares. I asked him if he got the letter you sent to Ibiza and he said no. Then he asked for your address in London, so I gave it to him 'cause I thought I knew it by heart. But when I got home I realized I'd given him the wrong house number. The right street, but the wrong number. I'm really sorry." Then she told me the house number she had given him.

So............this meant if I could identify a house numbered 29 on my former street in Golders Green, I might find a letter.

I *might*.

I grabbed a bus straight up there.

Nearly tiptoeing down the street, the numbers were diminishing: 35, 33, 31...... I half-expected to find a black hole where 29 should be. But, lo, there it was—not a park, not a subway station, but an ordinary house—number 29.

Like Gretel at the gingerbread house, I stared wide-eyed. Was it possible this unassuming dwelling contained the letter? Would this little housey give life to one more of Sylvia's predictions? I took a huge breath, then fourteen giant steps, and I was on the porch.

In London, many, many addresses were three-story houses divided into units. You could expect at least three doorbells at each address. This was no different. Good, more chance of someone being home to let me in. I pressed the bottom bell, heard it ring inside, and waited. Nothing happened. I pressed the middle bell, heard it ring inside, and waited. Nothing happened. Ditto for Baby Bell, the top one. How dare they all go to work on a Tuesday? Now what? I pressed all three bells again and pondered. Jumping up and down a few times, I then pummeled the door a bit.

Was there any way to get the thing open? I'd once started my mother's Carmen Ghia with a bobby pin, this door should be a cupcake. I scrutinized it for a weak spot. Ah-ha, the mail slot. I pushed in the metal flap located in the middle of the door and crouched down to peer in. Maybe I could somehow reach in there and get ahold of the doorknob. Expecting to see a long dark hallway, ten back issues of the London Times in a moldy heap, or perhaps the bespectacled eyes of an old pensioner squinting back at me, what I saw instead blew me away.

Attached inside the door, just below the mail slot, and only slightly out of reach, was a wooden shelf upon which the mail landed each day. Stacked upon it was a pile of letters. And on the very top, centimeters from the tips of my now-outstretched fingers, was a normal airmail letter...with my name on it, in Jonah's preschool scribble.

But only my fingers could fit through the slot and they were stumps compared to the set I needed to snag the letter. Now what, wait six hours for the residents to return from work? I rummaged through my handbag for some kind of tool. All I had was my hairbrush. Poking its handle through the slot, I jabbed at the letter, too aware that I was both tampering with the British mail and grappling with some crazy kismet. And what if my fumbling pushed the letter to the floor? Delicately maneuvering it into reach, I tweezered it with two fingers, and gingerly brought it to the light of day.

Having gone down onto my knees for that letter, what would it now say? Relocating to the seclusion of a park bench in the shrubs, I reviewed the envelope—good boy, he spelled my name almost perfectly. Inside was a minimal but veritable Jonah-authored piece. The gist was, "Let's get back in touch. Write to me."

Zeke, meanwhile, was overwhelming me with his own blitzed dispatches from insect-ridden French fields under starry skies. Fighting my way through his pick-up sticks penmanship, inventive phraseology, and spelling to rival even Jonah's, Zeke's letters exploded with color, images, and utter silliness. A month had passed and his London friend, Yanni, would soon be collecting him for the drive to Greece. Zeke implored me to ride down with Yanni, take this trip, don't miss this opportunity. But having succeeded in finding a job in a foreign country, I took my work and my luck seriously.

I wrote a couple of paragraphs back to Jonah, "I'm in London. If you come to Europe, stop by." But that ricocheted me back into the unholy ritual of waiting for the postman.... He'd write back, I knew that, but was I going to open the flood gates again? I mean, *one letter in two years?* Just because I was lonely, freezing, and living in a town I'd picked out of a hat was no excuse for emotional back-tracking.

Anticipating Zeke's return had been my energizer. But he was now in Greece, his mother's homeland, and phoning in offers for Cretan romance. Lying in my desolate bed with just the phone, I asked him when he'd be back. "Never," was the reply.

Never?

As August trudged by, I was secretly pleased when the Liquid Theatre audiences eventually began thinning.

Meanwhile, everyone was already returning to 48—Roger, Clare, Peter. I suddenly got the disgusted feeling that summer was over and I'd never taken off my mittens. I simply couldn't continue thumbing through the morning mail every stupid day—I'd thumb to Greece instead, and surprise Zeke!

I penned him a note in Athens, care of Yanni, saying I'd sent an important package and he must wait there for it no matter what. If he was still in Crete when I got to Athens, Yanni could direct me to him. And if I couldn't find Zeke anywhere in Greece, I'd still find BEACHES. All I could think about was salt water.

The show was closing exactly when I needed it to. It had been a stellar experience, and all those paychecks would pay for a lot of swimming in Greece. Purchasing a road map of Europe, I charted a course, as straight as possible on back roads. A peaceful, pretty journey would take me across sectors of Europe I hadn't yet seen.

- 41 -

The Alps

I sallied forth at the end of August, starting out on the sea-train from Victoria Station, crossing the English Channel to France. It was a tremendous feeling, quietly sitting in the plush compartment of an English train, knowing this was the start of a big solo adventure across unfamiliar turf. No one in the world knew where I was, and no one expected me in Athens—I was unaccounted for. It was as if I'd disappeared.

Standing like a road sign against what had to be France, I punched an extended thumb and fist meaningfully at ferry-disembarkers. Lucklessly, I then humbly walked onto the Continent, mildly embarrassed at my pedestrian status. But it was a short hike. I was soon in the back seat of a French family's car, trying not to shock the children with my plan of hitching fifteen hundred miles alone through five countries.

By nightfall, I was hurtling west in a semi, high above the minimal traffic flow in Rien de Tout, France. The driver, a pleasant if not adorable Frenchman, was trucking to Marseilles. He suggested I take the same route with him, but that would mean an extra day, plus I'd already been there. He'd be on my same course till about midnight though, before veering south. "I don't want to leave you on the road in the middle of the night," he said. "And I have to stop to sleep somewhere anyway. So instead of dropping you off and driving a few more hours, I'll just park for the night at my turn-off point and you can sleep in the truck with me."

Obviously I balked at sharing ten cubic isolated feet with an overnight male stranger, but, sensing my reservations, he assured me he wouldn't make any moves.

A hitch-hiker sometimes has zero options. I thanked him and accepted, under the condition that I could sleep in the front seat in my sleeping bag rather than in the bed with him. He agreed, but warned that sound slumber was unlikely for me. I could tolerate the discomfort, though; every hour of sleep was more than I'd expected.

After much camaraderie, we reached the junction. He pulled the mighty machine onto a shoulder, we staked out our respective plots, and couldn't sleep a wink. I couldn't because sleeping upright is a joke, and he couldn't because my endless shifting about suggested that any moment I might surrender. Every forty-five minutes, he'd re-invite me over, re-avowing of course not to touch me.

Exhaustion works like a voodoo doll against will. Sometime before dawn, I conceded. Intrinsically good-hearted, my host made only one all-encompassing seduction attempt. Not surprised that it failed, he then apologized boyishly, "I had to try." (Like betting a few bucks when you drive through Vegas.) "I won't try again. *Bonne nuit.*"

"*Bonne nuit.*"

We then got some shut-eye, and parted amiably next morning.

It was summer in rural France. I picnicked on bread and cheese between rides the next day and drew dumb drawings in my journal. Late that afternoon, someone dropped me off an eighth of a mile from the France-Switzerland border. Knowing I'd appear suspicious trying to catch a lift through the customs check-point, I opted to walk through border-control since it was so close, then hitch again on the other side. But borders simply aren't crossed on foot, it's bad form. And I definitely felt I was missing something, standing in line between a Mercedes and a Volkswagen—not unlike entering the Kentucky Derby without a horse. Smug Euro-voyagers and their kids peered out their sedans, discussing me in assorted tongues, and pointing index fingers until it was my turn for customs.

"PassPOOOR!" demanded the spokesman of three somber robots. I handed it over, for him to regard with a particular disdain known only to the French. ("I 'ave never in my life seen such an ugly passpooor, you slimy leetle worm.") Hey, I didn't deserve this, I was just out for an afternoon stroll through the Alps. "Where is ze car?" he then asked down his nose.

"I don't have one."

"WHERE are you going?"

"Lucerne," was the only Swiss place I could think of besides the Matterhorn. This was clearly no place for the truth.

He glared through me as though the hostility might provoke a perverse confession of some kind. I'd surely lifted more than my share of Lindt chocolate bars in days gone by, but it would take more than a filthy look to unbosom that disclosure. He had perseverance, though, "Let me search your bags."

Returning his evil eye, I placed my baskets on the table and he fumbled through my belongings like so many dirty diapers. "What is zees...and what is zees...and what is zees??" He pulled everything out, piece by piece, holding each item away from his precious self.

"That is a towel. That is a bathing suit. That is a notebook," I replied with tedium.

"And what do you write in zees nutbook?" he rolled his eyes and opened my sketchbook as if he was handling nuclear waste.

"It's just a journal," I told him squarely.

This was the last person to show my inept draftsmanship to, but the lame illustrations and little poems were exactly what he was interested in. "What does zees say?" he demanded accusingly, as if it might contain clues to the famous Edelweiss Mysteries.

"It's thoughts and ideas," I said.

"Translate eet for me," he meant business.

"It's personal and boring and I really can't translate it."

"I told you to translate eet."

"No. It's not necessary."

"Then you will go into ze office," he pointed to a closed door, "where ze madame will inspect you." His eyes became slits, "Completely."

Refusing to believe he was serious, I stood there looking at the other two to see if they went along with this. One did, the other wished he was in Tasmania. "I am waiting," said the metallic inspector, "to see if you will translate your leetle book or go inside weez ze madame."

I said nothing. These just weren't the intimates one shares a diary with…not quite the sisterly sorts to help resolve the Zeke vs. Jonah issue I'd been writing about.

"Okay," he whirled on his heels, "follow me!" And he headed for the office.

"Alright, alright," I was furious, "I'll translate the stupid book for you." Anything to avoid the naked Nazi party he had in mind. The three men clustered around as I attempted to give French definition to the pages before us. "This page is about a little bird I saw and a blue flower…. The bird flew over to the flower, sat next to it, looked around at the hills nearby, then looked at the flower…."

That worked. They looked at each other uneasily.

"Sank you," said the inspector, closing the book. "You will leave now."

Onward ever onward. Surrounded by mountains, it would get dark early. If I got a good, long ride, yippy, I'd travel all night; otherwise I'd scout for a cheap room in whatever town I reached at nightfall. I hoisted my thumb back up to half-mast. A few rides and a few raindrops later, I was in Lucerne. Night was falling.

The train station was right there…. Why not catch a night train to Milan? Keep moving and maybe get some sleep.

"The next train is in two and a half hours," said the stationmaster.

Nothing to do but wait. I took a seat.

"Good evening. Where are you trying to get to?" A man in a suit had overheard me questioning the stationmaster.

"Milano."

"That's two and a half hours."

"I know," I said gloomily.

"Why don't you come with me?" he suggested. "I live an hour from here on the same route your train takes. I can drop you off at the next station. You might have to wait, but I believe there's an earlier train from there."

Though nerdy and overtly Swiss, I decided he wasn't a Charlie Manson. I asked him the name of his town and found it on my map, then asked if he was going directly there, no stops along the way. "Yes, directly," he answered.

Anything was better than sitting in this station.

We set off pleasantly, chatting about Swiss cheese, Swiss Family Robinson, snow, and other apropos topics. To avoid small talk, I had said I didn't speak French, but now we were having even smaller talk in English.

Our route took us way up into the peaks where I lost all sense of direction and just braced both arms against the dashboard as we careened around hairpin turns. Louis, this starlight charioteer, had found roads that wound around the Alps like balls of yarn, and he seemed to relish terrifying me. Then, as our ears popped, and with no warning, he lit into a chauvinistic tirade against hippies and women—female hitch-hikers in particular. He ranted on, all the while doing a mad tango with the steering wheel. He didn't seem to care about our lives, but had grave concerns about women trying to get equal rights. "Who do you think you are?" he asked, "hitching alone through Switzerland? We don't like that. And you won't have a very nice time in this country if you think you can hitch-hike wherever you please. You're a hippie, aren't you? And you think you can do whatever you want! You American hippies come over here and travel through and never even learn our language."

"I'm not a hippie. I'm a person traveling from one place to another. You shouldn't have offered me a ride if you don't approve of me."

"You should be married, and you should travel with your husband if you want to go somewhere. It's very bad for Swiss young people to see people like you. They get bad ideas about trying to change their lives. They get bad ideas about sex, too, when they see young women like you traveling alone. You're not even married, but you still have sex with men, don't you? I know you do. All young people like you have sex whenever they please with whoever they want. You believe in free love, don't you?"

I was saying little in the hopes that he'd lose interest in this subject, but evidently he'd been trying to snag one of my breed for a good while. Louis' ranting and reckless motoring, together with the altitude and absence of guard rails, made a bad brew. Reeling around one hundred-eighty degree curves against the black mountain, I was thankful I couldn't view the sheer drops we were missing by centimeters. In the middle of one of those change-direction turns, when all concentration was needed to just hold the road, and as my eyes were averted from what I couldn't see of the abyss below, my escort executed a lateral sweep with both arms. His hands flew through the air, landing like meteorites on my breasts. "Louis!" I screamed, instinctively flailing across him for the orphaned steering wheel. My gesture reminded him that immorality and immortality were not synonymous, and he should save his tai chi for the straight-aways. He untangled his paws from mine, replaced them on the wheel and gearshift, and resumed the driving as though nothing had happened.

I was steaming though, and let him have it. In French. Was it a Swiss custom, I asked him, to take advantage of young foreign-ers under the guise of being helpful? And why was it only here in Switzerland that strange men had been disrespectful to me? "And, by the way, I AM married; my husband is meeting me tomorrow in Milano. He said he would come to pick me up but I assured him that I would be safe traveling alone in such a civilized place as Swit-zerland. Little did I know. As for hippies, you might learn some-thing from them if you weren't so aggressive. You shouldn't criticize what you don't understand." I then said he could drop me off right here or at the very next house or building.

At the first sign of life, Louis stopped the car and, without a look in my direction, disappeared into a gas station. I leapt from the vehicle and raced down the road. Spotting a well-placed inn just up the way, I figured I could rush inside its doors before Louis returned to his car. He was not to know, ever, what had become of me, but only to remember his own wretched conduct. As for me, I only hoped there'd be vacancy in this small hotel.

The Worst is Over.

You wouldn't know it was August up there in the Swiss night. And, noticeably under-dressed, I fell breathlessly across the reception desk. As luck has a way of returning, I was given a room for half price when I explained my harassment.

Arriving at night to new and beautiful places is especially wonderful because, after a good sleep, the morning produces travel posters in the window frames. Here, the mountains were collapsing into valleys of vertical pastures white with sheep scarfing pastel flowers. My eyes felt like violins, and I half-expected Johann Sebastian Bach (or at least Julie Andrews) to walk by with a goat herd. It dawned on me that those classical composers were really just good listeners, that the music lives up there, and they were clever enough to transpose it. They never could've written that stuff based in Sacramen-no. Up here, every image was from the story books—Heidi, brimming milk buckets, blondie children in suede shorts with suspenders, chalet charm farms with real men for fathers, fresh bread, and wood fences. Any doubt about the existence of fairies was forever vanquished. Good old Louis, what a guy to drop me off here— would've missed it all on the night train to Milan.

And for every lousy ride, you earn a good one. In front of the inn that morn, I was rewarded in seconds by a hitch-hiker's dream: a cheerful, retired gentleman. In his sleek Mercedes, we sailed along, tacking in and out of mountain shadows, to a Mozart soundtrack. This driver was going to Milan and wasting no time. Polished and scrubbed, friendly and interested, he had no ulterior motives. But he did validate the hunch I had that thumbing the five hundred miles from Milan to Brindisi in southern Italy, would make Louis a saint. "Don't try it. Take the train," he said paternally. For emphasis, he deposited me in front of Milan's depot.

Five hundred miles was going to take no less than twelve hours no matter how I swung it. The five p.m. train would reach Brindisi at six a.m., and would beat hitching all night through some back-street operetta in which I'm a pizza that gets eaten in scene one. So I'd take the train, then catch the Brindisi ferry to Greece. The worst was over! I'd sit back and enjoy the north Italian landscape until dark, consume some light fare, read a while, then tumble into rock-a-bye dreamland wherever I detected some empty seats.

But there were two virulent portents early on. One: The train was packed—in the Mediterranean sense—meaning multitudinous parcels stacked in unbalanced disarray, all oozing with life or re-cently-terminated life. Overseeing the transit of these eggplants and piglets was a talkative assortment of fat people eating bread. They had the trample-anything-in-your-way exhilaration of Cecil B. DeMille extras. The white-haired contingent was more subdued, causing the others to bury them under wailing bundles in swad-dling clothes. And the entire assemblage, as one, crossed itself at ev-ery bump in the track. Two: The track was so crammed with back-to-back stations that the highest speed we got up to was slightly faster than reverse; if the engineer exceeded four m.p.h., he'd miss three stops.

And there was a third unforeseen ramification: At every sta-tion (one every sixty seconds), there was a total reshuffling of each rooster, each grandpa, each set of triplets, and each picnic lunch for sixteen, as whole forests of family trees embarked or disembarked.

Even the scenery was intolerable. Do not, I repeat, do not go sight-seeing along the east coast of Italy. You know what's there? A railroad. And an endless grove of oil rigs along the rail-beach.

This is pretty bad, I thought, but it'll get better....

But the go-nowhere pace was set—the screech-grinding of brakes, harmonized with the hissing and whistling, hardly a lullaby. And where, at first, I'd been swallowed by the tribal imbroglio, as inconspicuous as a worm's wisdom tooth, eventually that demographic was replaced by Italian business men in twos and threes. In this mix, I was more like a centerfold in a prison camp.

"It's better to be looked over than over-looked," Mae West said, but there are moments when you'd really welcome some male anonymity. Knackered from travel, being looked over tonight felt like sandpaper filing my face. And when I'd look away from the current three sitting opposite in my compartment, I'd feel their six eyes grating my legs, chest, even hands as I reached for a book.

Okay, move to another compartment, there must be an empty one somewhere on this choo-choo. I'd seek out a fresh compartment with some room to stretch out. But instantly the train would stop and I'd be discovered by newcomers—where were all these guys going in the middle of the night?—and the new compartment, too, would fill up with men smoking cigarettes and cigars. They'd drink and play cards and nudge me every time I closed my eyes, hilariously jesting about what a party-pooper I was.

The only pleasure I could derive was a certain poetic decadence—not a soul from my life knew where I was. Not my father, not Zeke, not sisters, old friends, or new friends. These chimney-stack passengers scorching my retinas with their Gallois were the only ones who knew. But though I felt like a secret agent hard at work, unfortunately I was doing this for free.

Reaching Brindisi, in southern Italy, was too good to be true. It was a glorious morning, the port tap-dancing with sailboats and summertime. The worst was over!

Mid afternoon, the ferry loaded and detached itself heavily from the pier. Needless to say, I was traveling deck class. Amidst the chaos of bodies and bags strewn everywhere, catching up on sleep was out of the question. In desperation, I wandered into the second class area one level down and noticed some cabins with open doors and no occupants. Entering one, I locked the door and tuned out. No stops till Corfu, twelve hours up the road. In the blackness, I relinquished every cell of my limp frame to the rolling waves.

Refreshed the next morning, a little sleuthing on deck yielded a pleasant Greek couple who would be driving the four hours to Athens, then continuing on to where they lived. They spoke flawless English and readily offered to take me along.

From the moment the boat docked, the character of Greece—its sing-song conversation, the roundness of spirit, the contagious smile, and philosophic intellect—melted my psyche. My shipboard college had stopped in Greece, but only for a few days. Coming here again was obviously my smartest move in eons. Plus I'd be seeing Zeke. Might have to go all the way to Crete, but traveling in this country would be far from unpleasant. And Zeke knew Greek, so I'd soon have a tutor.

"Where are you going in Athens?" inquired the woman of the pair as we began the sunny drive. I dug for Yanni's address, that Zeke had written on the back of his last letter. This couple would probably know in just a glance what part of Athens to drop me off in. But with all these different countries and rides and trains (and nosy customs agents), I didn't know where I'd stashed that letter. I dug around in both my bags.

"You didn't lose it, did you?" asked the woman.

"I couldn't have," I said, now turning things inside out. But after ten minutes, I still hadn't found it.

"Did you leave it on the boat?" asked the husband, slowing for a u-turn.

"No, I'm sure I didn't do that. It would be with my passport which I still have." To quell the couple's fear that they'd have to house me, I made light of the situation, "It's no big deal, I'll just…I'll just… look through my stuff again. Don't worry." I assured them this was not their problem.

But it soon became clear I'd lost the address.

"What will you do?" asked the man.

"You're welcome to stay at our house while you sort things out," said the woman, sympathetically. "We don't live in Athens, but it's very nice where we do live."

I'd heard that Greeks were kind-hearted, and these two were proving it, but this dilemma wouldn't be remedied by retreating to a mountain village. I had about three hours to figure something out. I sank back against the back seat with a sigh. Now I was really anonymous. This disappearance thing was getting real.

- 43 -

Oops

The Athens telecommunications office, we all decided, was the sensible sanctuary for lost souls. The good couple left me with their phone number and their blessings.

I must have left Yanni's address back at 48, so my only hope was to call there, praying someone was home to answer the phone. Here in Athens, my only data about Yanni ('Yanni' being the Greek equivalent of 'John'), with unknown surname, was that he was staying with his parents and his father was a lawyer.

"Your call to London will come through within two hours," I was told in French. "Wait on a chair, *s'il vous plaît.*" It felt safe to gamble the first half hour in pursuit of a Greek dictionary. Better equip myself for social intercourse, it could be an interactive evening.

The Greek alphabet looked, at best, like fake Russian—at worst, like the New York skyline, including buildings that weren't built yet (like omega, Ω). I returned to my ninety-minute vigil on the appointed seat.

"Your call, *mademoiselle.*" Rushing into cabinet #4, I heard the distinct double ringing of a British phone. Oh, someone, anyone, please answer....

"Hello?"

"Peter?"

"Yeah?"

"Thank God you're there! It's Wendy."

"Where're you?"

"Athens! Listen..." and I described the whereabouts of a box in which Zeke's letter might be.

Registering the gravity of the mission and the cost-per-minute of the call, Peter flung the phone to the floor and shot upstairs to rifle through my possessions. Several minutes passed as he tore through flannel undershirts and Wellington boots. He then breathlessly returned to the phone. "Wendy?"

"Yeah?"

"I can't find it. It might be there somewhere, but I'll have to really go through everything. It will take a while."

"I was afraid of that. If I call you back sometime in the next two hours, would you mind continuing the search? I'm so sorry but I don't know what else to do."

"Okay, I'll go through everything."

"EVERYTHING. Shake out the notebooks."

"Okay," he said. "And when you call back, call collect."

"No, Peter, I can manage. It's my own fault."

"No, call collect. Don't spend your cash now, you might really need it," he laughed, "the way things are going. I insist." What a friend.

Ordering the second call without delay, I hunkered in for more worry and Hellenic study. Another ninety minutes passed and the second call came through. I held my breath as the ringing began.

"Hello?" answered Peter, expectantly.

"Did you find it?"

"Yes, I found it," he said slowly...

"Whew."

"...but it's in *Greek*."

"Right...well, um, just describe it to me, and I'll try to write it down."

"Okay, here goes: the first word, probably the name of someone, starts with a triangle."

"A triangle." I drew one.

"Then a script 'y,' a small one...."

"A small script 'y.'"

"Or it could be a small script 'n' with a tail."

"Got it. The tail down?"

"Yeah. The next one looks like a small script 'u' with a line through it, a vertical line going down like the 'y' tail."

"Oh God, this isn't funny, is it? Give me the next one."

"Next is an 'o.' Looks like a small 'o,' but it doesn't quite connect at the top."

"That's easy."

"This next thing is not describable. It's just a squiggle."

"Oh God. Try to describe it somehow. Is it 's'-like?"

Peter was absolutely silent for about fifteen seconds, pondering the squiggle. "It's a long horizontal line curving up, and attached to the end of it is a curved tail traveling southwest."

"Like half a smile?"

"No." Again he became funereally silent.

"Does it look anything like a smile?"

"No, not a smile or a mouth or any part of a face." We both had to laugh. "It doesn't resemble anything, but what makes it not look like a smile is that the end of the tail hooks back off to the east."

"Does it have any other distinguishing features?"

"Look, it's a hell of a character, but it's not a bank robber. We better move on because there's lots more to go and most of them are even weirder. The next letter, which could be part of the one after it, looks sort of like a backwards 6."

"Right, what's next? We're still on the first word?"

"Yeah, the last name. The next letter, which could be part of the one after it, is an 'o,' a small one with a hook on top. Like a six, sort of."

"Okay. Next?"

"The last letter in this line looks like a stretched-out S and is bigger than the others and hangs down farther."

Poor Peter gave that envelope his undivided attention for twenty minutes. At the end, what I'd written looked, at best, like the trimmings off a curly mustache. The chances of it being wrong ridiculed the law of averages. The chances of it having been written wrong to begin with—Zeke's Greek was half-learned, left-handed, and unpracticed since childhood—were even greater. Anyway, with my endless thanks and Peter's true good wishes, we rang off.

Night had settled in Athens. Clutching this if-y scrap of paper, I ventured into the city. The first thing to do was ask appropriate people if they'd ever heard of the street etched onto my paper. But there weren't appropriate people to ask, so I asked inappropriate ones.

One hundred percent of them had never heard of the street—was I sure it wasn't in Tokyo? And would I not rather drink ouzo than look for a Yanni in a haystack?

A new approach was in order. I'd have to narrow my search. I purchased an Athenian street map, then began seeking out English speakers in shops and touristy places. "Is there one part of town," I asked, "where a lawyer would be more likely to live?" The answer to this, miraculously, was yes. All the lawyers in Athens lived in one part of town. Thanking Zeus, I circled that sector on my map, thrilled that it appeared to be only a few square blocks. Surely one of the streets in that neighborhood would bear resemblance to one word of my squiggles. But, damn, the street names on the map were in upper case and my sad little figures were lower case (if anything). With map, Greek dictionary, pen, and paper, I sat under a street light and fastidiously reconfigured the map's street names into lower case. Completing each one, I'd compare it to the words on my paper. In time, sure enough, I honed in on the only street it could possibly be!

I then went to that street and saw, with elation, that it was only three blocks long. And the residences were all just two and three stories high. If I had to, I'd knock on every single door—a likely eventuality, as nothing on my paper resembled a number.

At the entrance of each apartment building were rows of names imprinted on glossy metallic plates. Possibly quite helpful. But three trips up and down the street only proved that the name I'd written was plain wrong. Nearly every building also had a doorman, and I had asked each one, pronouncing Yanni's last name every possible way, but had gotten nowhere. Now it was ten p.m. and my shoulders ached from the bags. Putting them down, I leaned against a lamp-post and scrutinized the chicken scratch in my palm one final time. "Can I help you perhaps?" an accented male voice asked in English. "I've seen you walking up and down. What is it you're looking for?"

With a look of despair, I slid down the lamp-post, landing on my baggage with a plop.

"No, really," the young man said, "I'll try to help you. Do you speak English?"

"Yes, unfortunately," I smiled.

The kindly stranger donated himself to my cause, and we repeated my previous effort, comparing my writing to the name plates. But even with a patient local helper, no luck. "There's only one thing left to do," the man said finally, "and we should do it fast because it's getting late...."

"I'm ready for anything."

"I'll translate for you and we'll go from door to door, and wherever there's a doorman, we'll describe what your friend looks like, mentioning the lawyer father. Probably someone will know them."

So we set up the street again. Moving from door to door, our descriptions were precise. But so were the responses: "No."

After an hour of interrogation, we shrugged dejectedly at each other, and rang the last concierge bell on the street. It was eleven o'clock and my new friend—to ease me into the Athenian way of life should I find myself stranded here permanently—now offered me a waitress job in his bar. Then we posed our tired question to this last doorman. "Yes, Yanni lives here," the man answered simply, as we stared incredulously at each other. "But he's not here now. He'll be back tomorrow morning."

Not fully buying this apparent good news, I described Yanni's every physical trait and had my translator get gold-bonded verification that we were getting the right Yanni. We wanted the London Yanni, the weird Yanni, the Zeke Yanni. "Yes," promised the doorman, "this is the Zeke Yanni. But Zeke isn't here either, you know, he's in *Kriti*."

But Yanni would be able to direct me to Zeke—that would be tiddlywinks compared to today's fiasco. I gave my tireless aide a meaningful hug then took his advice about a brilliantly-situated youth hostel at the end of this same street. I probably wouldn't need that waitress job, but thanked him for the offer.

Next morning I went back to Yanni's and rang the bell. A male Greek voice came through the intercom. "Yanni??" I asked it.

"*Nai*," said the voice. That sounded pretty negative. (Though I soon learned that '*nai*' means 'yes' in Greek.)

"Yanni?" I asked again, "Is that Yanni?"

"Yes," said the voice, now in English. "Who is that?"

"It's Wendy from London."

"Oh hello! Come up to the third floor." I was buzzed in.

Upstairs, the door to the apartment was ajar, so I quietly entered. No one was in the foyer, so I walked tentatively down the hall and turned a corner into a dining room. Standing beside the table was someone reading a letter. The letter was from me, the reader was Zeke. He looked up and stared at me for a second, then looked back at the letter. He then dropped it and crossed the room to scoop me off my feet and swallow me in a hug that seemed to magically neutralize all the trials of my trip. Yanni then appeared, laughing; he hadn't told Zeke it was me at the door.

"What are you DOING here?" Zeke wasn't convinced I was real. "I just this minute walked in the door from Crete and was reading your letter. What are you DOING here??"

"I don't know," I laughed, "but I'm here. And I'm glad."

Zeke looked oddly at Yanni, "Well, it's just great—we're ready to go back to London. That's why I came back from Crete...so I can drive back to London with Yanni. To see you."

"Oh.... You said you were never coming back and I believed you."

"How'd you get here?" Yanni asked.

"Yeah, how did you get here?" echoed Zeke.

"A wing and a prayer."

PART V ~ ISLANDS

- 44 -

Zeke

September 1972

Zeke was brown, strong, and clear. Seeing him again was divine—his arms more home than ever. We'd fallen in love in London, and three months hadn't changed anything. He had curly, shiny, blue-black locks and a smile without borders. He laughed and took care of people and made me a lady by being ever a gent. He expected too much from everyone including himself, and was consequently disappointed by everyone including himself. He could see three colors where everyone else saw one, and was constantly pointing out things that at first I couldn't see. He saw beauty and novelty everywhere, saw circles and lines and white spaces where others saw just another day. He uncluttered my vision by sharing his, and I thank him still. Anyone who really got to know Zeke had their eyes cleaned by him.

We rested up in Athens that first day. The sun was hot and everything fabulously foreign to me. Zeke had exaggerated about staying in Crete 'forever'; he meant 'four weeks.' In truth, he'd promised Yanni to share the driving back to London, as Yanni's school was starting again shortly.

Hardly a scenario one would hitch across Europe for. "Well, when do you have to leave?" I asked.

"Soon. But Yanni's just learned that the car needs attention, so a few extra days have materialized."

"Zeke, let's get out of this city. I need some peace and quiet. Let's go to the islands. Any island. Let's just go somewhere beautiful till you have to leave. Let's take the next boat wherever it's going."

"Okay. But what about you? Are you going to ride back to London with us? I wish you would."

A shudder traveled my spine at the thought of all those countries again. "It's unlikely that just a few days of clean air and sea will be enough," I said, "but we'll see...."

The Mimika was sailing at noon for Mikonos, Zaxos, Naxos, Plaxos, and Saxos. "I don't want to go to Mikonos," I told Zeke. "Wonder what Zaxos is like."

"We'll ask Yanni," said Zeke, "He knows all the islands."

"Zaxos?" a far-away look moved across Yanni's eyes. "It's beautiful. Go there."

The Aegean is a color all its own. And a feeling. To look upon that sea is to feel elevated—something emanates from the water and lightens the mind. Zeke and I felt we'd stolen time and stopped it— every second described by a dictionary of blue around us, each hour growing bigger than the one before. We sailed and sailed and sailed, an intimate zephyr and perfect temperature serenading the whole Aegean, our eyes seeing twice as much, our noses twitching like rabbits. It was crazy obvious that something, some invisible THING was present....

With Zeke as a buffer, finally I was protected from the disruptive surprises sprung on the lone young female, safe at last to simply absorb. And Zeke assured me that my sense of well-being was not imagined. "It's in the air. Nobody can pinpoint it, but the Greek Islands have something extra that you feel the minute you're here."

Midnight, without a moon but a thank you hanging between the stars, revealed a great shadowy hulk sliding by the port side of the ship. Zaxos. (Pronounced Zak-zos.) It held a power all its own. We sailed in close to the looming mountain silhouettes and were enticed further by all we couldn't see. Were there homes and towns and roads and pastures? Or vicious cliffs of cruel inaccessibility? The Mimika continued steadily, past quiet black masses and vague inlets. Tiny on the map, Zaxos seemed mighty now. The clock struck one and the calendar struck September, and the few of us on deck felt the sea's sudden placidity as we entered Zaxos' sheltered harbor. The horn sounded roundly, practically bumping the big dipper out of the sky, and then we glided in silence. Dots of light flicked off the still water, but nothing else happened. And we slid into...lost time.

All I saw was a necklace, a string of luminescent pearls in the blackness, where evenly placed streetlights curved around the bay, with lamp-lit homes glowing behind it. I drew in a long and certain breath—this was my place, I'd found it. Having stopped looking for Paradise, I'd now stumbled upon it. Not at all what or where I expected. It mattered not at all to me what was revealed on the shores of Zaxos by day—sandy beaches, cactus jungles, or Long Island duck farms—I was irrevocably smitten from the moment I sensed its unassuming holiness. Even in the middle of a moonless night, before getting off the ship, I knew.

Zeke knew too, and we put those first moments in our hearts forever. The smallness of the serene harbor, with the soft and reassuring candlelight, fit the night and the time of my life utterly and completely. "I'm never leaving," I whispered to Zeke as the boat floated in.

Drawing up to the quay, a cluster of islanders could be seen below, waiting to meet passengers and help unload cargo. Half a dozen foreigners, too, waited to board the Mimika to make their way back to Athens. For most travelers, the season was ending.

Once on the pier, Zeke chatted to a robust, cubist matron, who we then trailed to her ancient stone house where she rented rooms. Her home was only a hundred steps from everything else in the tiny town.

As Zeke lay down on the bed, mesmerized by the oleander scent riding the night, I tiptoed back out into the stillness. Through the unlit pathways, I moved like the Sandman. We had landed on a sleeping angel's wing, so my treading was lighter than a feather.

The next morning, all I'd suspected about being helplessly in love with the island was so overpowering I became almost giddy. Could it be? All I knew was that I'd stay here, it was my place, I was committed. Zeke saw what happened, felt it too, but was already committed to Yanni. In three days, he'd have to re-board the Mimika.

Zaxos was kind to our relationship. I had déjà vu at first, recollecting that arrival in Ibiza two years earlier with Jonah. Here was another enticing Mediterranean island, and another not-too-familiar lover who knew the language. Zaxos, too, had sun-blessed beauties decorating the port cafes, and I was certain Zeke would disappear, as Jonah had, and I'd be fending for myself. "What's the matter?" Zeke asked innocently, as we sipped ouzo the second evening in the village square.

I didn't say anything.

"Tell me."

"Look Zeke," I began, "if you want to go off with someone else, fine, you can do what you want. But don't just disappear. Please have the good manners to tell me to go to hell."

"*What are you talking about?*"

It was Ibiza again, the whole nightmare. "There are all sorts of attractive women around," I said, "and I'm sure you want to meet them."

"I came here with you."

"I know. But that doesn't necessarily mean anything."

Knowing about the Hispanic chapter of my life and its leading man, Zeke realized my wounds were talking. "Look at me," he said firmly, taking my shoulders, "I'm not Jonah. Do you understand that? I don't know what kind of weird guy he was, or all that happened in Ibiza, but I'm Zeke. Look at me." He lifted my chin up till my eyes were level with his. "Who do you see?" He brushed a tear off each of my cheeks.

"I see Zeke," I said softly.

"And I love you," he said. "And we're here together."

- 45 -

The Gods

Apprehensive about leaving me floating in the Aegean alone, I had to convince Zeke I'd never felt safer in my life. You can hardly feel dubious in a land where rocks and boulders say good morning, where the sun throws kisses, the sea is a hammock, the goats little cherubs, the stars dance around your head, and the days do grapevine steps past you like lazy hours.

And the clincher, the most unusual feature of all, was the people—they were beautiful. And happy. Sure they probably had their troubles. But something in their eyes was stronger than the humdrum ways of the outside world. They loved their island and cherished every stone. They knew God lived upstairs on the mountain and they liked having Him around. It was no accident that Saint John had his revelation on that hill; everyone who went up there had one. You just don't come face to face with God Himself every day. And when you do, it's cause for a mild revelation—as shooting stars whiz past by night and fresh figs fall into your mouth by day.

To immerse myself completely, after sadly watching Zeke's ship slide behind a far chunk of mountain, I moved to Lipoi, a cove of beach a twenty minute walk from the port. And for the next month I forgot the meaning of indoors. It was the largest, fullest September ever. Without needs or cares, I moved freely around the island—a vast palace. And the trees, rocks, mountains, beaches, and waves were obliging servants, silent joyous children. I had never partaken of the world so openly, so rightly.

After two weeks of living in my sleeping bag at Lipoi, I relocated again. To a giant stone. Kalikatsou was a massive hunk of barren rock about three stories high, situated in the middle of a bay, in the exact center of the universe. Like the skeletal head of an enormous prehistoric lizard, it looked foreboding, but upon closer approach, one found it was climbable.

Kalikatsou was extremely isolated. And the solitude would've been overwhelming had I disregarded the infinity of stars and the million natural goings-on twenty-four hours a day. Therefore, I found the place packed; and it was there I discovered the glorious companionship of nature. With no people around at all, and no machines, it was quiet…but far from empty.

Winding steps had been carved into one side of this giant rock, said to have been inhabited by monks long ago. Another curious etching was a rectangular incision on the very top, just the size of my sleeping bag. With that perch as base camp, I spent a week just watching. Equipped with watercolors, camera, pen, and paper, I found all mediums useless, and couldn't even manage a postcard home. I simply existed spellbound inside the minutes, exclusively trusting them.

The Greek gods all made themselves known. They entered my eyes and lungs and skin and heart—came in through the wind, the smells, the smiles of villagers, and the bleating of the goats. They wiggled in reflection around my ankles as I stood in the lapping waters, rolled over my tongue in the taste of tomatoes, jumped around the night sky as constellations, and slid down the domes of the tiny white chapels one found at remote overlooks high in the hills—all in a resounding 'yes.' Replaced by openness and invitation, 'no' had vanished.

There was nothing subtle about what was happening to me. The table was set, the feast laid out, I simply took the seat that was waiting for me. I spoke to almost no one that month. I hardly had time to breathe. Everything about life and about God—the real one(s), not the church guy—was seeping into my pores. This I could believe, this was personal, this was holy.

I now knew, in my cells, that—despite my mother's death, my longings for more chocolate than I could afford, my talent for ticket-less travel and girlie disguises, and even being jilted by Jonah—I wasn't an underdog and I wasn't forsaken by the greater good. Just because I didn't bow to Jesus, comprehend Judaism, or find my peace through Buddha—just because I had never subscribed to other people's religions, had found joy and sacrament in candy, and had had to go it alone for much of my life till now—by no means was I hung out to dry.

In light of all this, instinctively, not even consciously, I put scamming behind me.

One day, after having walked hours and hours to the far reaches of Zaxos where I'd heard there were breaking waves, bigger than the Aegean norm, I arrived at a perfect crescent-shaped beach, a body-surfer's dream. Alone, I peeled down to bare skin, plunged into the surf, and rode waves to satiation. After the cool water, I stepped drenched onto the warm dunes and sprawled on my belly across this Eden. With my index finger, I wrote in the sand:

> To God's hill
> in God's hand
> I stretch my naked body
> across God's hot sand
> and bleat in birth,
> God's lamb

♥ ♥

- 46 -

Townsfolk

Under this hex with me were all the islanders. As joyous as I got, they were right there. My 'contacts' were the goat-herding set, shopkeepers in the port where I scored provisions, and farmers I met on day-long hikes up and down the goat paths. All honest, cheery, and bright, I wanted desperately to understand their language. So I quickly learned: Hello, Goodbye, Please, Thank you, and the numbers one through ten. Plus, Zeke had taught me seven sentences that I'd rehearsed till his last hour: How are you? What's your name? What time is it? I don't speak Greek. I don't understand. What did you say? Where's the post office?

The nice thing about these un-garnished queries was that they could be used in almost any situation, in almost any sequence. Though limited, this store of remarks let me initiate conversations then chug along until I ran out of lines. So I'd pleasantly approach someone, like Phillipa.

Phillipa was a twinkly diminutive man with a bowed walking stick and two faded donkeys as cute as he. I thought of him as 'the man who's tied in the middle,' as he always wore blouse-y shirts and billowy trousers belted with an old rope. His aged garments were clean and neatly patched at the elbows, knees, and seat. Even the patches were patched. Though nearly extinct, everything about him was in working order.

"Hello, how are you? What time is it, please?" was how I made myself known to him.

He sweetly told me the time (that I, of course, didn't understand).

"What'd you say?" I asked.

He repeated it.

"I don't understand."

He then indicated manually that it was ten minutes before three.

"Thank you. What's your name?"

"Phillipa," said he. "What's your name?"

I told him mine, then had to ask where the post office was. He pointed to it, sixteen feet away, then said something incomprehensible, forcing my final play, "I don't speak Greek." But after the lengthy exchange, he didn't buy it. So more discourse followed, with me totally faking it by alternating, "What'd you say?" and "I don't understand." But at least I'd made his acquaintance.

Overall, my approach to the language was successful. Because I could at least open a conversation, I gained access to the wondrous Greek Island world, a superlative culture. And through these encounters, my vocabulary doubled daily.

A couple of weeks later, I entered one of the few local *tavernas* for a bite of lunch. "Sit down, sit down," someone called out. Phillipa patted the chair beside him.

"Phillipa! Hello. How are you?"

"Beautiful," he nodded his head happily, removing his cap with panache. "Very beautiful. And you, how are you?"

"Very beautiful." (The customary Greek answer.) By then he had poured me a glass of retsina, a merry yellow wine from pine resin, and obligatory hydration for male islanders. "Thank you very much," I said and raised my glass.

"To us," said Phillipa, lifting his glass.

"To us." (Another customary expression, now part of my repertoire.) But from here I had to let him lead the conversation because he'd already told me where the post office was. So I just beamed happily at him, privileged to be in his company, perhaps the most authentic individual I'd ever befriended.

"I'm eighty-two years old," he then confided.

"What'd you say?"

"Me. Eighty-two. Eight, two. Me."

"Oh-h."

"I'm a strong man."

"What'd you say?"

"STRONG!" And he flexed one forearm and shook a tight fist meaningfully.

"Oh-h-h."

"Very strong," he shook his fist again. "I have eight children."

"Eight what?"

"Children!" And he indicated little people of assorted heights. "And grandchildren!" And he illustrated an army of smaller people still.

"Oh-h-h."

"Very strong." Little Phillipa watched for a reaction and waited for me to reply which I couldn't. We sat in silence for a while, gleaming at each other. Then matter-of-factly, he broke the silence, "My place or yours?"

After Kalikatsou, I went back to the beach at Lipoi. There was a chill in the air as September ended. But to leave the island was out of the question. "Will you get a house?" asked the acquaintances I'd made. But, still feeling safer, more serene, and less worried than ever before, I had no plans. A house would find me if Zeus willed it.

There was a band of young local guys who gathered in the evenings, laughing and drinking ouzo and coffee. Six or seven in all, they got around on motorcycles and had keen eyes for foreign females. Luckily I'd arrived with Zeke, and had been regarded by them as off-limits. By the time they realized Zeke was gone, I was familiar enough with the village to dodge or ignore them. Though there were other non-Greeks also sleeping on Lipoi Beach, I was still solo and in no need of unannounced visitors at three a.m.

One evening at sunset, as I strolled through the port on my way back to the beach, one of these dark-haired young men approached. To my surprise, he spoke English, "Are you staying at Lipoi?"

"Yes," I answered coolly.

"Do you know Marguerita, the German girl?"

"Yes." The last few foreigners were all familiar by now.

He held out a letter. "Can you take this to her? She said she'd translate it from German to English for me."

Seemed on the up and up. "Okay."

I took the letter. He thanked me. Then we turned in opposite directions. As I climbed the donkey path leading to Lipoi, I realized I'd hardly even looked at the guy—how would I know which one of the bunch to give the letter back to?

Buying tomatoes, olives, and feta the next day, the friendly shopkeeper who spoke some English asked if I was planning to stay a while, and I answered affirmative.

"Do you want to rent a house?"

"Maybe."

"I have one in Lipoi. The girl who lives there is moving out tomorrow." He produced a snapshot of a traditional old white farmhouse with blue windows that I'd often seen, then quoted the fair price of thirty dollars a month, mentioning that there was no electricity or running water but a good well and a toilet. As the first autumn rain fell, I moved into that two-room farmhouse, more joyfully than I'd ever moved anywhere. The structure was fashioned of white stone, and a small hillock rose behind it. A hundred steps from my front porch, across a cucumber patch, was the row of Ironwood trees that protected Lipoi Beach. Each sunrise, what I opened my double blue wooden doors to was Heaven, with a well and three cows.

Several days later, while shopping in the village for household staples—kerosene, "Nescafe," olive oil—I suddenly noticed the guy who'd given me the letter. Having given it to Marguerita, I'd forgotten about it when the weather changed and the nesting instinct took over. Now I told him that I'd delivered it but hadn't seen Marguerita since.

"No problem," he said, "Marguerita gave it back to me. But thank you for taking it."

"Any time." And I resumed my errands. Being a home dweller was a full-time responsibility after living out of a basket. I was ripe for domesticity, though; October was colder and wetter, and the four weeks of undisturbed meditation were enough to inspire some letter-writing, or even another gospel for the New Testament.

Theologos

Having entirely avoided western civilization, the cooler weather made me receptive again. One evening, as I passed the lively *taverna* on my way out of the village, I paused in the doorway, for the first time forgetting my love affair with the island and considering the crowd of carefree foreigners eating, drinking, and laughing. But no…I didn't want to come down to humanity. I continued on, passing the next *taverna*, a smaller one enjoyed more by locals. Hearing bare footsteps behind me then, I turned around. There was the guy who'd given me the letter. He invited me for a glass of retsina, but automatically I refused. He then disappeared into the light shower of the eatery.

I walked slowly on into the darkness.

…A glass of wine sure would be nice, and even some noise to compliment all the peace. I'd easily shared Greek coffee with the grand-daddied townsfolk, yet I shied in the eyes of a young-shouldered man…. Turning around, I traced my steps back to that last *taverna*. I saw his legs standing casually beyond the crowded table and chair legs. Entering slowly, I walked over to where he leaned against the counter. "I changed my mind," I smiled.

He nodded warmly and ordered another glass. Leaning sideways, he had one forearm on the counter-top and one foot stretched to a straw-seated chair. Putting my elbow on the counter as well, I faced him. The proprietor placed a carafe of retsina on the counter between us. And as the Greek guy poured it into the two glasses, I quietly observed him for the first time. He was wearing gray corduroy pants and a black t-shirt, no shoes, no belt.

He was lean, taller than me, and much stronger. He had black, uncombed hair and…he lifted the two glasses of yellow wine and handed one to me…aqua eyes. "To you," he said.

I had to hold tightly to my glass as I raised it. My hands were unsteady and my knees about to give—he was the most beautiful man I'd ever seen. He had the angular cheekbones and straight nose of a Greek god. There and then, I fell completely in love with him. His eyes contained everything the island had revealed so far. "To you," I answered and looked down.

The wine seemed to escape the glass and bottle, and encircle his hands, his head, and eyes. The moment was stolen from me as he drank my thoughts in one movement, then refilled his glass and drank my passion, too. My own glass stayed motionless in my hand, my mouth wordless. Once again, the ancient mythology was reaching across centuries, the gods still at play.

We passed some hours and fried fish around, easily surmounting the language barrier, our communication always way ahead of any words. His English, created as he spoke, was crazy poetry, with ad hoc word choices like Bob Dylan abridged for third-graders. But there was more in the air, something between the words.

Then he told me, fairly, of his woman. Calling her 'my girl,' he explained how they'd met and how much she meant to him. Just as well, I thought, and told him of my man—inventing a Zeke-Jonah blend rather than peeling back the layers. The field was leveled, at least. I wondered where his girl was.

A moment arrived and in long loose threads we held it between our faces. "Tonight, will you sleep at my house?" he asked after a silence.

"All three of us?"

"Three?" he looked at me blankly.

"Yeah. You, me, and your girl."

"My girl is not *here*." There was slight annoyance at having been misunderstood. "She's in Vienna."

"Oh."

"Did you think I would ask you to sleep at my house if my girl was here?"

"I didn't know what to think." We looked at each other oddly for a minute then both laughed. "Well, you told me about your girl but you never mentioned that she went to Vienna."

We slipped out into the street. With our honesty, a trap had been neatly laid should pain perchance trail us in the night. Proud of our simple trust, our feet strongly overtook the stones. The night had many dimensions but we were transported through them and past the black sea by a narrow, winding pathway between stone houses that were white-washed together. We took the swept stairs by twos to the top where his small painted doorway slowed our breath to a stop. As the night settled around us, the stillness placed his arm across my shoulders. The harbor lights swam beneath sleeping boats. He whispered that the fourth one, green by day, was his and that he was a fisherman.

Our love was a balanced and equal discovery, a kind of dance lasting half the night. Our joy was mutual at having found each other. I owed him an apology though, "I'm sorry that I didn't see you when you first spoke to me."

"It's okay, I saw you."

"And I'm sorry I didn't see you the second time."

"It's okay, I knew."

"Knew what?"

"That we would come to my house."

The room was tiny but daybreak remembered it. Vine-like dawn coiled through the keyhole with the voice of a rooster. Two lips touched mine. In the shadows of sunrise, two eyes looked to the eager boat below. Two bare feet found the doorway while his hands pulled swiftly at sea-washed clothing. The open doorway let in a call from the shore. I felt a smile covering my whole face as his palms warmed my shoulders. "Tonight I will see you again?" he asked.

I nodded.

- 48 -

Retsina Wine

Every now and then you don't love anyone at all. Usually, though, there's someone you care for. And very occasionally, your heart-strings are pulled in numerous directions. This latter scenario might seem problematic, but compared to no love or bad love, it's hard to brutally condemn it. I exuberantly adored Zeke and was a permanent student in his visual school; I was addicted to Jonah's will and spirit and compelled by the game we were playing (plus he was a Long Island home-boy); and I was now totally enraptured (gaga) over Theologos the Fisherman.

Zeke had sent a letter saying he was now residing in my old room in 48, and the house was full again with everyone back from their travels. "But if you're staying in Zaxos forever then I'm coming back!" He also forwarded my London mail, including a postcard from Jonah: "I'm in Ibiza. I want to see you. Come visit." (I pretended that Zeke hadn't read it.)

And Theologos was right here. But he was accounted for by his 'baroness'—he'd be leaving soon to join her in Vienna.

Zeke was accounted for by no money in London. And Jonah, oh my God, was in this very Mediterranean.

My forwarded mail also contained a dispatch from Mimi, who—together with Sonny, back again from Nova Scotia—was at long last taking the truth-seeker trail overland to India. Via Zaxos. "Expect us soon!" Good thing I had a house. They were more than welcome, but no more predictable or communicative than before.

I returned postcards to Jonah ("My island's better than yours, you come here") and Zeke—who knew too much about Jonah but, thankfully, nothing about Theologos—("No definite plans, I'll keep in touch").

My most powerful pull—pretty strong when you considered the others—was for Zaxos. I was learning purity, elementary Greek, fishing, joy, wine-drinking, mountain climbing, folk-dancing, solitude, long-distance swimming, endurance, even math—because when you get down to the fundamentals, you discover simplicity, rhythm, circles, triangles, squares, music, and other things that categorically can only be called mathematics. (Pythagoras himself, the ancient Greek philosopher and mathematician, was born one island east.)

Theologos the Fisherman, who it took me three meetings to actually *see*, was one of the finest people I've ever had the fortune of knowing. Without falseness, he was sharp, quick, ironic, and personal. Nothing contrived or sophisticated in him, his life was a song, his wisdom piercing. And, though generous beyond calculation, there was nothing 'nice' about him—he wasn't someone you 'liked,' wasn't soft, didn't care about the smooth functioning of social intercourse. He was someone you loved, because he wanted the best for all, and made that known, usually through humor or silence.

Things went his way, and his way was a kind of law. It took time for me to see that Theo ruled. Maybe the entire island. He walked like it was his place. Loved it like it was his. He moved his eyes selectively over the people, the boats, and the stones, as though they, too, were all his. "I never saw that stone before," he said one night, stopping in perplexity on the donkey path back to my house, staring at one of hundreds of boulders along the way.

"The life of a fisherman is freedom," he told me. "I want nothing but to fish. Other men must search, but I know now." And though uncluttered by doubt, there were dark traces in his ocean eyes. His balance and munificence of soul were at such an apex that it rendered him almost fragile. I treasured the innocence of both the island and him. I feared European invasion of Theologos. I never wanted to see him in city clothes.

But his transit through my life was so fleeting I could only cherish him, not consider his ultimate reality, his struggles, his complexities…there wasn't time. He wasn't a lover to adjust one's own character to. He created no space for another half. Even his mistakes were so subtle they might've been somebody else's. His simple manhood was rare. His palms were leather, worn by miles of net. He sang and danced and steered a room's mood. He was a sensitive child that all his friends, new and old, adored and spoiled. As though he were handicapped, we couldn't give him enough. The odds were against knowledge as pure as Theo's. And sorrow? I tried not to see it, but it cornered his eyes when he laughed, and when the leaves of the fig trees turned brown in October. Our time together was short....

But I was caught. And for all Theo's integrity and responsibility, so was he. Zaxos was a spiritual spot, okay; there was something in the air and everyone could feel it. Even the Bible mentions Zaxos. There were churches in every nook and cranny, monks swarming all over the place, bells ringing morning, noon, and night, and celebrations for different saints almost daily. Not to mention endless thanks all around for the privilege of living there. However...the Greek Orthodox Church, who sort of sponsored everything, did not sponsor sex before marriage. Even after wasn't recommended. It could overlook little scenes between Greek boys and foreign girls passing through—boys will be boys—but after a week or two, it preferred the girls to please move along. Unmarried couples did not reside on Zaxos.

Well, there had been one couple not long ago, who took a house together. And the islanders gave the girl hell for many months, even stoned her. But the man was strong, was sure of their love, and fought hard to convey to his kin that marriage was unnecessary. Finally, when the girl stayed the whole winter, proving her sincerity and learning the language and ways of the island, she was accepted. And by the time she left Zaxos, after a full year, she'd earned a unique place in their hearts as an outsider who'd found her way in. That couple was Theologos and 'his girl.'

Now, just six weeks after she'd left, he was serenading *me* in the port town twilight. The townsfolk, in their cafe chairs, sat unmoving like turn-of-the-century portraits as we strolled past. But their eyes moved with us and their heads leaned together once we were out of earshot. The village was tiny—anyone who stayed more than a week was under scrutiny; people-watching was the evening entertainment.

But not only did I treat Zaxos as an awesome university cum monastery, I also adored every man, woman, child, goat, and sacred cove. And Zaxos loved me back. The people knew I'd spent a month by myself, climbing goat paths, sleeping on Kalikatsou, learning Greek, asking everybody where the post office was, and being probably the most gung ho tourist in Hellenic history. And when they saw me with Theo, they didn't quite know what to think. Instinctively, they actually liked us together.... But it couldn't be right...because of the other girl, tradition, the monastery, everything. They felt cheated; finally they'd found a place in their pews for her, and now, just as he was preparing to join her in Vienna for the winter, he was with me. (I, of course, was clueless that I had a starring role in the final act of a Greek drama.)

But Theo and I were crazy about each other.

"Your face..." he said to me, shaking his head in confusion, "... your face. Since one time I saw...since two...since ever I saw...your face." And our happiness was contagious. In accord with another Greek custom, we drank retsina with abandon. Theologos and his friends informed me and my friends (Jim and Steve, two brotherly Americans who rented the house next to mine) early in our Greek island lessons, that retsina was essential to all good things and left no hangover. Put to the test nightly, the info proved accurate, so Steve penned a ballad called "Retsina Wine."

> retsina wine
> makes you feel fine
> costs a few drachs
> will fill in your cracks....

The blond drink guaranteed an infectious silliness by the second glass, and what transpired next was anybody's guess. "Somebody help me, I'm dancin' in the streets" were some of Steve's lyrics, sung while dancing with a wooden chair. By the fourth glass, we'd be begging Theo to dance, if he hadn't already.

To watch him dance was to get what Greece was all about— passion. His agility, vibrancy, and spontaneity literally spun the room. With total balance and control, he'd do handstands as part of the dance, or leap to the food-covered table on one foot. Expecting wreckage, we'd hold our breath, but he'd somehow contain himself in grace, continuing the dance balanced on one foot atop the food-covered table. Maybe he'd bend one knee all the way down, straightening the other leg inches above the plates of fish and olives, and pour some wine into my glass or eat a fish, then rise up again and spring from the table with a cry of "OPAH!" Then we'd all smash plates to the floor at his feet. And Thonassi, the proprietor, would grab a few more from the shelf and hurl them, too. Nobody could dance like Theo, nobody had the skill or the celebrity. His dance was heroic and liberating, benevolent, and joyful.

Theologos was all-seeing, he never relaxed. Knowing nothing went past him, you automatically sat up straight when you saw him coming. This was the hard part for me, I wasn't used to behaving. Theo didn't give commands or even readable hints, but expected some unspoken protocol I knew nothing about. "Are you my woman?" he'd ask sternly, as though I'd done something wrong by dancing with someone's grandfather.

He meant, "Don't step out of line," but I didn't know where the line was, and wanted to scream, "No, I'm NOT your woman! Your woman's in Vienna. And the second your passport comes from Athens, you're leaving me. Forever!"

"Somebody arrest me, I'm dancin' in the streets," sang Steve, watching Theo and I arguing with our eyes.

I loved Theologos. He was a story. Like an adjective—red, hot, boiling…or blue, clear, exceptional—he gave more to everything he touched. Little children rode on his shoulders and old ladies cooked him food. And during our madcap soirées, he took total responsibility for the well-being of all of us. If Theo was at the table, everybody ate and drank to incapacitated merriment. "Somebody help me," Steve howled, "I'm barkin' with the dogs!"

"Next summer," Theo announced one evening, like a statesman, "maybe I will marry. You will all come to dance."

"I'm not dancing at your wedding!" I was furious.

"Why don't you want to dance?"

I said nothing. But later, alone with him while the others chain-danced around the chards of broken plates, I asked, "Theo, how can you get married? What am I supposed to do?"

"You think I should marry you?"

It was a yes or no question and I couldn't honestly say no. "Yes."

"You want that you and me marry together??" He didn't believe me.

"Yes."

Somebody help me, I just proposed to a Greek fisherman.

- 49 -

Fare Thee Well

Money wasn't seen at Theo's table. At the end of the evening, we'd all just dance straight out the door and frequently right off the pier. "Theo, Theo, who paid?" I'd ask, wringing out my skirt.

"Don't worry," he'd say with finality. "You live in my country."

So we'd do what we could when he came to our houses, but since our houses were also in his country, he'd arrive with grapes, fish, tomatoes, feta. Like the day after the proposal, when I thought he was out fishing. There was a knock on my door.

I opened the blue wooden doors to the gleaming world outside. Framed there was a pinch-yourself prince. White light flecked off the Aegean behind him, and he stood glimmering, barefoot and square-shouldered in a blue plaid shirt and weathered, rolled up jeans. My hand went to my heart at the sight of his eyes, matching the sea behind him. A black beret pushed his salty hair against one cheekbone, and he held toward me a leafy branch with cherry-like fruits. "For you. Something new." He plucked one and put it in my mouth. "In October only is this fruit. From the other side of the island. Now you know. I missed the boat this morning so I ran across the island to catch it. But no boat there either, only fruit."

It was delicious.

"Are you still drunk?" he smiled.

"No," I laughed.

"Were you serious last night?"

"About what?"

"Were you serious when you said that you and me should marry together?"

Maybe he didn't realize how much I cared. Maybe I didn't realize. "I don't know," I told him honestly. (Maybe he was better off on the pedestal.)

"Can you fish?" he asked.

"No, but I can dance." We both laughed then made love all afternoon beneath the straw and wood ceiling of my silent house.

Theologos. I will always love him. May he crinkle to a stubble of a withered branch of that fruit tree, he'll be beautiful to me—his crystal blue spirit, his eyesight seeing both inside and out, his quiet knowing, and his devotion to the sea, to his bloodline, and to the white God that lives on Zaxos.

He was prime for military service. But his political views were as adamant as his social ones and he had no intention of serving. To dodge the Greek armed forces was no easy feat, though. Great compromise or high-powered string-pulling was required. Theo elected to leave the country instead. But to avoid service, he'd have to stay out of Greece for twelve years—until he was beyond military eligibility. And only if he could get a passport, something that was close to impossible. His decision was extreme, but actually made sense. He loved the baroness in Vienna. She loved him too, but couldn't stay indefinitely in the Greek Islands. Her father, the baron, could pull the political strings to arrange a legal passport for Theo. And along with the passport, he'd be sent a train ticket to Austria. When he got to Vienna (his first trip outside Greece), he'd look for a job and study language and philosophy. Such was the plan he conveyed to me.

Well, none of us, lastly his mother, liked the sound of it. We couldn't even imagine the guy in sandals, let alone a suit or, God forbid, horn-rimmed glasses. To all who cared, the whole endeavor was counter-intuitive. His mind was made up, though: he was in love and opposed to military service. And, all things considered, a little worldliness never hurt anyone. So his passport would arrive, and he was waiting.

"Theo," I said sadly, "you and me are just two ships passing in the night."

"No," he said, "two ships crashing in the night."

Sonny and Mimi never showed. November did though. Zaxos was cold, damp, and gray. "The weather is two," said Theologos, and took me under the covers. But our love would be ending soon—and the waiting for his passport was a slow torture for all concerned. I kept reminding myself about my much less complicated love for the island itself. Couldn't that flame keep burning when Theo had gone? My Greek was getting quite functional after two and a half months; I should fight the winter, see it through. I should overcome the weakness and dependency Theo had unintentionally kindled. Yes, I must transcend emotion and get back to my education!

Every week, Steve and Jim packed up and waited on the pier for the great Mimika. Then, realizing they were about to re-enter the big bad world of cars and trucks, they'd chicken out. Back at Lipoi, as they unpacked, they'd congratulate themselves on their soundness of mind, "It's too good here, we'd be stupid to leave so soon." But eventually they'd have to. We all would. We couldn't stay forever.... We hated to admit it, but ideals alone can wear thin. Zaxos was the end of the rainbow, but if we stayed too long and consumed too much, we might put out the spark. 'Enough' is a hard one to recognize.

Anyway, after Theo left, the island would feel empty despite its fullness. Plus, without him, I'd freeze.

One evening, wearing several layers of t-shirts, plus one as a scarf and another around my head as a cap, I went to the village. Finding Theo bent over a game of backgammon, I knew winter was upon us—he was wearing shoes. Like seeing Zorba in a lace nightie, it was jarring. Boots maybe, swim fins, even sneakers, but black lace-up shoes?

"I'm leaving this night," he said quietly as I walked up.

Oh terrific. I had all of sixty minutes before the boat abducted him. What could I do? The town was already humming as everyone prepared for the Mimika's arrival and the bustling exchange of passengers and cargo that would follow. What could I do? I stared at the floor, fighting back the waterfall behind my eyes. All Theo's friends were sitting inside the dusky *taverna* with him, chain smoking and pondering the shoes. Theo wouldn't cry, but he was not crying so beautifully that it was tearing the rest of us to pieces.

Jim and Steve were leaving tonight, too. Again. I'd be alone in the world. What would I do? I'd never see Theologos again. Well, maybe in twelve years we'd see each other again, with our husbands and wives and kids and stooped spines and old memories.... For all intents and purposes, our love had fifty minutes to go.

I couldn't look at him, couldn't bear the unwieldy blackness that hung in the cigarette smoke around him. I couldn't sit there in the room and drink a silent ouzo while he bore his eyes into the backgammon board. Suddenly I spun round and careened out the door and down the street. A shout followed me, but I kept slamming my feet against the stone pavement, racing through the village blurred by tears.

I had to find my reason, had to find a way to say goodbye.

He loved me, but he didn't love me most. Did I love him most? I had never had to decide. Arriving, winded, at the small beach near town, I sank heavily onto the sand and pierced the boat-less horizon with hating eyes. The distant islands were waiting. Like a row of people in a train station, they were looking down the track. Any moment that great white whale would swim in and devour Theo like a herring. Even the Aegean seemed cruel now for taking him from me. His departure was a cliff I was falling off, and there was nothing below except twelve years, his girl, winter, European cities, and knife-point poetry.

Where was my goodness, my grace, my...understanding? Why was I being selfish and thinking small?

...I remembered something my mother had often told me. "If you really love someone, if you really...*love*...someone, you want them to be happy."

I did love Theologos. I did want him to be happy. Tonight he was doing what he wanted most to do. To go to Vienna would make him happy; he loved his girl there. And he would leave his homeland and see new places. This wasn't a bad thing, but good. Lost in subjectivity, I'd had it all wrong.

I sat quietly for a long moment. My eyes were drying. Not much time left—I'd just blown half an hour. Better blow my nose, too, and get back to the *taverna*. I watched the last of the sunset, just a red thread sewn into the night.... We'd had a perfect love and its end had to fit the rest of our story. I could let him go, he'd made me wealthy indeed. He'd given me the glorious Aegean and every God in it; he'd given me Greece, the real thing, soaked with retsina and salt water, fortified with fish, friends, and mercurial mischief. He'd given me the Greek twist, to laugh instead of crying and to cry instead of laughing. I'd laugh now. I ran back through the village to find him.

Head down, I crashed straight into a couple of donkey-esque pedestrians, stumbling toward the dock. Jim and Steve. "Theo is leaving tonight," I wailed. "You guys can't abandon me, too. Not in my hour of need!"

They looked at me sympathetically, then at each other. "We don't really *have* to leave," said Jim to Steve.

"No," Steve smiled, happier already, "we don't have to. We could wait till next week. Nobody believed we were going tonight anyway, they wouldn't even sell us tickets."

"They sold Theo one," I said. "Will you really stay?" A great horn resounded in the distance. "Oh God, the Mimika!" I fled on to find Theo.

I met him and his hang-dog gang in the square. "Where did you go?" he asked me. They were crawling toward the quay, Theologos alone propelling a group that was really trying to drag him the other way.

"I went to the beach," I said breathlessly, avoiding his eyes while squirming through his friends to my privileged position under his arm. All entwined, glued together at the shoulders, arms, and waists, our human mass struggled through the village like a wounded caterpillar. Only Theo's eyes looked at the boat that was now docking. As the others moved along, looking frantically for another hour or even a freak fifteen minutes, he held me back a moment under a quiet archway. This was our last second because the final goodbye would be dominated by mother, father, brothers, and nieces. It wasn't my place. I'd stand back with my friends and just watch.

Two fingers under my chin, Theo lifted my face and looked into my eyes. "I will write to you," he said.

But tomorrow had never been our concern. "Perhaps," I said. What mattered was that he'd taken these last minutes to confirm all we felt.

Clenching his jaw, he stared hard into my eyes. And reaching all the way through my heart, he said, "I will remember your face."

"I will remember yours," I answered and took a final drink from his infinity. He kissed me then, and I let him go.

A bit stunned, I hung back from the quayside chaos. Though no longer demolished, I could recall kinder occasions. Then Jim, Steve, and all their earthly goods chugged up to me like a freight train. "Retsina?" they said.

"You're staying!!"

"Of course we're staying. We wanna be near Turkey for Thanksgiving. And near retsina. Retsina?"

"Costs a few drachs, will fill in my cracks," I started singing.

The boat was moving sluggishly from the pier. We walked to the edge, watching Theologos up on the aft deck in his black beret and pea-coat. Then sounding its hollow horn, the Mimika pointed herself seaward and picked up speed. "Retsina wine..." a Greek voice sang out louder than the horn, as the boat was sucked away, "makes you feel fine...."

♥

- 50 -

Echoes

It was the village more than anything else that echoed Theo's absence. Going to town just to buy halvah and check the mail was a tad meaningless.

Also, my immune system was finally losing ground to my dextrose diet. My father had said I'd be diabetic by thirty-five, but I was only twenty-two so it wasn't that. I pondered the symptoms.... My lungs felt like the Grand Canyon when I coughed, and trying to get oxygen back down there afterwards left me a shade of scarlet that readied onlookers for mouth-to-mouth. And any minor injury, like a needle prick from sewing, swelled to alarming proportions overnight. Was I going to meet my maker? Even my vegetarianism had backfired. Replacing meat and fish with white sugar, white bread, butter, ice cream, candy, cheese, halvah, yoghurt, pastry, Retsina, and coffee, is like divorcing one's immune system.

Meanwhile, if my under-supply of oxygen and oversupply of mucous didn't eighty-six me, poverty would. I was down to forty bucks, and my dwindling stash in London was three weeks away by Mimika-mail. I couldn't hold out indefinitely for Sonny, Mimi, or word from Jonah....

But could I live without this island?

A week after Theo, even Jim and Steve tore themselves away. Now, a short think on a sunset boulder led to the realization that if I stayed here and died "for love," it would probably be recorded as a halvah overdose. All things considered, the most sensible action might be a visit to the island doctor.

Pleasant enough but disappointingly un-fazed by my condition, he handed me a band-aid for my infected thumb. My worse-infected toe, he painted red and told me to bask in sunlight for twenty minutes. A second opinion here would prove useful, but there was no second doctor, so I settled for a second band-aid. For the lungs, he prescribed cough syrup.

While in town, I then wheezed my way to the post office and found a letter from Spain.

"I would come to visit you," Jonah wrote, "Zaxos sounds beautiful, but I'm in a hospital in Barcelona with a broken leg. A motorcycle accident in Ibiza. I'm not too well. I've had two operations. Write or call collect. Much love, Jonah." He included a phone number.

Limping double-time to the outhouse-sized telecommunications office, I placed a call to the Barcelona hospital, then hunkered in for a half hour wait. "Spain!" piped the operator eventually.

"Hello?" I began....

"Hello?" answered a voice.

"Jonah?"

"Yeah?"

"It's Wendy."

"I can't believe it. Where are you?"

"Still in Greece. I just got your letter. Are you okay?"

"I'm a mess, but I'm in one piece. How are you?"

"I'm a mess, but I'm alright, too. Is that really you?"

"Yeah, and it's really you.... It's nice. Been a long, long time...." There was a silence, as we remembered each other's voices, his warm and sweet today.

"So what happened, and what's happening?" I asked him.

"Blew out my leg in a bad bike accident on the island. Had an operation there. It went wrong and they were talking about taking my leg off, so I grabbed a helicopter to Barcelona and had another emergency operation. They saved my leg I think, but they had to put nine screws in it. Now I've got one more operation coming which will decide whether I'll walk again."

"Jesus, Jonah...."

"Things are looking up...it might work out."

"Oh, Jonah...who's taking care of you?"

"Who the fuck's always taking care of me? I'm taking care of me."

"Do you want me to come?" I asked quietly.

"Oh, would you?"

"Yes."

"I'd be so happy if you'd come."

"How long will you be at that hospital?"

"Uncertain…. A while longer."

"A week?"

"Yeah, probably a week or more. They won't tell me anything. I'm going nuts in this place. When can you get here?"

"I'll leave immediately, but it will take a while, with boat connections and stuff. A few days. Don't leave till I get there, okay?"

"Okay."

"I'll come as fast as I can. I'm on my way right now."

"It'll be good to see you…. We'll get our whole show back together."

"Mmm. Take good care, Jonah. See you very soon."

"Love you."

"Bye."

I stood numbly in the phone closet. Zaxos had come to an abrupt end. But at least the immediate future had been decided. And thoughts of Jonah made it easier to surrender thoughts of Theo. (Thoughts of Zeke were more like calming background music, since he was living in the same room as all my possessions back in London.)

The next boat to Athens wasn't for three days, but checking at the port, I learned there was a *caïque* (smaller one) to another nearby island next morning and from there I could connect more quickly to Athens. That left little time to close the house, say my goodbyes, and have money cabled from London to Barcelona. Before leaving the village, I scribbled a sketchy postcard to Zeke, "Moving east. Destination unclear. Under-dressed and coughing. Next address—c/o American Express, Barcelona." He'd always known there'd be another round with Jonah, here it was….

Dizzy with romance and emphysema, I hustled up the donkey path toward my house. Halfway back, I nearly collided with a bright young man coming from the other direction. "Oh!"

He smiled broadly and opened his arms. It was Sonny, looking wonderful. A small boat had quietly unloaded him as I was phoning

Spain. Following my written instructions, he'd found my house, but not me, so was returning to the village. His face was full of joy. We hugged tightly a second time. "Is Mimi here?" he asked.

"I was about to ask you that. I haven't heard from her. I thought you two were coming together."

"We were, but you know Mimi—the last minute she was struck with a burning desire to see Portugal. So she took off for Lisbon and said she'd meet me here."

"How's she getting here?"

"Hitching."

"Alone from Portugal?" (This should surprise me?)

"Probably not, with her faculty for meeting weirdos."

"Well, looks like I'm gonna miss her…and I sure wish you had come sooner, because I'm leaving tomorrow morning at six o'clock."

"For good?" His face fell and I felt horrible.

"Oh, why didn't you come sooner?" I asked. "I've waited so long, and you missed so many good times and good people…. But the island's the best thing, and it's as beautiful as ever."

We had just that afternoon and evening together. Zaxos was dressed to kill that day and Sonny had the eyes for the place. He appreciated everything and I was pleased to bequeath my house to him—the rent was paid for another ten days. There he could comfortably await Mimi before alighting on their pilgrimage.

At dawn, Sonny walked me to the *caïque*, on which I was one of two travelers, the other the captain. Leaving both Zaxos and Sonny was heartbreaking, and leaning off the stern as they became smaller in our wake, I added to the salt water below. But leaving something as precious as Sonny there, like a part of myself, in the place I loved, calmed me. It was good. And I'd be back.

51

Barcelona

After several small boats, a lot of waiting, one bus, and two big boats, Zaxos was now forty-eight hours behind me. Things were pretty empty and casual around the old Med this time of year, so scoring a sly second class berth could be done in your sleep. (Irresistible backslide into badness—old habits die hard.) As Italy blossomed on the horizon next morning, so came the opportune moment to see who of the vehicle-owners was going where. As perky passengers sniffed the early air on deck, I approached the approachable ones and was soon tipped off. "There's an American Navy guy who might be going your way," someone said. "In fact, that's him standing by the railing."

With no false humility, I arrived at the side of a super clean-cut man of approximately my age. "Do you have a car?" I asked him.

"Yeah. Where ya trying to get to?"

"Bar-ce-LO-na," I moaned, knowing my ordeal was just beginning. "Where are you going?"

"Barcelona," he smiled. "Even farther, actually, but I'll be driving right through Barcelona."

Too good to be true. "But…?" I asked, waiting for why he couldn't take me.

"But what?"

"But…you've got thirty crates of something and there's no more room?"

"No. In fact the car's almost empty."

"But…you have to spend a week in Rome with your uncle?"

"No. In fact I'm in a hurry and I can only stop for food, gas, and sleeping."

"But, I know, you have a lot on your mind and you need to be alone."

"No, I'd actually appreciate some company. I've been thinking it's going to be a strenuous trip by myself."

"But you never pick up strangers."

"No, I like strangers."

"Well, I'd be ecstatic to ride with you, but I'm not the most ideal passenger because I don't have much money and I do have a dramatic cough."

"No big deal, I have a lousy cough, too. And I don't need any money from you as long as you can pay for your food. And believe me, I won't be stopping anywhere fancy."

"But if I'm traveling that far with you I should chip in. I can give you fifteen of my twenty dollars and eat sparingly."

"Don't worry about it. I get paid to be in the Navy, and there's nothing to spend the money on. I'll be real glad to have your company and that's enough. Now, do you have any other problems? Stops along the way you have to make? Morphine in plastic bags? Anything I should know?"

"No, everything's on the table. How long do you think the trip will take, and where do you plan to sleep?"

"I estimate two full days, and was intending to sleep in the car, parking along the road somewhere. Both front seats fold back like beds and are quite comfortable. Are you good with that?"

"No problem. I have a sleeping bag, so I can sleep anywhere. Also I drive, and would be glad to help out that way."

"Great."

No question where this match was made.

We drove off the ferry together and just kept rolling, hugging the shoreline the entire way up the west coast of Italy to Genoa, along the Italian and French Rivieras to Marseilles, then crossed the Spanish border and continued to Barcelona. Our two nights in transit, we simply pulled off the road, cranked down the seats and slept like bears. In the morning, robot-like, we cranked ourselves upright, turned on the ignition and cruised on. The American car was a rocket and we floated in music and easy conversation. Perfect companions, it was the smoothest imaginable drive. Free of mishap or misunderstanding, I was astounded at my good fortune.

It was evening when I disembarked in front of my dependable old hotel near the port. Wishing my new friend the best, he (familiar now with who I was meeting) earnestly wished me good luck, too.

I had had no time to register the changes since Zaxos—Greece, Italy, France, now Spain—but my small-island mentality was definitely thrown akimbo by this churning mainland. Securely in my hotel room, finally I could just lock the door, peel off the layers of summer clothes, and wash all those roads, cars, and boats from my Greek essence. Since Jonah didn't know I'd arrived, I could also sleep in the next morning. I'd need all possible fortification for this reunion. Though, knowing Jonah, he had probably split for New York three days ago.

Next morning, I did what I could with my road warrior looks. What to wear wasn't an option—brown rubber Greek sandals, shell jewelry, and a giant t-shirt (as a dress) previously owned by Phoebe who got it from Peter, belted by my dead grandfather's canvas pouch. I packed my shoulder basket with a Spanish dictionary, meager coin collection from four nations, extra t-shirts in lieu of a jacket, and Jonah's address (that I'd managed not to lose). I then set out like Florence Nightingale.

A long taxi-ride through up-market suburbia delivered me to a small, modern medical facility.

Boldly approaching the reception desk, I stated Jonah's name. It felt red and foreign coming out my lips. Had I changed or were the feelings all still there?

"That's room twenty-three," said a nice nurse. "I'll take you there."

What would he look like? Sick, weary, older? (What did he look like before? I couldn't remember.) I followed down a long corridor. What would he be like? Warm, reassuring, and confident about the importance of our lasting feelings for one another? Or cool, punitive, and clandestine? Had our understanding of each other matured? Were our needs less opposing now? The nurse and I turned down another corridor. Was this a meant-to-be love that was finally to become, or were we something different from lovers really, something only a lot more years would ever define? The uniformed lady knocked lightly on the white door marked "23" and a low voice said, "Come in." She opened it and stood aside letting me enter.

It was a sun-flooded room, with one entire wall a sliding glass door open onto a spacious terrace. Two people sat talking in the sunshine outside, both with the bathrobe air of patients. A dark-haired woman spoke familiarly to the other, who had a white telephone pole hinged to his hip. The phone pole rested on a metallic support. Accustomed to the routine come-and-go of hospital staff, neither looked our way. "Jonah," the nurse got his attention and he looked up.

Our eyes met, his as dark and bottomless as ever. A smile radiated across his face, "You came."

I could only laugh—the relief of being there, seeing him again, and at how well he looked despite the injury. "Come and kiss me," he opened his arms, "carefully."

I obeyed, then backed away from his delicate condition. Locked into looking at each other, we forgot the others present. Then, snapping out of it, we saw that the nurse had vanished, as nurses do, and the woman on the terrace, much at home, was sunbathing. Jonah introduced me to her, then, uncharacteristically, asked her to please leave, "because I'd like to be alone with this lady. I haven't seen her in a long, long time."

"You look good, Jonah," I said when she'd gone. "You look exactly the same."

"So do you. Like your haircut." He squinted, "How are you, woman? Sit and talk to me...tell me what you been doin'."

I sat but was at a loss for words. Here we were having this grand reunion and we'd never known each other to begin with. "How are you feeling?" I asked, gingerly touching the outrageous cast. "Pretty serious-looking piece of leg there."

"Yeah, pretty heavy-fuckin'-duty. I really did myself in this time. Look at me. But this isn't me, man, no way. They've had me pretty scared, but I'll beat this one. Nothing's got me yet, not hepatitis, not cancer, not motorcycles. And I'll be damned if I'll be beat by a busted leg. Even if I'm a cripple for the rest of my life—and it's a possibility—" a cloud crossed his face, "I'll be one hell of a bike-riding, skiing cripple! These hospital people around here, they want me to hang around and recover slowly under their surveillance. Well, fuck 'em. The minute, the very minute, they give me crutches, I'm outta here. And I told 'em. They don't believe I'll grab those things and walk straight out that door, but I told 'em. What about you? What are you gonna do when they give me my crutches?"

"I doubt I'll stick around after you're gone."

"You want some crutches too? It'll make me feel better if there's two of us."

"Then who's gonna carry the suitcases? Or do they get crutches too?"

"Crutches all around, crutches for the whole family. Seriously, what are your plans?"

"My immediate plans are to lie down and die, I'm deathly ill. After that, I have to go to American Express to pick up some money, and other than that I just want to help you."

"You're a good girl. And with all my heart I appreciate your coming. Whatever happens between us, thanks for coming. I'd do the same for you."

"I know you would." (Right.)

"Do you have anywhere you have to be? Work? What about London?"

"London? It's sitting there if I want to go back. I left some things there, and some good people, but I don't have a job. Besides, it's freezing. I'll wend my way back there eventually."

All afternoon we stroked hands and heads and didn't believe we were together again. We had a bland lunch, then at Jonah's insistence, I was given a chest x-ray and some medicine, and advised to take up residence in the bed next to his. But I could hardly be a conscientious sick person with him in the next crib. Nor would I be much assistance to him. Another option was the "guest" bed in the room. "Just stay as a guest instead," Jonah offered cordially, since a Spanish custom permits visitors to stay with patients. "Then if you happen to need treatment, you can just press the buzzer." But, despite invitational reclining places in every direction, a starched sterility held the space. Jonah's mummy leg was imposing, and the old shyness I'd felt before was back. The combination of our past and his cast made this less than a honeymoon. And, as history tends to repeat itself, an emotional retreat could be necessary—better keep my hotel room.

For the moment, though, I was floating. Suddenly it was worth two whole years to recapture the good feeling with Jonah. Time had taken away the pain. Together again, we were an amazing twosome, matched only by each other. He, and he alone, seemed constructed of identical stuff. Needing no external nod to formulate his next move, Jonah walked the line. He alone had the will and independence I sought, plus humor and agility to offset what might otherwise read as stubborn determination and arrogance.

I wafted back to my hotel on a cloud.

♥

52

Memories

Jonah had opened a door for me—taken me from my father's home and given me keys to the world. I'd survived every journey and every city. The experience gap would be closed now. I was ready for him, we'd be equals.

But with half his body in plaster, we weren't likely to work things out sexually. Though a bolder or more imaginative girlfriend might've found this medical backdrop stimulating, I found it austere and restrictive. Another reunited pair might have picked right up where they left off, ignoring phone poles and wheelchairs, but Jonah and I had nowhere to revert ecstatically back to. We were now basically re-estranged, so we drank tea and wordlessly pondered what would become of us.

"We're going to Ibiza," he chirped upon my arrival the next day. "As soon as I get my crutches."

"Oh dear."

"What?" his smile faded.

"Ibiza?"

"Yeah, a happy little island in the Mediterranean."

"Why Ibiza?"

"Well, I have to go back there. I left all my things, including a car. I thought we'd go to Ibiza, collect my stuff, then take the car back to the mainland and drive to my parents' place in Madrid. My parents are in New York." This was all in sing-song, like the refrain of "Old MacDonald had a Farm."

I didn't say anything.

"What's wrong?"

"I can't go to Ibiza, Jonah."

"Why not, it's a charming little spot."

"Too many associations, not all pleasant. And, I hate to tell you, I've seen islands more charming."

"Well tut-tut…. What associations?"

"Well, I don't know if you remember, but you and I didn't have much fun together on that happy little island. In fact, we had so little fun we didn't communicate for the next two years. Besides, you can't drive."

"You can."

"Can't someone else bring your car over?"

He thought a moment. "No. I have to get it myself. I have to see a couple of people over there, too. I left pretty suddenly. Ha ha."

"Who's got your car?"

"It's at Missy's." This chorus was more familiar.

"Who's Missy?"

"The woman I was staying with at the time of the accident."

"Splendid. Are we going to her house?"

"It's not what you think, and we won't be staying with her."

"I think it's exactly what I think."

"She's a very understanding lady, and she knows that she and I are essentially friends."

"Essentially?"

"It's really no big deal, believe me. But I have to see her, she's done a lot for me."

"I don't doubt it. Look, Jonah, you're in bad shape and no one expects you to take care of business right away. Can't Missy hold onto your car a while? Why don't you leave things till you're better?"

"Can't. Gotta close up shop on the island so I don't have go back there later. But if you can't find it in yourself to return to that hor-ri-ble place, I'll go alone."

"Don't be ridiculous. You can't even walk."

"No one walks to an island. I'll manage. You did say you'd help me, but we all have our petty limitations."

"You're not being very understanding." Returning to the scene of the crime seemed fatal to me.

"*You're* not being very understanding. You offered to help and what needs to be done is to come to Ibiza, it's simple."

So I'd be a jerk if I went and a heel if I didn't. "Okay, I'll transcend my petty limitations, but I sure hope it ain't like last time."

"It'll be real different," he said grimly, "I'm a cripple."

"How long will we go for?"

"Just a few days."

Next morning, I entered Jonah's room carrying the new suitcase he'd requested so he could fly the coop. "Good, you brought it," he nodded, "'cause we're leaving today."

"We are?"

"Yeah. They promised me my crutches after lunch. I tried them on this morning and they look adorable. If we really step on it, I think we can catch the afternoon boat."

Nothing like homemade panic—leave it to Jonah to cook some up. Anticipating my response, he said, "There's no boat tomorrow. And I'll lose my mind if I have to stay here two more days. So right after lunch, we bolt like a couple of thieves."

"I haven't had a chance to go to American Express yet though."

"We'll hit it on the way back."

"Whatever you say, Kimosabe."

The doctor appeared on schedule. And standing between us, Jonah balanced himself on the chopsticks. Since normal clothes couldn't accommodate the cast, he was sporting short shorts, designed for the occasion by none other than Missy. "Right," he said squarely after sixty seconds of crutch lessons, "Ring the nurse and tell her to call a cab."

"Don't you want to hop around a little?" I asked, as the doctor swiftly dematerialized so as not to witness Jonah's escape.

"Gotta conserve energy, it's really strenuous. No time now anyway, we still have to stop and pick up your stuff."

"That's easy, my hotel's by the port."

"Should've known your hotel would be by the port," he smiled. "You haven't changed."

"Yes I have."

"No you haven't."

"Yes I HAVE. Should've known you'd drag me to Ibiza. You haven't changed."

"Yes I have."

"No you haven't."

"No, I haven't," he giggled.

He didn't bother to learn how to crutch, just bashed along down the corridor. Rather than having one leg, it was more like having three. And with only half the normal locomotion, he also had to transport the dead weight of the plaster limb. Carrying his suitcase, I trailed him ineffectively, then sprung ahead to open doors. "Don't you have to check out?" I asked as he passed the front desk like a soldier going AWOL.

"They'll figure it out."

I opened the cab door and he flung in the crutches, then, with difficulty, situated himself across the back seat, wiping sweat from his brow. I climbed in the front, then turned to him and had to laugh. He didn't see the humor in the unwieldy cast though, or the short shorts, or the thought of limping through the rest of his days. But it was his will that humored me. Where another invalid might have respected the injury, yielded to it, slowed down, Jonah hated and fought it. The leg would just have to keep up with him, nine screws and all—he wasn't slowing down. Would hate to see him as a father, I thought, he'd give his kids about ten minutes to grow up.

The gangplank was another trial, all eyes on him. Jonah, clearly, was going to make a lousy cripple, reeling in humiliation whenever well-wishers offered help or pity. All I could do was be there, proving to society at large that at least he wasn't a lonely cripple. But he didn't need my assistance; any stranger could've and would've carried the suitcase.

As the late sun gilded everything on deck, Jonah and I engaged in conversation with a young guitar player who'd recently been to India and was talking about gurus. Jonah was eager to hear how these gurus actually functioned in practical terms. The fourteen-year-old Maharaj Ji was the current rage, and this musician told us how the young swami had recently chartered five 747's to take the whole club from India to London. Everything had gone swimmingly until they reached English customs, where it was revealed the teenage guru had more than hare krishna up his sleeve: twenty gold watches, to be precise, ten on each arm.

I had to chuckle. But Jonah glowered, "You think that's funny?"
"It is funny."

"Well, I don't think it's funny. And I don't think it's funny that you think it's funny."

"Well, I think it's weird that you don't think it's funny." Who on the planet but Jonah would side with a teenage smuggler moonlighting as a savior, over a long-lost lover? I went below to our stateroom to get away from him. I felt imprisoned and foolish being there at all. He was as abrupt, insensitive, and off the wall as ever.

Soon he, too, came down, to brood on his bunk. The jaunt from hospital to ship had worn him out, and he withdrew into depression. Then, eventually emerging from that, he donned a cold aloofness for a few hours, then moved on to brittle meanness. The Spanish Siddhartha so glad to see me must've tumbled overboard, and I was now superfluous to this wounded beast who'd once again flung me off like a sweater in a heat wave. A difficult silence thudded between us.

"Jonah, what is it?" I finally asked him. "What's wrong?" Maybe he'd admit frustration and fear, maybe he'd apologize.

"You're a bit of a child," was his answer, said gently as though I really needed to know.

I did not need to know.

"And I'm a man," he concluded.

With that exchange, I left the stateroom.

Late that night, I stood alone on the top deck as the ship glided into the still Ibiza harbor, the old clock-tower welcoming in the boats. I remembered it so well, but it meant nothing to me now. Zaxos superseded it all. Still, something out of my past was creeping toward the ship. And, though trying not to, I was already reliving inferior memories. Tears fell as the port embraced the boat. Ibiza had always symbolized Jonah to me, and now as the anchor dropped...I couldn't believe we were both on the same boat.

Jonah appeared at my side by the railing. "What's wrong?" he asked.

"Nothing. I'm just crying because I'm a child."
"Tell me."

"Oh Jonah! I just can't believe that here it is, Ibiza again, and you and me sailing in, just like before...but two whole years have passed and *nothing's changed*. We're as far apart as ever.... It makes me sad, that's all."

"I don't know why you think it was so bad before...."

"I know you don't."

53

Straight Talk

We took a hotel room near town, and stayed on the island three days. It was rainy and bleak. Sleeping in our twin beds at night, physical contact was reduced to nothing. Taxiing hither and thither by day, Jonah tied up loose ends and loose affairs. Invited to meet Missy, I chose to forgo the pleasure. I'd already more than filled my quota for adventure this week. I could use the alone time for serious reflection.

Every second thus far, I'd been trying to give Jonah the benefit of the doubt: he had a broken leg, his life had come to a full stop and looked pretty sketchy from here, he needed help, he was proud and independent so it was even harder, and...he was wacko to begin with. But my dream of us was running out of days, months, and years. After all my travels and compelling love affairs, I knew that real love actually delivers. Maybe not what you thought you wanted or needed—maybe you're stood up in Tangiers, sleeping under a truck in the Bayou, or left dancing with a wooden chair on a Greek island—but real love also delivers what you never knew existed. Real love is not *over there* like half a rainbow. It may be imperfect and complex, like its owners, but it continually regenerates through kindness, touch, generosity, sweetness, support, beauty, memories, surprise, and little twinkles between two people. I knew this, and I hadn't before.

Before, I'd been waiting for Jonah to show me what it was he seemed to know and I didn't—"Fill my heart, it's so empty right now." But my heart was no longer empty. Nor my confidence, nor my grasp of the great wide world. I'd made decent use of my time these few years, and knew what it felt like to be loved in return. I'd learned that love doesn't have to last forever, but it has to be cherished by both lovers. It has to be mutual or it's doomed. The mutuality is what seals the deal.

My heart was not empty at all now. With the help of Sylvia, who'd reconnected me eternally to my mother's unconditional spirit; with the help of Gilbert, who'd taught me to inhale love fully—it's the best high; with the help of Jules, who'd shown me about bedrock, being there, being equals, and sharing animals and a home (or tool shed or van); with the help of Zeke, who'd illustrated how humor, devotion, willingness, and creativity keep love ever playful and alive despite anything; with the help of Theologos, who'd proven that love is as breathtaking and poetic as the ocean full of fish and the blues of the Aegean; with the help of my father, who taught me that love can retrieve you from unbearable grief, sometimes save your life, and that love's tender union can never be known by outsiders; and…with the help of Great Spirit itself, who gave me Paradise, Harmony, and Forgiveness, showing how life is friendly and we're never alone—the trees are breathing, the sky fills us with awe, the animal kingdom is bleating, birthing, and making us smile—life is wealthy and…full; never, never empty.

Now, with Jonah, everything was muddled. Who knew why, but we seemed to miss each other at every opportunity not to. I didn't know how to be more 'all in' than to still readily hitch across a continent for him, at the spur of the moment. I thought I'd made that fairly clear (twice now, two continents). But perhaps in the end we each needed someone more grounded.

By the time we were waiting on the pier for the boat back to Barcelona, just standing side by side felt awkward.

A friend of Jonah's agreed to steer the car, a sporty red Fiat convertible, onto the huge ferry, after Jonah insulted me for not driving while simultaneously forbidding me to. Even the friend couldn't figure that one out. "Don't mind him," he winked at me sympathetically once Jonah had boarded the boat, "he's like that to everyone—a little hard to handle."

"I know," I said flatly.

"How do you like Ibiza?" he changed the subject.

"Not much."

"Really?? How long have you been here?"

"Three days."

"That's not really long enough to get the feel of it. What brought you here?"

"Jonah."

"Oh. You came with him from Barcelona? Did you meet him there?"

"No. New York."

"Oh. Is that where you've just come from?"

"No. Greece."

"Oh. Is that where you live?"

"No. London."

"Oh. Is that where you're going now?"

"No. Madrid."

"Oh. You're going with Jonah?"

"Yeah."

"Bravo, you finally said yes to something. That's pretty courageous of you to stay with Jonah, considering the foul frame of mind he seems to be in. Think you two'll stay together?"

"No."

"Don't be so pessimistic, you might make a nice pair if you both cheered up."

"This couple's not big enough for both of us."

"Oh come on, give him a chance—how long've you known the dude?"

"Four years."

As we put to sea, I stared out to the horizon—something had to give. We were preparing to drive to Madrid together where he would recuperate, and where I as yet had no function. With the status of our relationship presently downgraded to an F-minus, whatever love we had seemed unworkable. Jonah and I were going to have to talk it out from the heart or say goodbye. I was still more than willing if we could find a way. And he could still save it if he'd just say something kind, show me this mattered to him.

But resenting each other was nonsensical. Sure, we were both under-achievers at communication and truth-telling, but why forfeit any good feelings we still might share by indulging in these funky ones?

The Greeks have an expression they use in parting, "*Sto kalo na pas*," meaning, "Go to the good." And the good is everywhere. That's what I learned in Zaxos.

Going down to the stateroom, I found Jonah performing that boredom act. With additional years of practice, he was now a master, barely distinguishable from the walls and floor. "Jonah?"

"Yeah," only his eyes turned in my direction.

"Do you want to try, or do you want to just forget about it?" His eyes moved from mine, once around the cabin, pausing on the relaxed crutches leaning against the sink, then back to me. I went on, "Either way's alright with me. As long as we both know what's going on."

"Well," he said after a time, "you said you'd drive with me to Madrid...so why don't you stay with me till we get there? Then we'll rest up at my parents' place, and you can make your plans."

"Fine."

I left quietly.

It was a little like being assassinated.

Wow...he didn't want to try. I really thought he'd at least want to see if there was any common ground.... I found my way up to the top deck. In the salty blackness I tried to digest the death of whatever it was I'd been holding onto for so long....

Oh well...trying to be his girlfriend was beyond my skill-set. With that officially canceled, perhaps there was the freedom to be friends. I watched the bow dipping into the waves. For a long, long time. The heaviness of foolishness and failure clung to me like the anchor to the ship.

But eventually it lifted. If there was one thing I'd confirmed since leaving Jonah in Spain the last time, it was that I could survive.

A while later, I smiled as he hobbled toward me in the strong wind. "I feel much better now," I told him. "How are you?"

"I'm okay," he said with traces of sadness and apology.

I didn't want him to feel sorry though, or sorry for me. Love takes two and he wasn't in. "It's alright, you know," I said. "It's really better this way. For both of us…. I'm really not capable of being your woman. So I feel relieved now. Maybe we can actually have a nice time." I kissed him on the cheek, "I love you."

He rested his crutches against the railing to free his arms for a hug, "I love you, too."

54

Old Habits Die Hard

With me at the wheel next morning, we headed from the pier to American Express. But Jonah, feeling fit enough now for fresh histrionics, decided to have a nervous breakdown over my driving. He viewed my caution as cowardice and my inexperience with Spanish traffic as idiocy. Within moments of setting out, he was shouting, writhing in his seat, and operating both the gear shift and steering wheel for me as though driving required two people. "Jonah, will you please calm down before you cause an accident? Otherwise I'm gonna drop you off at the next insane asylum. You've said, yourself, on several occasions that I'm a good driver."

"If I said you were a good driver, then you BETTER drop me off because I AM crazy. LOOK OUT! LOOK OUT!"

"Look out for WHAT?"

"I thought you were going to hit the curb on that turn."

"I'm gonna hit you on the next one."

We then stopped at a red light, as Jonah shouted, "GO! GO!" while shoving the gearshift into first.

"It's a RED light, Jonah!"

"It's almost green."

Then, moments later, he grew livid as I slowed down for another red light ahead, "*Why* are you stopping?"

"It's a red light. Are you color blind?"

"It just *turned* red. You don't have to stop if it just *turned* red."

"Jonah, I'm amazed only your leg was broken."

Somehow we got to American Express. Jonah came in with me to get a road map, knowing I was incapable of the task, then joined me at the mail window. Aside from some money and a couple of letters, I was also presented with two telegrams. "Oh dear," I opened the first one, "what could it be?"

We both stared at the message:

CALL ME IMMEDIATELY. I LOVE YOU. ZEKE.

"Who's Zeke?" Jonah asked.

"A friend in London. Gee, I hope everything's okay."

"Open the other one," said Jonah.

We both stared at the second message:

COME BACK HERE IMMEDIATELY. I LOVE YOU. ZEKE.

"Sounds like a pretty good friend," said Jonah. "Who is this Zeke? You haven't mentioned him."

"He's, uh, somebody...who loves me, I guess. I better call him, maybe there's trouble of some kind."

"If there was trouble, he'd say so. It'll take ages to call from here. We'll be in Madrid in eight hours, call him from my parents' place. Eight hours won't make any difference."

No sense in unsettling this human time bomb any further. There were still three unbroken legs among us that my agitated companion was itching to sacrifice to the patron saint of Frenzy. So we made our maimed way back to the Fiat, Jonah swinging right along now as though the crutches were ski poles. Reaching the car, he tapped the shotgun side authoritatively with the rubber nib of one crutch, "You get in this side."

I stood glued to the sidewalk, refusing to be party to this. "Jonah—" I warned, as he bopped around the car to the driver's side.

"Get in," he nodded to the co-pilot position, feeling utterly rejuvenated at the prospect of endangering not only us but everyone else on the road. Plus there was the logistical challenge (he was climbing in now) of operating the accelerator, the clutch, and the brake with one foot. The broken leg would have to be 'cast' aside completely, wedged between the gearshift and the other passenger (the one rooted to the sidewalk, considering bus travel). "Let me just try it," Jonah coaxed with boyish appeal, as though my permission mattered. He was smiling broadly, "Come on, get in, we're leaving." He started the ignition. (He'd been keeper of the keys, of course.)

I didn't move. "You're obviously self-sufficient, Jonah. You don't need my help, so goodbye."

"Look," he conceded, "I know it's far-fetched, but just let me try it for a couple of blocks to see if it's possible. I might need to drive at some future time when you're not with me. You know? Just a few blocks. We'll go real slow."

"I don't know, Jonah...."

Knowing he'd won, he flung open my door.

"Just a few blocks," I stated firmly and strapped myself warily to the seat.

It really isn't possible to drive a sports car with one foot. And I didn't know what Jonah had in mind as we pulled into the throbbing municipal traffic. My left foot was ready to be called into service, but there was quite a pile-up of human and car parts blocking its way to the dance floor.

"Grab the wheel!" Jonah shouted, as we picked up speed, then dove head first under the steering panel. He was using his left hand on the clutch pedal. "Second!" he called up from the floor. I moved the stick into second. Jonah popped up for a quick look around, then burrowed back down. "Third," he sang out jubilantly, thrilled with the operation's success thus far.

"That's two blocks, Jonah—very good—I think we should stop now."

He reappeared in time to see a red light ahead. Then with a sharp cry of "Second!" he dove back under.

"We don't stop at red lights," I reminded him.

"I know, but we'll just stop for this one because I need practice down-shifting."

"You mean WE need practice," I said, as we came to a stop and Jonah slipped the stick into first.

"No, you can take a rest, I think I can handle the gears now; I've got the clutch under control."

"Yeah, Jonah, this situation is really Under Control, my feelings exactly. Come on, that's enough. Let me drive."

"I think I can make it to Madrid actually," he said, and vanished again as the light turned green. "Second!" We both shifted it this time. And he didn't need to say "third" or "fourth" because we'd worked out the rhythm. "Yeah," he surfaced, "no problem, we've got it sorted out." He turned a smiley face to me as we cruised leisurely along in fourth. "See?" he took both hands off the wheel, "Nothin' to it. Aren't you relieved you don't have to drive for eight hours? You want to see the sights—Spain's great. You'd miss everything if you had to drive."

"You're very considerate, Jonah, thank you."

Once outside Barcelona, on the open road, Jonah became relaxed indeed. We shot along in the sunshine like a couple without a care. Zooming down rural Spanish roads in our fiery hotrod, who'd have guessed the driver was minus one leg and all his faculties? But, with his penchant for pandemonium, Jonah felt bone idle now with no shifting or clutching to do. What could he conjure up for the remaining seven hours?

Velocity. For his audience of one, he would attempt to make highway history.

Recognizing my helplessness, I could only abandon all fear. As he careened around the cliff-side roads with his head under the steering wheel, I knew my anxiety would further incite him, so I sat serenely back and watched the mountains hurtling past like they do in cartoons. From time to time, when he wasn't perilously overtaking a faster vehicle, Jonah would shoot me a devilish glance. But his wickedness fell flat against my yogic demeanor; I just smiled pleasantly like he was rowing me down a lazy river.

"Aren't you scared?" he asked finally.

"I'm having a lovely time," I replied sleepily. "Scenery's magnificent."

"Oh…having a lovely time…."

Another hour passed. The only way to shock me further would be to crash. With cast, crutches, and a leg with titanium parts, though, Jonah wasn't quite his old self. "You're really not scared, are you?"

"I'm beyond fear, Jonah. What am I supposed to do, jump out?"

"No," he reflected momentarily, "but you could gasp a little."

"What for?"

"Good question. I'll think about it," and he floored it.

Stopping only once for gas and a quick lunch, this outing was an all-day exercise in faith. Madrid was The Promised Land when we arrived.

Since relinquishing all romantic notions aboard the ship, we'd been, emotionally at least, in blissful accord. Our union was moribund and we were gleeful. Of course I had some reorienting ahead, with no more Jonah capers to anticipate.

His healing was probably all physical, but adjustment would be required of him, too. Our conclusion wasn't dreamy, but—without liking it much—we understood it. The courage was in saying goodbye. A part of each of us wished to be side by side, but our souls couldn't swing it. We detracted from each other, competed, while withholding encouragement, support, and love itself.

Jonah's parents' apartment in Madrid was ornamental and delicate. On good behavior now, he hopped into a spare bedroom and collapsed from exertion. This was a neutral and safe place for him to rehab a while. There was a full-time housekeeper if he needed her, and he knew the neighborhood.

Wasting no time, I phoned London. Jonah could probably hear me and I didn't have a lot to hide. "What is it, Zeke? Is everything okay?"

"Everything's excellent HERE, but what are *you* up to? You're not with who I think you're with, are you? You're not stupid enough to be traveling backwards in time, are you?"

"No, not really. A little relapse maybe, nothing too retro. Why? What do you think I should be doing?"

"I think you should be here. What are you doing with him? I'm the one who loves you, you silly twit. Haven't you figured that out yet? And I miss you, dammit, when are you coming back?"

"Tomorrow."

Exhale Poem

Churning across the Continent
letter in hand
clutching his address like a full canteen
you reach for that far-off land...

The map is like your grandma,
too slow, but you must sit tight
sit until the 'pizza' signs
change to 'omelettes' in the night

And in that mountain valley
where liras turn to francs
too many short rides eat up your time
and fill your mouth with thanks

Then stumbling under eyelids
reddened by the strain
you point your thumb to a darkening sky
and demand it not to rain

As one more night subtracts itself
from the mileage on the map
you're jerked out of monotonous sleep
awakened with a slap...

The final car door slams
and the highway rides away
but you're all unwound, so a place is found
to rest this Spanish day

The map goes in the garbage
the letter is reread,
and disbelief becomes relief
in the comfort of a bed

The morning shines in yellow
  beneath the down-pulled shade
your face is washed and teeth are brushed
  hotel bill quickly paid

A taxi takes you uphill
  to the street spelled on the page;
the door is white, the number right,
  you're just a knock away

"Come in." That's it, the same old voice
  You walk into his eyes,
"You haven't changed." "Nor have you."
  Just donned a new disguise

You share with him your journeys
  and loves you've had since then
you swear you would have written
  but you didn't have a pen

And round and round the words go
  confessions flow in tears
until your arms absorb him
  your one love through the years

"You'll never know," you tell him,
  "how far you've made me go"
"Oh, no, my love," he shakes his head,
  "it's you who'll never know."

But the chorus of the love song
  is always just the same
He's once again the player
  and the driver of the game

"A bit of a child you are," he speaks.
"And I, I am a man"
Without a why or a single reply,
  you let him take command:

"I have for you a ticket
  on the Paris train at ten.....
  Of course, of course I'll write to you
  if I can find a pen"

"Oh God, oh Death," escapes your lip
"What's that?" says he, perplexed
"Oh never-mind—I'll be just fine,
  I know it's for the best."

Half his mouth turns upward
  and he blinks you from his eye
"You've an hour and a half, now take your bath
  or your hair will not be dry."

And one more time you're on your way
  and he's where he fits best
  inside your brain on the ten o'clock train
  Amen. Farewell. God bless.

November 1972,
written on the train, Madrid to London

- 55 -

Rear-view Mirror

It was the following year when I spotted Jonah in New York's Penn Station, then rode to Long Island on the same train. I was living in East Hampton again and waiting for Zeke to join me from London. Jonah had always made me nervous. Something seemed to lift him a few feet off the ground.

He was older, mobile, half European, and generally quick. His snappy bounce and unpredictability had perennial charm, but essentially he was a ramblin' bad-boy with an allowance. He really only wanted to make love and make music, and Spain was where he could afford to. At 19 though, or even 22, that simplicity evaded me—he seemed complex, unknowable, anguished, also splashy, romantic, and free.

What I really needed was a durable traveling companion, and mistook Jonah's restlessness for wanderlust. Regardless, we were never to merge or really know each other even as friends—not in New York City, Long Island, Venice, Austria, or Spain—though the electricity always crackled. It was a love that couldn't continue because it never actually began. But it was my first love.

Words from Simone, 2015, Northern California:

Looking back forty years, I marvel at how innocent we were, children of our own time—the assassinations, Vietnam, Woodstock. We were so full of our youth, mere propinquity, the present was everything.

Now Wendy and I are again in touch. The beautiful young woman with the blinding smile who came into my kitchen and my life with her hopes and cheer. I remember how we were friends from the start, and our culinary adventures were many and, in retrospect, rather terrifying. We took on crazy things—like catering a huge film party, and baking a seven-tiered wedding cake—that somehow turned out all right. It was actually a bit plucky taking on a restaurant like that. I can probably lay a mild claim to our little eatery being the first pop-up on the east coast. We worked endless hours as only the young can, kept on moving into our future as only the young do.

In the year-round culture, few had cars or if someone did, it was a pickup truck or some working vehicle. We rode bikes, lived in basements or spare rooms (or tool sheds). There was a wild old culture there, oblivious to the class gap and the summer people—who occupied a world of rambling stone houses with emerald lawns and roses climbing the walls, with fathers who appeared on weekends and sons who dealt dope.

Thinking back, I see us in perpetual motion, laughing, picking blackberries for the restaurant, riding bikes, sleeping on the afternoon beach, catching a wave. It's always summer and we're young and beautiful. And like a thread through it all, I remember the exact feeling and smell of my skin on awakening from a sleep on the sand. Through it all, I remember the blue Atlantic, the white sand, the sound of the waves crashing against the shore, and the smell of salt in the air.

Words from Dad (almost 94), 2015, Long Island:

I have mixed feelings about that time in our family. One feeling was that I felt I abandoned my kids. Another was that the loss of my wife was so absolutely strange…there was no way I could prepare for it. Charlotte passing on was the worst experience of my life. I don't expect ever to get over it. I'm still learning to accept it and not have it in the destructive mode it was in in the beginning—a terrible period that lasted a long time.

I never doubted that I'd somehow pull through, but I sure felt like a wandering nomad in a wind-blown desert.… And Nadine saved the day for me. Because I absolutely had to go to the college and teach my classes. I had to get food on the table every day, had to pay the bills, and keep things functioning. So I continued working and managed to hold onto everything. And Nadine was there at the school and aware of what I was going through. And I needed her support—at the beginning platonically, just enough not to feel alone in the desert.

But I couldn't really help my kids. I seemed to feel that they disappeared.… But I disappeared. And they found out that I was distant. I wasn't doing anything to support them that I can remember, except seeing that there was food on the table every night. And I tried to get them to go to college. The rest of the time I didn't know where they were. And I felt badly about it. I left a lot to Nadine…but I don't think she knew what the hell to do. There was really no one in charge. It was a period of absentee management and I was fully aware of it. But my first responsibility had always been to my job, because that was my bread and butter. And with six kids, I needed that bread. So the little strength I had went to the college.

When the kids took off for the far corners of the globe and were gone, I actually felt some relief that they didn't need me, and that they weren't in trouble. I wasn't getting messages back that anyone was hurt or wounded or impoverished. It was a relief to believe that they were able to take care of themselves.

And here was a woman who loved me, and it was the support I needed. I remember once saying to Nadine, "How would you feel if I decided not to marry again? It's occurred to me that maybe I shouldn't marry again." And she looked at me and said, "It would kill me." I can see the look on her face to this day. I never brought it up again. I don't think it would have killed her, but it showed me how much she loved me. And I don't think she's ever wavered. Even now, every night when she leaves the nursing home, she says "I love you." It's rock solid. And it's a relief.

Regarding organic farming way back then, there weren't many others into it. I didn't notice though, because I gave every bit of my spare time to it. Organic farming was always a strong part of my character and is to this day. I always found good literature, certain little books by the leaders of that movement and others who were interested in right eating. A magazine called "Organic Gardening" kept me right on the money. But even way before that, we used to eat tomatoes and corn from the garden. And we were composting.

Words from Sonny, 2015, Long Island:

Regarding our home life back then, well, I remember the summer of '69 there was a whole topless period that was kind of cool, when all my sisters were always weeding Dad's garden with no tops on. My friends loved to come visit. The summer of '69 was pretty frickin' wild. I remember going to Smitty's and drinking. I was under-age but nobody seemed to care how old you were. You just had to know someone, like your sister, who they were letting in for free, and you'd just follow her in. I don't think they ever carded me—and I didn't look old, I was 17. Was that the summer of The Case of the Prude Drood Rude—the crude dude rude nude...? Yeah, nudity was a big theme that summer. I had just been to California where we had a nice nudist scene on the roof of the house I stayed in, the

Del Mar Degenerates Sunbathing Society. Anywhere from two to ten people on a Wednesday afternoon—playing cards, drinking, smoking dope, listening to music. They were all college students at UCSD, and I was like their little mascot. Stealing the food was my value to the little commune, and I was very good at it because I didn't have any money. Until, of course, I got busted: "You're spending a lot of time in this store and we've never seen you buy anything. You get fatter when you leave than when you came in."

We rationalized stealing, or doing anything completely worthless because we were "being oppressed" by the state, the cruel government. And I thought I was angry at the United States, when I was pretty much just angry at Dad.

The spring of 1970 was a crazy time in Southern California. Patty Hearst. They fire-bombed the Bank of America. One day we were at some girls' house for dinner, and knock-knock-knock, three officials in suits come in, "F.B.I." They had badges, so we let 'em right in. It was crazy times. And the girls were like, "Hey, how are ya? Y'all want some spaghetti?" "No, we're looking for outside agitators, the SLA (Symbionese Liberation Army)." We had a whole bowl of pot right on the coffee table, but they had bigger fish to fry. I had paratrooper boots on, and they said, "Where'd you get those boots?" I said, "Army Surplus." They said, "Are you a deserter?" I'm like, "No, but I'm gonna be. I'm not 18 yet, but as soon as I am…."

When I came to Greece, I was on the ferry in the middle of the night and missed the stop for Zaxos, so I got there two days late. And I was coming up the goat path, walking over the hill, and you were coming up the other way. And then the first thing you told me was you had to leave the next day for Spain 'cause what's his name…Jonah…had had a terrible motorcycle accident. And of course I was a little upset by that. But you said that I could stay in your house.

And then I had the best three weeks of my life by myself on Zaxos. There was nobody around—it was idyllic. I did yoga and swam and walked, and ate cheese and carrots and olives, and drank a little wine. I went all over that island, always walking. And the sun came up right in the center of the cove right off your front porch. The weather was perfect, and swimming in that bay was crystal clear. There was no one around except the few locals that lived nearby, who I rarely saw. I just read books and slept and walked and played my little flute. I felt like a lot of things were kind of settling, coming together. In fact, as incredible as the trip to India was, I think I said when Mimi eventually got there, "We should just stay here. At least for a while." But we already had this plan to get going....

We went overland to India, completely winging it. I was 19, Mimi was maybe 17—we didn't even know you needed visas for these countries. We took every kind of transport—plane, trains, a boat, buses—basically just following the people ahead of us.

I remember one little harrowing bus through the Kyber Pass in Afghanistan where there were four-thousand-foot drops on the sides. The guy drove like a maniac and there were no guardrails. And a train in Pakistan which we literally jumped off while moving. We slept in a rice paddy that night, then hitched a ride on a truck full of apples all the way to Bombay. Then a bus to Goa in Southern India. A full month on the road.

I spent two months in Goa, and Mimi stayed on much longer, but I was sick and had lost 35 pounds, so I flew home to get well.

Dad was happy to see me.

Words from Dale, 2015, Long Island:

The whole family transition was really all a blur to me. When your mother dies and your family falls apart, it just becomes a blur. It was all reeling, everything changing so fast. I didn't have conscious feelings of betrayal or abandonment, just emotional upheaval. There was a new situation to deal with, a new mother in the house, and my dad wasn't around. It was just...turbulent.

But when you're young and there's no structure, you don't really mind because you have freedom. I was doing pot, I was doing LSD in eighth grade. At night, I was taking Dad's Jeep Wagoneer out for joy rides with my friends. I didn't have a lot of time to feel bad when I'm out driving around—12 or 13 years old, hair down to here. Plus I was thrust into like a Lord of the Flies school. Wild, not a lot of control. The worst things you can think of happened in that school. (Not murder.) (That I know of.) Just kids running amok, molesting people—all the time. Molesting girls, and a couple boys. Daily fist-fights on the playground. There was a real collection of characters, with a few dominant ones. I was friends with most of them so I wasn't victimized. But I wasn't behaving particularly well myself. In the eighth grade, I was going home at lunchtime and smoking hashish then going back to school.

My older siblings would show up from time to time to drop off some drugs or pot. Sonny and Mimi turned me onto pot. They were there for a while. Mimi and Lily were there at that private school for a year or two.

My friends and I would go out drinkin'—we used to drink a lot. I remember going to Smitty's when I was 13, in eighth grade. To get in, I borrowed a friend's ID who was 18. I was like five foot four, prepubescent, long shaggy blonde hair. A little boy. Somebody had given me a wallet that had a stack of those plastic sheets you put your photographs in, and I put the ID in the top one. So, at the door, I take out the wallet, open it up, and all the plastic sleeves unfold all the way down to the ground. So I roll them up. The guy at the door looks at the ID and says, "Okay, go in." I was a little boy, but I went in. Then a few minutes later—I didn't even make it to the bar—he comes up to me and he goes, "You know, kid, I'm sorry...." he was crestfallen, "I'm sorry, kid, but you just don't look 18. I gotta ask you to go."

I said, "Okay." It was like 11 o'clock at night, so my friend Billy left with me and we hitch-hiked home.

Words from Peter, 2015, Los Angeles:

It was all so long ago I can barely...it was forty-some odd years ago.... Well, I'd left America, was living in Europe. It was a very free time when things we worry about now weren't even on the horizon. We were a little naive back then, I would say. We had no worries, we had no kids. We were really at the beginning. So it was pretty easy. You could just do stuff—you know, if I wanna go to Greece, I'm gonna go to Greece. It was a time when you could be immature and still survive. It was fun.

I didn't really associate with being a hippie, I was more of an artist, more into film and photography. I didn't go to Woodstock...I was more interested in art as opposed to making a socio-political statement. I spent a lot of time in Spain. I loved that sort of earthy environment.

I was on a fellowship and we were gonna do a film. I was co-directing and we were casting in Paris. I remember that's when we first met you and Phoebe.

That flat in London was an interesting dynamic. There were a couple of generations. Roger was much older than the rest of us, and Daniel was sort of, I don't know, making connections. And there was Zeke. And Kip...and you and me and Phoebe and Clare and a bunch of other people. Daniel moved in later. Yeah, it was a great time, one of those magical, golden little moments when you could kind of just do anything and it all seemed possible. There was a lot of fluid social interaction going on. And fluids. A lot of... fluids.

Regarding Phoebe.... I thought in a way we all were more of an impediment to her life. She sort of wanted something different, I don't know what. You know, she had limited resources and all of us were kind of an option—she could grin and bear it, pretending she was all in, but I didn't think she was. And of course she obviously wasn't 'cause she just left one day and I never saw her again, or ever even heard from her. She was going through some personal crisis—I don't know what it was. I don't know what ever became of her....

...I vaguely remember when you phoned from Greece. I had just come back from Amsterdam where I did that movie. It was some crazy thing where you left a piece of paper, a letter or something, in a language that no one reads and we gotta figure it out. You must've told me where it was. I ended up describing Greek letters—a backward E? And after we hung up, I figured, "Well, she got most of it... she'll figure it out." And you did find the address, right?

Words from Mimi, 2015, Australia

When I was 17, I decided to make a spiritual pilgrimage to India. I worked hard and saved up that summer, and by the end of October, I was ready to go. I had talked Sonny into accompanying me on the overland journey, and met him in Greece where he was visiting Wendy (who had unexpectedly gone to Spain because one of her true loves was in hospital there, having crashed his motorcycle).

Sonny and I had no clue about what we were in for. We flew from Athens to Istanbul, where we stayed in a cheap hotel right across from the Blue Mosque. I was shocked—not by the beauty of the mosque, but by the multitude of hippies heading east from there. Hippies from everywhere—all on their way to India. It was the first time I humbly realized most of my 'bright ideas' were nothing more than generational group-think.

Many years later, watching the Steve Jobs movie, I laughed at the scene where he is walking barefoot across his college campus, holding the 'Be Here Now' book under his arm, saying he was going to India to find his guru. I smugly told whichever of my kids was watching with me, "I read 'Be Here Now' when I was only 17 and went to India a year before he did!" Group-think may humble one... but not that much.

Words from Zeke, 2015, Long Island:

We actually met at Belsize Gardens, through Phoebe. I recall that Peter and Phoebe had a party or something. You were a very attractive girl, and you were American—foreign, you know—which made it more interesting. You were energetic and your Liquid Theatre thing was interesting.

I remember you and I danced a lot. And there was a lot of pot—not marijuana, but hashish, laced with all kinds of stuff—that brown paste. I think we actually got together soon after that dinner party at some kind of art opening. Then we went back to where I was living in that dilapidated old house on Harmood Street, an absolute wreck of a place, where a carpenter friend and I were squatting.

I wasn't focused on getting a career going, apart from just being an artist and working for artists—money didn't come into it. And I think you had the same disposition. Money wasn't important to us for a long time. But we had to survive—I mean, I had to get to the islands. But I don't remember how I got the money to do that.

I originally met everyone in Belsize Gardens when I got the job with Daniel, who had his studio there. And Roger lived in that space—a total inspiration. I loved the community in that place. It was great being around people who were doing something. I remember we built a large studio in an old milk factory in Camden Town. Then they had two big shows at the Hayward Gallery, which had just opened. And I was building the sculpture for Daniel, and hanging the show, then going to the opening. The place was packed with all these glorious artists. It was just a perfect time.

…That morning in Athens, I had just come from an all-night ferry from Crete and arrived at Yanni's early in the morning. He and I were planning to drive back up to London. And I was just standing in the dining room reading a letter from you and suddenly there you were. I was amazed at the story of your journey and that you found Yanni's address, and that you turned up on me literally when I was about to leave.

Then, of course, we went off to Zaxos together, which was incredible. The Mimika. Women in their dark shawls, black clothing.

…And then I came back to London because I needed money and work. I moved into Belsize Gardens when you were in Greece. And you stayed on and had an affair with a fisherman, that I found out about later, and that was quite upsetting. And you also had an affair with a guy in Spain, and went off to see him. I remember you had mentioned that he was important to you. So your delay made me a little jealous, to tell the truth. Yeah, I've actually met him around here a number of times. I think your name came up once— not much was said, I don't remember—but he's aware of who I am and aware of you.

Yeah, he lives somewhere right around here. I was out walking two or three days ago and he waved from his car.

Spring 2015, Long Island.

It was 43 years since Jonah said goodbye to me in Madrid. Our paths crossed maybe twice in the following years, and briefly.

Now it seemed only fitting to let him know he'd play a role in an upcoming book, and even to let him see the manuscript. In telling this story, my intention had never been to slight or discredit his colorful, powerful force in my young life. And our higher selves had always been kin. So, if there was anything he wanted deleted, added, or corrected (within reason), I wanted to accommodate.

And so much time had passed, the subject matter seemed much less volatile, much safer than it once was. But even now, I didn't doubt his heart would pause a second at the sound of my name. As mine did at his.

Finding him again wouldn't be hard; mutual acquaintances had told me he'd ultimately settled in East Hampton with his wife, Katrine (the woman with him on the train that day). So, on line, I found him listed as owner of an East Hampton house. Boom, done. Next time I went to visit my ancient pop, now 93, I'd knock on Jonah's door.… I'd have to leave any alleged comfort zone for this flier, but that wouldn't be hard either because I'd never had a comfort zone.

A few months later, I found myself stepping onto the front porch of a quiet house on the outskirts of East Hampton. With half a lifetime having marinated the miserable failings Jonah had prophesied, at least I didn't have a hubby and kids out in the car hoping his offer still held. ("Okay, everybody, it's a go, here's our new home!") Nope, just me on the porch, pulling pluck from the soles of my boots.

Looking way too normal for someone having hitched her wagon to Jonah, Katrine answered the door.

"Hi," I pretended this was no big deal, "is this Jonah's house?"

"Yes, but he's not here. He'll be back a little later.'"

"Oh.… Are you Katrine?"

"Yes." She opened the screen door, "Come on in."

"Thanks," I stepped inside. "My name's Wendy. I'm an old friend of Jonah's from way back. I'm in town to see my family and thought maybe I'd catch up with him—I haven't seen him in years."

Katrine was my age, pretty, and endowed with European charm. Though she didn't recall an evening get-together we three once had (nor that chance meeting on the train, that I didn't bring up), she immediately treated me as a friend. She poured tea and (with no prompting from me) then began sharing surprisingly personal family details.

She commenced by relaying how Jonah (and his brother) had inherited their parents' house, "and with that money, Jonah bought this place." Then, exhibiting no conflicted emotion pertaining to her spouse, she said, "But then he ended up moving out because he wanted to have an affair."

"Moved out to have an affair?" I feigned surprise.

"He found some all-consuming attraction to another woman and believed he needed to be with her."

"But weren't you married?"

"Yes. And I was really hurt, of course, and really angry. I mean, he not only cheated, but lied about it for a while first. So I broke up with him."

Jonah untrue? Our own Jonah?

Maybe Katrine needed to vent, or wanted more people to know her side of the saga…. More likely, she figured any female 'friend' of Jonah's could probably relate to her tale. She continued, "So he rented a place of his own, to have his affair. But in the end, it didn't pan out as he'd hoped. So then he wanted to patch it up with me."

"Oh man…."

"So, probably to win me back, he gave me this house."

"He *gave* you the house? He must've really regretted hurting you."

"Well…he said it was so I'd always know I had a place to live no matter what happened between us. And that worked for me."

"So you got back together?"

"In some respects. But I won't let him live here."

"Oh, I thought you said he'd be back soon."

"He will. He comes over for meals. He'll be here for lunch at 1:00. But he doesn't live here. He'd like to…and we never actually divorced…but it's just not the same for me anymore."

"So, he wants to live together and you don't?"

"Maybe," she laughed. "But this set-up works fine for me. I'm really happy living here alone. And we see each other every day. Plus, he's really good to me now and we get along well."

"Where does he live?"

"He rents a house a few miles from here."

"Really? He rents?"

"Yeah, and drives over here three times a day for meals."

"Three times a day?"

"Yeah, he buys the food and I make the meals," she shrugged as if this arrangement was commonplace. "Y'know, he was the one who moved out, he was the one who wanted to live separately. Now I'm the one."

"He's lucky you didn't divorce him."

"He is. And he knows it. And there's not much he can do about this situation. Getting me back sort of cost him a house, I guess. So he comes over for meals. And it works fine…."

Continuing amiably, Katrine peeled back more decades of the marriage, recounting next how they'd lived in France a number of years.

I just sat like a priest taking a confession, quietly amazed how unconcerned Katrine was about how I knew her husband or why I was looking for him. 'Old friend,' apparently, was a good enough explanation for me to materialize on her porch. But the conversation remained one-sided, and I'll never comprehend what compelled Katrine to cheerfully answer all my questions without me asking them.

"What about kids?" I did ask that one. "Did you have any?"

"Jonah couldn't have children," she said.

"Oh, I didn't know that." I concealed my astonishment as the 'other shoe' dropped squarely on my head, about 43 years late.

"Yeah, he always knew that.... He'd had cancer when he was young. But I didn't really need to have kids—we were both okay with children not being our thing. Plus, we were really into skiing for a long, long time."

"I never had kids either," I offered. (Just ignore those rug-rats out in your driveway.)

"Anyway," she said, as we finished our tea, "Jonah will be here for lunch, if you'd like to wait."

Despite Katrine's hospitality and likability, I couldn't stay—was en route to visit my bedridden dad on Long Island's North Fork. So she said she'd tell Jonah I'd stopped by and pass along my number. Then she invited me to visit her again next time I was in town.

I had to conclude that whatever status this marriage had morphed to, the pair had clearly worked out some kinks, buried some hatchets, and molded a symbiotic lifestyle.

As for me, I was hugely thankful so much time had passed.... Some pieces of some stories come together shockingly late in the game.

Jonah called me that afternoon, stunned and pleased to hear I'd dropped in. And I admit to feeling a touch light-headed myself—even decades past all the madness—that we were actually talking on the phone in real time.

We set a rendezvous for the following morning.

At the chosen spot next day, Jonah parked a small white sedan rather than a motorcycle. And, as we walked toward each other, he carried nothing where the guitar case once was. Sporting a baseball cap and jeans, he looked just like everybody. And at 71 and 64, we could've passed on a street somewhere and never known the difference. To me, his maturity read well—though more low-keyed than expected. Any eccentricity still lurking in there was masked by a sedate, unassuming air. No unfiltered cigarette dangling from his lips, no scent of hashish.

"All grown up," I said, as we warmly hugged.

We stepped back to take each other in. It had been half a lifetime. And not once had we convened or spoken about those highs and lows, the shooting stars, or the final act. I guess we both knew we gave it our all.

Now there was this book I had to spill the beans about....

We took his car to a sandy, bay-front overlook where we parked for a chat.

It wasn't small talk, more like large talk, as we rolled over and through a mix of personal histories, faith, and philosophy, all punctuated by jibes about who was to blame for our shortcomings and miscommunication, plus admittance by both of immaturity, fear, and plain survival instincts ruling us back then. Now we were looking back, passing the long lens back and forth. We took several revolutions through the subject of 'us'—once sore, now painless—about where and how we messed up and missed each other completely. We were still in agreement that, despite the attraction and our dreams, we didn't function as a pair.

"Well, you know," I tried to sum it up, "for me, it was my first love...for you, it was one of many."

"No," Jonah looked at me sharply, "it wasn't at all one of many for me. You were...a big, big thing for me." His eyes held mine... and in that moment our truest feelings zinged back and forth again. There was just something between us that would probably never die. You couldn't call it 'love' anymore—but we once did.

So here we were, a good way down the road, and both doing fine. Back then we were taking life by the horns, now we were gliding along it, like the river it is. And I'd say our 43-year reunion was just about right. The spark we once saw in each other is essentially the spark of life itself, a spark we each still live by...that never goes out.

Regarding the book—that one stone unturned—when I mentioned it, he almost pretended not to hear me. Either not proud of his past, still emotionally guarded, or realizing—legitimately— that the book was obviously my story, not his, he said he had no interest in reading it.

I could sympathize. But needed to lobby my case. I conveyed how all names are changed, how his strong suits are also given air time, and, most of all, that his input was welcome and important to me. His perspective might even enhance the story, I said, who knew? And I explained how my intent had never been to dis him, just to portray his role in my story. I said I could re-work any scenes or descriptions he remembered differently, and that I sincerely wanted him to green-light the manuscript before it went to press.

No dice. Jonah declared he's a very private indivual these days, keeps to himself, and is content that way. Wanted no part of this sort of thing. So I dropped the subject (momentarily) and we rolled on.

No one mentioned children or fertility. Nor did I reveal anything Katrine had unleashed like tear-gas.... But in sharp contrast to her State of the Union address, Jonah now began waxing almost sing-song about the glory of the marriage—apparently airtight in his view, blissful, a treasure to possess, something to live and die for. With no mention of separate dwellings, he proclaimed how meaningful, all-important, this marriage continues to be.

To an innocent bystander hearing such contradictory, back-to-back, spousal testimonies......well, someone was fibbing. And it seemed like the whole jury was in now. In fact, that case was adjourned and the courtroom empty. Finally. Just in time for the end of my book.

So, circling back to *my* case, the literary project in question, I reminded Jonah how he used to say, "I don't care if people are saying bad things about me, as long as they're talking about me."

"I was hoping you still believe all publicity is good publicity," I threw one last pitch.

He gave a half smile, then reiterated how he's a quiet, private person now and will remain so. But with a tad more gentle prodding, he agreed I could send him a copy of the manuscript, and wrote down a P. O. box number to mail it to. The post office he notated was two villages over, where his parents' house had been, but since he and Katrine had also lived in that town a number of years, I figured he'd kept that address for practical or nostalgic reasons.

My work was done! I'd reached out to Jonah and invited his input. I now had total solace and just one final task.

When I got home, I whisked off a copy, then awaited his reply, not anticipating anything earth-shattering, but pleased the book was nearing completion.

However, the response I got, about three weeks later, wasn't what I expected. And it shouldn't have surprised me...but it did. The same package I'd mailed out reappeared in my mailbox, with a postal note now attached. The note read: "No such person at this address."

So this one's for you, Jonah.

End

Other books by W. M. Raebeck:

Expedition Costa Rica
Some Swamis are Fat
Stars in Our Eyes — true stories
Silence of Islands — poems
Nicaragua Story — Back Roads of the Contra War
Ta Ta for Now—the Movie

~ all in paperback, ebook, and soon in audio ~
~ more books to follow ~

At WendyRaebeck.com, read excerpts, see photos, sign up for email notifications of news and new releases, and submit comments. The site's calendar also lists book-signing dates and locations, and has links to buy books, ebooks, and audio books.

If you had even 1% as much fun reading this book as I did living it, please encourage my habit (writing, not sugar) by:
- *posting on-line reviews*
- *giving copies of this book as gifts*
- *reading my other books*
- *recommending my books to other readers and book clubs*
- *asking your library to carry my books in paperback and ebook*
- *join my email list through my website (and get 2 free stories)*

Most of all, I want to thank you for accompanying me on my journey. It has been my pleasure having you along. Sto kalo na pas —Go to the good.

Peace and love,

Wendy

Printed in the USA
CPSIA information can be obtained
at www.ICGtesting.com
LVHW090257251123
764662LV00005B/880